Chulo

Bil Gilbert

Chulo

A Year Among the Coatimundis

The University of Arizona Press
Tucson, Arizona

About the Author

BIL GILBERT is a native of Kalamazoo, Michigan, and was formally educated at Northwestern, Michigan State, Georgetown, and George Washington universities. He was informally educated by many wilderness trips and investigations into the lives of animals. He has written six books and hundreds of articles that have been published in national magazines, including *Audubon*, *Sports Illustrated*, and *Smithsonian*. His essays have won four national magazine awards. Mr. Gilbert and his family share their time between Fairfield, Pennsylvania, and the Huachuca Mountains in southeast Arizona.

THE UNIVERSITY OF ARIZONA PRESS

First Printing 1984
Manufactured in the U.S.A.

Pictorial maps by David Lindroth

Library of Congress Cataloging in Publication Data

Gilbert, Bil.
    Chulo : a year among the Coatimundis.

    Reprint. Originally published: New York : Knopf, 1973.
    Includes index.
    1. Coatis—Behavior.   2. Mammals—Behavior.   3. Mammals
—Arizona—Behavior.   I. Title.
QL737.C26G54   1984   599.74′443   83-18299

ISBN 0-8165-0842-9

Contents

Maps of
Chulo Country

Southeastern Arizona
The Huachuca Mountains
Montezuma Canyon

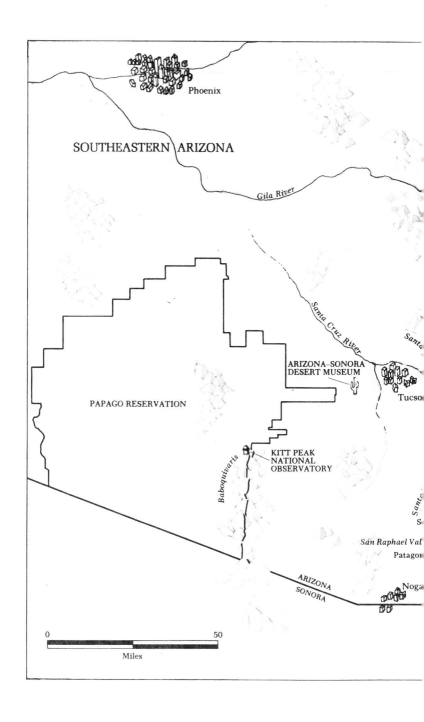

SOUTHEASTERN ARIZONA

Phoenix

Gila River

Santa Cruz River

Santa

PAPAGO RESERVATION

ARIZONA–SONORA
DESERT MUSEUM

Tucso

Baboquivaris

KITT PEAK
NATIONAL
OBSERVATORY

Sant

S

San Raphael Val
Patago

ARIZONA
SONORA

Noga

0   50

Miles

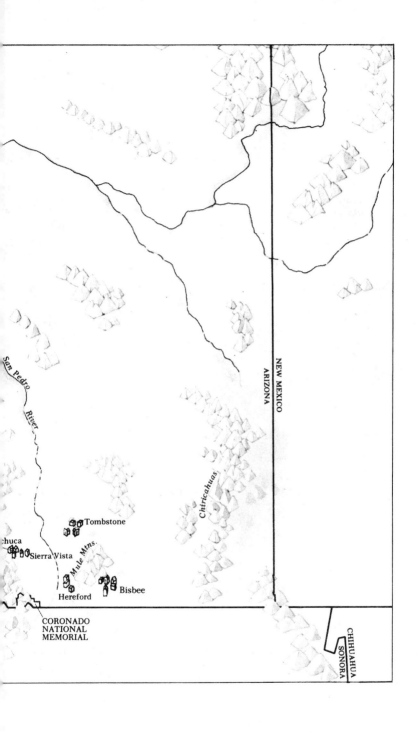

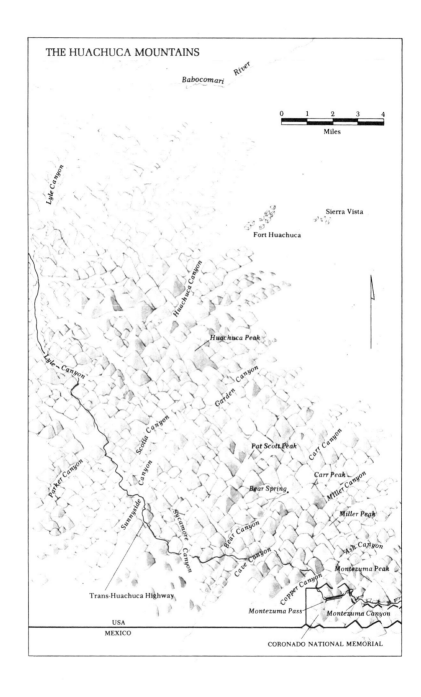

THE HUACHUCA MOUNTAINS

Babocomari River

0 1 2 3 4
Miles

Lyle Canyon

Sierra Vista

Fort Huachuca

Huachuca Canyon

Huachuca Peak

Lyle - Canyon

Garden Canyon

Scotia Canyon

Parker Canyon

Pat Scott Peak

Carr Canyon

Carr Peak

Bear Spring

Miller Canyon

Sunnyside

Canyon

Sycamore Canyon

Miller Peak

Bear Canyon

Ash Canyon

Cave Canyon

Montezuma Peak

Copper Canyon

Trans-Huachuca Highway

Montezuma Pass

Montezuma Canyon

USA

MEXICO

CORONADO NATIONAL MEMORIAL

MONTEZUMA CANYON

CORONADO NATIONAL MEMORIAL

Montezuma Pass

Den cave

Spring

Spring   The Wedge
West Ravine   East Ravine
                Spring
            Grub Stake cabin
            Clark's Ravine

Den cave

Joe's Canyon Trail

State of Texas Mine

Montezuma Peak

Den cave

Spring

Blue Water Ravine

Den cave

Den cave

Memorial Headquarters

Trans-Huachuca Highway

0   1000   2000   3000

Feet

Author's Note

This book is an account of a year spent in southern Arizona observing, intimately associating with, thinking about a mammal called the coatimundi. The central fact of existence for the coatimundi is that the animal is thoroughly communal. Thus this is principally an attempt to describe the dynamics, life style, traditions, and routine of a non-human community.

During the course of the year, the four of us involved in the study collected a great mass of information. Much of it is original, since no one had previously been able or inclined to spend much time with these animals along the Arizona-Sonora border. At present, some of this material is being analyzed and organized for publication in technical reports and journals. However, it seemed appropriate that the first statement should be in the narrative form of this book. Prolonged association with a community such as the coatimundi tribes inevitably leads to speculation about many matters which cannot be summarized statistically, which do not fit into a conventional technical format. These speculations, feelings, impressions about the coatimundi communities with whom we lived are included without apology in this narrative. In a sense, it is intended as a kind of traveler's tale, describing not only where we went—into these remarkable mammalian tribes—but how we got there and the effect of the passage on us.

Chulo

1

The Beginning

In the summer of 1970, we set about breaking up our household, a pleasant, pastoral life style which was centered in an old rambling house located at the mouth of an Appalachian valley near the Pennsylvania-Maryland border. In August, we finally succeeded in arranging a van and a sedan so as to accommodate seven people: Ann (my wife), myself, Ky aged 17, Terry (Ky's long-time friend) 16, Lyn 15, Lee 13, Kate 10; three animals: a ninety-pound dog named Dain, an excessively active spider monkey called Bobo, a despondent black cat, Christy, who because of either their virtues or their frailties had made the traveling squad (other arrangements were made for the remainder of our small menagerie); a formidable pile of baggage. Eventually the caravan crossed the continent, arrived in Tucson, Arizona. The move, all the aggravation, exhaustion, and sadness which inevitably accompanied it, came about because I had the notion that it would be an instructive, constructive thing to spend a year or so in the mountains along the Arizona-Sonora border trying to find and study a communal, raccoon-like mammal called the coatimundi.

All of us involved in the move, and a good many others who observed it with curiosity, doubts, even alarm, wondered why we should do such a thing. Our ostensible objective, mingling with coatimundis, was an exotic, quixotic, profoundly unnecessary one. In pursuit of it, we were trading very comfortable circumstances for others which would almost certainly be less comfortable in a measurable way. For example, anyone who in August leaves the cool green Appalachians, a trout stream with a swimming hole, and the shade of big maples, willows, elms, white pines, birch for the blazing pitiless sun, the searing heat, the thorns, and the dust of the Sonora Desert is, at least physically, behaving in a peculiar and impractical way.

For good reason, I expect I had thought—thought while we were in the process of relocating, have since thought—more about the reasons for our behavior than anyone else. The others had various motives for going with me, among the best being that it would have been very difficult for most of them to have done otherwise. However, in the beginning the coati scheme was not the result of group discussion or decision. The original plan was exclusively mine, and therefore all the subsequent disruption was more or less my doing.

That men's motives are various is a truism which has been frequently noted. However, there is a corollary less often invoked. Our motives may be various but seldom do they seem as remarkable or interesting to others as they are to ourselves. Thus my personal, subjective motives in this matter were common—common to my class—and can be stated briefly. For some years, combining certain training and a lifelong interest in natural history with an ability to write, I have earned a pleasant and easy living as an essayist, a commentator on the affairs of other species. Being moderately successful at an agreeable trade, being forty-three years old, I was consequently restless, feeling now and then that my life was too agreeable, that the soft sheets were getting me, that it would be a good thing to send out the laundry and pick up new challenges, physical, intellectual, emotional. Also I believed or had convinced myself that change would be good for the entire family, that the children would benefit from getting out of their cozy life in the gentle Appalachians, from poking about for a time in the larger world.

Especially I thought a drastic change would be good—was, in fact, necessary—for Ky and Terry, who had been close friends all their lives. Both were in their middle teens and their sap was flowing vigorously. Both were excruciatingly bored with and increasingly hostile toward school, their schoolboy status, the village life style. I thought they had good reason for being bored and hostile. In the interests of an almost worthless education, small-town gentility, their natural exuberance and vitality were being suffocated. Their legitimate ambition for adventure, real work, freedom was continually thwarted by petty tyrannies and tyrants. It seemed that if I stirred my stumps, got out of the soft sheets, I could release them from the prison to which I had helped commit them, in which they had been left too long.

Such itches, irritations, desires might have been partially soothed by sailing to Australia, packing through Patagonia, moving to Belgrade, or by one of the other ingenious activities designed to alleviate middle-class, middle-aged angst. However, given my tastes, it was inevitable that we should, if not watch coatis, do something similar. For as long as I can remember, I have been a kind of animalcoholic addicted to associating with other beasts. Money and time that might have been spent more conventionally have always been invested in animal studies and expeditions, in maintaining an establishment that is often more of a preserve, sanctuary, cageless zoo than a household. The extent of my addiction to other species may be somewhat special, but again I think the motivation for it is a common one. What C. S. Lewis once elegantly identified as "the love of other bloods" is a general human response. It does not seem to me to be a trivial, aberrant passion any more than is a passion for music. It is deep rooted, a continuing stimulus to speculation, a persistent source of pleasure for most men. It is in a sense an innate behavioral characteristic which serves to identify and define man. Rather than considering myself handicapped by my inordinate love of other bloods, I am usually grateful that I have had exceptional opportunities to express, consummate it.

So far as the coati specifically was concerned, several happenings had directed my attention to this animal and ultimately sent us packing across the continent to find them. For several previous years, I had simultaneously been working on a book about animal communication and a study of what might simply be called the emotional responses of raccoons. Inevitably these two interests merged, creating a new one. I yield to no one in my admiration for the raccoon. If, as the old literary test goes, I were to be marooned on a desert island and could share it with only one other species, I would choose (or would have before meeting coatis) the raccoon. However, despite the many virtues of this instructive mammal, the raccoon is relatively solitary and in consequence is not especially communicative. Therefore after a time I began wanting to become acquainted with a raccoon-like mammal who was also social and would thus presumably be more demonstrative. Selecting such a creature was not difficult, since the coati is the only such animal existent.

There were other attractive features about the coati, apparent even from a distance. The animal is diurnal and terrestrial, which meant we could deal with it in our own element, would not need complicated equipment or facilities just to locate the creature. The range of the coatis made it obvious that if we were to see them in the wild we would have to travel to and live in a new, un-Appalachian-like country. Also, search of mammalian literature confirmed a background impression that very little was known about this creature, virtually nothing about it in the United States. Therefore an obvious objective and attraction was to learn what we could of this mammal, perhaps contribute something to the knowledge of its natural history.

There was or we hoped there would be another purpose and value to our year. Despite the current fashionable interest in such subjects and causes as conservation, environmentalism, we generally find it difficult to believe truly in the fundamental ecological principle: that the planet is inhabited by a multitude of separate but equal and interrelated communities. The fact that other species, societies of other bloods, are our peers is perhaps less easily accepted now by our consumptive culture, in these exploitative times, than it was by men we call primitive but for whom biological egalitarianism was a fact of life, a matter of firm faith. Long before we met one, it seemed that the coati, being a tribal, foraging mammal (and thus closer, more comprehensible to us than a fish or an insect), might clearly illustrate the point that our peers exist, that the social organizations of other bloods are not failed, flawed, emerging human societies but may be rich, subtle, successful, if, to us, foreign communities. We had the notion that if we could find coati communities, remain with them for a time, the experience would be satisfying and instructive for us; that the description of the experience might be vicariously satisfying and instructive for others. As it happened, we were successful in finding coati tribes along the border and were able to associate with them far more intimately than we had thought or hoped we could. Whether or not we have been successful in other matters—e.g., demonstrating reasons for our belief that we share a world with many peers—remains to be determined by the following.

RECONNAISSANCE

The coati scheme had simmered, so to speak, on the back burner of our minds for several years, during which time Ann and I flew to southern Arizona three times for domestic logistic purposes, to scout about the country, talk to local residents, game and wildlife men. So far as the coatis were concerned, the information we were able to collect was scarce, poor, and generally discouraging. Despite its being the only place in the country where the animals were theoretically in any abundance, we could find no coati gurus in southern Arizona. Ranchers were thinking about cows, coyotes, and mountain lions; state game agents about deer, javelina, turkey; field biologists about masked bobwhites, Sonoran antelope, desert sheep. The casual consensus was that there had been many coatis along the border in the late 1950s but they had died off in a distemper-like epidemic (which proved to be true) and were presumably very scarce or nonexistent (which fortunately was untrue, or at least untrue by 1970). Our ambition to find and stay with groups of coatis was viewed with varying degrees of scorn, amusement, sympathy. As to the crucial matter of where was the best place to look for coatis, the answer of all hands was usually to the effect "If you'd been here ten years ago, I could have showed you a pack almost anytime you wanted, but I haven't seen any in a long time. I suppose if you really want to try, your best bet is to look around in the Huachucas, talk to some of the old-timers over there, but I doubt if you'll have much luck."

The Huachuca Mountains, which rise on the Mexican border between Nogales and Bisbee, being so often suggested as the best of a bad lot of possibilities, I decided during our winter trip of 1970 to get into this range at least briefly, to spend a day and night hiking up, camping in Bear Canyon, a big, tortured gorge cut out of the western flank of the range. Like so many other subsequent happenings, the choice was a lucky one, based on nothing more substantial than that my topographic map showed a road, passable by car, intersecting a pack trail going up Bear Canyon. Now having become more extensively acquainted with the Huachucas, I still think that Bear Canyon, into which I first accidentally stumbled, is the most attractive spot in these mountains, one of the most attractive places I know in this country. Had I first wandered into one of the dry, chaparral-choked canyons, my interest in and enthusiasm for the Huachucas might have been less, my attention directed elsewhere.

On the February day I was in Bear Canyon, the temperature was in the seventies, the air dry and clear, the cloudless sky so blue as to be almost black. A year later, we would have seen, lived in so many such winter days as to consider them ordinary, but the first time, fresh from Pennsylvania, the weather seemed remarkable, virtually perfect. I started walking from the gravel road, at 5,000 feet of elevation, at about the eastern limit of the San Rafael Valley, where the short-grass prairie, golden brown in the winter, began to thin out, give way to open thickets of oak and alligator juniper. Within less than a half-mile, I was well into another life zone, a mixed deciduous forest of oak, sycamore, walnut, madroña, mountain mahogany, manzanita, grape, a few maples and piñon and a great many plants, bushes, trees which I did not know. Bear Creek, a clear, musical little stream, spilled down the canyon in a series of gentle steps. Underneath the lip of the ledges there were deep pools fringed with aquatic plants in which there were chub minnows, leopard frogs, turtles. All of which delighted me for no better reason than that it was familiar. The ravine, the brook, the woodland, with a few additions and deletions, could have been Tom's Creek Valley, in which we live in south-central Pennsylvania.

When it comes to natural aesthetics, most of us are strongly conditioned in favor of scenery such as that inside Bear Canyon: a brook, soft grass, shady glades. A principal reason for this preference may be that it is similar to the scene which so appealed to English Romantic poets and landscape artists of the eighteenth century and their cultural descendants, the nineteenth-century New England essayists and naturalists. For better or worse, these critics have largely shaped the notions of many of us as to what is beautiful and what is ugly in nature. You can see their Atlantic taste reflected in many of our contemporary activities and preoccupations: the kind of parks we build and use; the green, open wilderness land we battle to preserve; the forsythia bushes and birdbaths we buy to create bosky glades on our half-acre lots; the way we mow our grass; the sort of postcards we send; the colored slides we take. In Phoenix, Tucson, Nogales, communities located in an environment as different from that of Avon or Concord as it is possible to find on this planet, there is everywhere evidence of the strong preference for the English park, the New England countryside scene. In these desert towns, those who can afford it have installed ingenious hydraulic systems so as to cover little patches of desert gravel with swatches of greensward, to support a few trees which will cast a dappled shadow or two under the fierce sun.

All of which is not to argue that aesthetic standards and prejudices are silly, much less wicked, but only that the mythical boob who says he doesn't know much about art but knows what he likes may not be so silly as critics with a stake in some particular system of aesthetic values have led us to believe. I liked the Appalachian floor at Bear Canyon better than I did the desert country, not because it was formally superior but because of what I am and have been made.

The best sight of the day came in midafternoon while I was sitting on a ledge on the side of the canyon taking the sun and listening to the peculiar whirring noise Arizona blue jays make when they fly. I heard some snuffling and scuffling in a scrub-oak thicket across the creek, and shortly thereafter nine javelinas, including two young animals, appeared. They were scruffy, dirty grayish-brown creatures who blended in cunningly with the weathered rock behind them. Javelinas are long-legged, with nothing of a barnyard pig's waddle about their movements. The two young ones particularly were skittish. Every now and then they would become alarmed—sometimes alarming each other—give a couple of little skips and disappear, a few stones, a scraggly bush or two being enough to hide them. Seconds later, they would move again, and a spot that was apparently empty would suddenly have a little pig in it.

Javelinas have a ferocious reputation, there being many stories in the Southwest about them treeing all sorts of animals, from mountain lions to men. Unquestionably these wild pigs, which usually travel in herds of a dozen or so, are formidable. Adults may weigh forty pounds or more. They are equipped with sizable tusk-like teeth, and they are physically capable of defending themselves against virtually anything they may encounter, except a man with a gun. However, there is no reason to assume they are any more pugnacious or aggressive than other wild animals.

Lyle Sowls, an Arizona zoologist who has spent considerable time watching javelinas, believes poor vision may account for some of the horror stories about them. Though they possess relatively good hearing and a keen sense of smell, javelinas are notoriously shortsighted. According to Dr. Sowls, a typical reaction of javelinas upon hearing or smelling something that alarms them is to rush about trying to locate the trouble and get close enough to recognize it. If a man stands still, says Dr. Sowls, who has practiced what he preaches, the pigs, after coming up close enough to identify him, will normally turn and run in the other direction. If, however, the source of the alarm starts to run, the javelinas are very likely to pursue it, right to the foot of a tree if necessary.

Whatever they may have been capable of under other circumstances, the band I watched were placid. The wind was blowing away from them and they seemed unaware that I was sitting only a hundred yards off. They nuzzled and skipped about the thicket for twenty minutes or so, and then, simultaneously, completely disappeared. I did not see or hear them again. After they left, I crossed the canyon and stream to look at the place where they had been working. All day I had been seeing little holes and piles of dirt dug up by some foraging animal. Anyone with even a casual acquaintance with the area could have identified these signs but, being a complete stranger, I had wondered about them. The obvious answer was the javelinas, whose tracks were plentiful. However, more wishfully than otherwise, I did not want to exclude entirely the possibility that coatis, who with their strong forepaws are also habitual diggers, might have made the holes. The matter was settled conclusively, there being fresh diggings in the thicket where I watched the javelinas.

At about 7,000 feet, I climbed out of Pennsylvania into Vermont, or maybe Colorado, a dark forest of tall evergreens: ponderosa, white, Apache pines; blue and Engelmann spruce; Douglas fir. There were snowbanks under overhanging cliffs, water trickling over moss, and the footing became sloppy, boggy. Stellar jays screamed in the pines and I came across mountain-lion tracks in the snow, scats—droppings—along the trail.

I camped that night at Bear Spring, a big, deep, all-weather outflow which rises in a grove of mature pine and fir. In the woods behind the water there is an old corral, built and used years ago by cowpunchers, prospectors, other trail riders. Beside the spring is a wide ledge, now a foot or so thick with accumulated pine straw. I spread out a poncho and sleeping bag on the needles, arranged in a circle around me everything I could possibly need during the night: two avocados, a piece of cheese, some hard rolls, a can of beer, a chocolate bar, tobacco, a jackknife, a flashlight, and my boots.

The sensual joys of bedding down outside—lungs full of fresh air, with starlight, moonbeams, owl music, wind tunes —have been persistently touted to the point that they have become clichés suitable for cigarette advertisements. These pleasures do exist, but the enjoyment of them rests upon another condition, one which is implied but rarely specified. If you lie down at dusk and plan to be there until at least daybreak, you have time and are in a mood for something in addition to the little death of an eight-hour sleep. In such a twelve-hour period, you may wake up half a dozen times and stay awake for five minutes or an hour, not as an insomniac but because there are a lot of pleasant, entertaining things to do: eat an avocado, sip on a beer, chew a little tobacco, listen to a large unidentified animal walk on the mountain-side above, look for constellations, and above all let your mind run free. During the night at Bear Spring, in a lei-surely way, I wrote a novel, a long essay on the play of dogs, made up spring workout schedules for the members of the girls' track team I coach, catalogued the equipment I would need for the coati project, and visited the Scented Grass Hills, an arctic peninsula in Great Bear Lake. There are always a lot of people around during these dreamy night watches. The people who stop by are the ones you have loved or admired or been interested in, never the fools, rascals, and monsters you have known. A park ranger who had told me about butterflies in the Huachucas, a twelve-year-old quarter miler, a Jamaican botanist, a college room-mate, and a girl I had not seen in twenty years were among the group who stopped by Bear Spring.

In the middle of the night, I was awakened by a light snow squall. Directly overhead there were heavy clouds, but elsewhere the moon and stars were visible, reflecting brightly off the rocks below. It was a nice scene and a sort of funny one—traveling across the continent, out of a Pennsylvania winter, to lie on the ground and be snowed on in Arizona. It was the kind of thing that amused my father, who had a lot to do with developing my tastes, and who has been dead thirteen years. So I told him about it, and then we talked for quite a while about other matters of mutual interest.

During the night, it occurred to me that it would be a good thing, as soon as light came, to climb up from the spring to Bear Saddle, on the topmost ridge of the Huachucas, and wait there for the sun. When it got light enough to do this, I had to reconvince myself of the merits of the plan, arguing against the warmth of the sleeping bag. I finally did so by applying the logical crusher—how was I to know if I would ever again have a chance to sit in Bear Saddle at dawn?

The sunrise, from the vantage point of 8,200 feet, was—as I had advertised it to myself—well worth seeing. The sun came up behind me, from the direction of Tombstone. The light spilled through the saddle, changing the blues and grays in the canyons below to reds and burnts, then progressed across the San Rafael Valley, up which Coronado, looking for the golden cities of Kansas, had marched some 155,000 mornings previously. I waited until the sun lit the Canelo Hills, the Patagonia and the Santa Rita mountains, across the valley, to the north of Nogales and the Mexican border.

When I left Bear Canyon that day, I had decided that—come heaven, hell, or distemper epidemics—I would return to these mountains by fall, that they were where I wanted to watch coatimundis.

2

The Chulo

Since the coatimundi is not well known, either popularly or scientifically, it seems appropriate to introduce this creature at least casually before proceeding with an account of how and why it so engaged our interest. The coati (*Nasua narica*) is one of a family of four medium-sized carnivores found in the New World, the Procyonidae. The other members are the kinkajou, the ring-tailed cat, and the more familiar (to North Americans) raccoon. In South and Central America the coati is widely distributed, being relatively common from Argentina to northern Mexico. In the United States, the coati is rare, designated as a peripheral animal by the U.S. Bureau of Fish and Wildlife. It is occasionally reported along the Rio Grande Valley in Texas and New Mexico, but many of these sightings may be of escapees, since imported animals are often stocked in pet shops. The only place where the coati is found regularly and in any abundance in this country is southern Arizona. There, when conditions are right, a resident population of from 500 to 1,500 animals inhabits a series of wild, isolated "mountain islands" which rise on or straddle the Arizona-Sonora border. In these mountains the coati is a newcomer, according to the records of collectors, having pioneered north and entered the United States within the last century.

Even in the southern Arizona bush, the coati is an uncommon animal, regarded as something of a curiosity. Prospectors and cowpunchers, who see the animals most often, sometimes call them Mexican monkeys. Others believe the coati to be a peculiar kind of arboreal anteater. More generally in this region, coatis are called "chulo bears" or simply "chulos," and will be so referred to hereafter. The derivation of this name is obscure, but because it has a triple meaning along the border, the complications can confuse and embarrass the newcomer. "Chulo," the name of the animal, is usually slurred in conversation, pronounced "chula." "Chula" means "pretty, nice, attractive" and also, depending on the circumstances, refers to a wild girl, not a professional but an easy and willing pickup. Thus innocent strangers, poking about Lochiel, Palominas, Naco, and other border villages, cowcamps, and mines, inquiring soberly about chulos, their natural history, provide local residents with considerable good, clean ribald fun.

There is a family resemblance between the raccoon and the chulo. Both are medium-sized (the coon is a bit heavier, the chulo longer) animals. Technically they are carnivores, but in fact are economic opportunists foraging for and enjoying a wide range of foods—vegetable, invertebrate, reptilian, amphibian, avian, and mammalian. Both are plantigrades; that is, they walk more or less flatfooted, as do, among other beasts, bears and men. The distinctive rolling gait accounts in part for the name chulo bear. Both chulos and coons have facial masks, though they are the reverse images of each other, the chulo having white facial markings set on dark brown fur, while the coon's bandit mask is black on light gray or silver. Both animals have considerable tails, the coon's being bushier, the chulo's longer, both of which are marked with lighter rings.

Despite vaguely resembling the more common animal, the chulo looks to most Americans like an exotic creature, quite different from any of our other mammals. The most distinctive features are the nose and the tail. The nose—in fact, the entire muzzle—is long, slender, flexible, somewhat like that of the anteater, and is often used in anteater fashion, for grubbing, gouging, poking about in the earth and litter. The tail is about two feet long, as long as the rest of the body. It is slim, furred, looks somewhat like that of a spider monkey. The tail is used with great expertise as a balancing pole, a bracing rod when the chulo climbs in trees and on rocks. However, it is not, as has sometimes been claimed, prehensile, cannot be used for grasping objects or looping around limbs.

The foreshoulders, the forepaws, which are tipped with heavy blunt claws like those of a skunk or a badger, are very strong. While looking for edibles, a fifteen-pound chulo will work through a rockslide, rather casually flipping over thirty- or forty-pound rocks. The long chulo jaw is set in front with small, sharp incisors with which the animal seizes, nips and dispatches small prey—insects, lizards, and snakes. The canine teeth are exceptionally large, larger than those of a raccoon, and are used for killing prey and in self-defense. A cornered chulo, being a remarkably quick and well-armed animal, is a formidable opponent for almost anything. Dale Lee, a veteran and the best-known mountain-lion hunter in southern Arizona, has lost two of his lion dogs to chulos. Both were lead dogs who ran ahead of the pack and into a tribe of chulos. They were slashed to ribbons, apparently without being able to kill a chulo. Since Lee cannot break his pack of running chulos as he can break them of chasing deer and javelinas, he is one of the chulos' sworn enemies along the border.

Chulos are shortsighted, as are many animals of the heavy undergrowth. They hear moderately well—about as well, it seems, as a man. They have an exceptional olfactory sense, at least as good as—maybe better than, it sometimes seemed to us—coyotes or hounds. Chulos are almost entirely diurnal, most of their foraging and other activities taking place between dawn and dusk. In the more southern part of their range, in the tropical forests, chulos build nest platforms in trees, where they rest, sleep, bear their young. In southern Arizona, however, they den at night, have their cubs in small caves and crevices, generally in limestone outcroppings. Also during the day they often nap, socialize, groom each other on sheltered ledges projecting out from cliff faces.

As such things are currently measured (by men, using tests based on human value systems), chulos are regarded as being, like the raccoon, animals of considerable intelligence. They learn quickly from experience, adapt readily to new situations and stimuli: i.e., experiences, situations, stimuli which men can conceive of being important. Though it cannot be demonstrated on a bar graph, there is much circumstantial evidence indicating that the chulo is an animal whose emotional reactions, inner life, are, again from our viewpoint, rich and varied.

The most unusual characteristic of the chulos, that which sets them apart from all the other procyonids, from most other carnivores, is not physical but in a sense psychological. The chulo is a truly communal animal; now that the wolves have been all but exterminated, the chulo is the only communal carnivore in the United States, one of the few in the world. A chulo tribe, as we came to think of and refer to their social unit, is made up of animals of various sexes and ages, from infants to ancients. Most of the animals in a tribe may be rather closely related, but the tribe is more than an extended family group. For example, the protection, education, and entertainment of the young are the principal occupations of the tribe during most of the year and engage all the adults, not just the parents of the young.

At least in southern Arizona, a chulo tribe is made up of fifteen to forty individual animals who operate throughout the year in a territory of some five to ten square miles. Usually the tribal activities are confined to one large canyon complex. Occasionally two neighboring tribes will meet at a good food source and for a short time commingle without hostility. These infrequent tribal conventions probably account for local reports and stories about chulos foraging in packs of several hundred. Such accounts are unquestionably exaggerated, since even in their best years (like most species at the margin of their ranges, the chulo population in the United States declines and increases periodically, in cyclical fashion) it is unlikely that there are ever two hundred chulos within visiting range of each other. Also, unless one is completely familiar with the individual animals, it is difficult to count chulos accurately in the rough, rocky bush of the southern Arizona island mountains.

A chulo tribe is one of the more intricately, subtly organized mammalian social groups, less complex than most human societies, comparable perhaps to those of the chimpanzee or the baboon. There are certain innate behavior patterns corresponding figuratively to human laws, traditions, rituals which are common to all the tribes. However, no two tribes have precisely the same life style, since in addition to the genetically fixed responses, tribal activities also reflect the individual wisdom, ignorance, idiosyncrasies, learning, and experience of the principal adult members of the group.

Sketchy as this introduction is, it is still somewhat more comprehensive (since it is fleshed out with our own field observations) than was the chulo information which we brought with us to Arizona. There are, in fact, only two important studies of the natural history of the species. In 1961, Arthur Risser, a candidate for a master's degree at the

University of Arizona, selected the coatimundi as the subject for his dissertation. Unfortunately, Risser came to the border country during one of the periodic low points in the chulo cycle, when there were very few animals in Arizona. Though he worked hard, as his paper indicates and local residents confirmed, Risser, during a year and a half of intermittent field study, caught only brief and rare glimpses of chulo tribes. Beginning in 1958, John Kaufmann, a graduate student at the University of California, spent parts of the following two years observing chulos at the Barro Colorado Research Station in Panama, and in 1962 published a doctoral dissertation based on his experience there. Kaufmann's principal interest was in the ecology of the animal. While both his paper and that of Risser provided us with useful background information (as perhaps our work will be useful to subsequent students), the tribal life of chulos in the United States was for practical purposes a virgin field of study.

That so little is known about such a common, curious, and eminently studyable animal as the chulo illustrates a peculiar situation in the field of natural science. Though the neatly organized guide and reference books might indicate otherwise, the truth is that there are very few feral animals in the United States whose natural history is adequately understood. Furthermore, those we know most about usually belong to one of two classes, both of which in a real sense represent the least important elements of our fauna. These two classes are: the game animals, creatures who have been studied so as to provide better, more abundant sport for gunners; and the rare and endangered species, sad sick animals who are so near extinction as to have virtually no ecological influence, but about whom a good many people are now feeling guilty and remorseful. In between these extremes is the bulk of our fauna, species for which we have found no direct economic or emotional use, and which we therefore have not been seriously motivated to study or understand. The chulo is one of this large mid-band of creatures.

The lack of information presented obvious problems as to where and how to begin our study, but there were compensations, principally the rare and exhilarating sense of being explorers, of feeling that we were seeing or knowing things that others had not looked for, or had overlooked. During our eleven months, Terry, Ky, John (who joined us several weeks after we arrived and became the fourth permanent member of the chulo cadre), and I spent 290 days and nights in the Arizona bush, during the course of which we put in some 8,500 "man observation hours," as they are called in the field naturalists' jargon. During these hours, we recorded 5,000 observations of chulos, some being only brief sightings, others representing many consecutive hours, even days, spent with the same animals. Most of our observations were made of two chulo tribes, one in the Baboquivari Mountains, the second in the Huachucas, that we were fortunate to locate, in a sense privileged to associate with intimately. In some ways, we were comparable to students who take themselves off to strange places and become absorbed in the culture of Bushmen or Irishmen. But in a fundamental way ours was a more foreign trip than any which an anthropologist or a sociologist can take. We and the chulos with whom we lived are, of course, of different bloods.

One evening toward the end of our year, an evening like so many summer ones in these Southwestern mountains, clear, cool, quiet, bugless, we were sitting on the stoop of the cabin which we used in the Huachucas, watching a gang of juvenile chulos, the young of 1970, tribal teen-agers, helling about the premises. Despite the splendor, the satisfactions of the moment, we were all suffering from twinges of depression, thinking that there would be so few other such evenings, that our days as chulo watchers were very much numbered. In an effort to put a better face on the situation and on us, I said something to the effect that while it might not be much, like being the best snowshoer in Saudi Arabia, we almost certainly knew more about chulos at that moment, were closer to being adoptive members of a chulo tribe than any other men in the world. I said that whatever else happened to us, I thought we should be able to remember that moment—the whole year—with true pride and satisfaction.

3

Chulo Country—
the Huachucas

HABITAT AND INHABITANTS

Though we are glad we did not have to test the hypothesis, we should have been able to have a good year in the Huachucas had we never seen a chulo. For anyone with natural-history interests, these mountains (as well as three similar border ranges, the Chiricahuas to the east, the Santa Ritas and the Baboquivaris to the west) are extraordinary wilderness areas. For example, Donald Hoffmeister and Woodrow Goodpaster, who twenty years ago compiled the only checklist of mammals of the area, identified seventy species in the 150 square miles of the Huachucas and their environs, more species than are native to the entire state of Illinois. Ornithologists have discovered that 25 percent of all the species of birds which nest in the United States nest in this small range. The reptile, insect, plant life is comparably plentiful and diverse. There are students (catering to zoological and botanical field parties is something of a cottage industry in the area) who claim that the flora and fauna of these southern Arizona mountains is richer, more complex than in any similarly sized region of the New World.

The unusual abundance and variety of plant and animal life is the result of an unusual combination of geographic and geologic phenomena. The Huachucas rise on the Mexican border, extend northward some twenty-five miles, and the range varies between four and six miles in width. The principal peaks, Carr, Huachuca, Miller, are more than 9,000 feet above sea level, with the elevation of the main ridge being generally about 8,000 feet. The range is a new, rough, sharp one, appearing to be—in fact, being—an island rising up abruptly from the surrounding ocean of desert.

Being high, these mountain islands of southern Arizona are relatively moist and cool. The peaks in a sense draw down water, creating rain shadows behind them. Thirty inches of water, as rain, snow, mist, may fall in a year on the upper ridges while the desert below receives only a third as much. The water trickles and seeps down the slopes to the grassy valleys at the foot, wetting the land in between. Even in late spring and early summer, the annual drought period, there are always places where there is open water in the mountains. For the same reason—elevation—temperature on the peaks is some 20 degrees lower than in the desert flats, mean annual average being 50 degrees as compared to 70. This combination of southerly location and elevation (the Huachucas are the most southerly highlands in the United States) is responsible for an extraordinary number of microenvironments being compressed into a small area. Commencing in the desert south of Tucson, proceeding toward the crest of the Huachucas forty miles away, one passes through miniature replicas of virtually every major environment, except coastal, to be found in the adjacent forty-eight states. Just above the desert ocean are what amounts to the beaches of the mountain islands, the short-grass prairie valleys, mile after mile of knee-high grass. The prairies are cut by ravines, mouths of the mountain canyons, the floors of which are tropical in character and vegetation. Above the prairie, from roughly 5,000 to 6,500 feet, is a broad band of mixed, largely deciduous forest in which oaks, of which there are fifteen species in the Huachucas alone, are the most prominent tree. Depending on the local conditions of soil, shade, water, and temperature, the nature of the woodlands varies considerably from place to place, a hundred yards sometimes being enough in which to pass from one microenvironment to another. Above the deciduous zone is the evergreen forest, which also gradually changes in character, culminating in a Canadian zone at the summit.

This variety of environment is translated into a variety of habitat for plants and animals. Species whose typical range is far from the border country have, permanently or temporarily, found suitable niches in these mountains. The large, various mammalian community of the Huachucas is an obvious example of this phenomenon. There are, or were in the recent past, some thirty species of rodents, including such diverse creatures as deer mice, prairie dogs, porcupines, and beavers. There are four rabbits, two jacks and two cottontails; four skunks, spotted, striped, hooded, and hog-nosed; sixteen bats; two shrews; and an opossum. The javelina or peccary, the mule and white-tailed deer, the pronghorn antelope range the area. Carnivores are especially well represented. Mountain lion, bobcat, black bear, coyote, timber wolf, kit and gray foxes, badgers hunt the mountains and adjacent prairies. Three tropical cats—the jaguar, the ocelot, and the jaguarundi or otter cat—occasionally wander in from Mexico. Three of the four procyonids—the raccoon, the ring-tailed cat, and our chulo—are permanent residents.

An ecological factor accounts for the continued existence, if not origin, of so many diverse, relatively exotic species in these mountains. They are, always have been, sparsely inhabited by man. The Huachucas (the name is Apache, meaning Thunder Mountains) apparently constituted a natural boundary between the Apaches to the east, the Papagos to the north and west, and the Yaquis to the south. They were used as open hunting land but never permanently occupied by these tribes. After the coming of the Latins and Anglos, the mountains were used, but because of their isolation, difficulty of the terrain, they were not used hard or regularly. Ranching was and remains the principal occupation in the area, but most of the cattle are kept in the prairie ranges and on the lower flanks of the mountains. The high meadows are small, fragile, and it is costly to move stock to and retrieve it from them. Some timber was cut late in the last century but the more valuable trees—ponderosa pine, Douglas fir, Englemann spruce—grow in scattered groves and again were hard to get at or get out. For a century, prospectors have scratched about in the Huachucas, which are only thirty miles west of the once rich lodes and mining towns of Tombstone and Bisbee. They have found a variety of minerals, gold, silver, copper, zinc, molybdenum, and others, but never in sufficient quantities or in accessible enough places to pay for large-scale mining operations.

At the north end of the range there is a sprawling 75,000-acre military reservation, Fort Huachuca, established as a cavalry post during the Apache wars and now serving as an electronics center. Though the reservation extends up to the crest of the range, most of the installations and activities are in the flat arid lands below and the military has little direct effect on the ecology of the mountain. At the gates of the fort there has sprung up in the last decade an ugly, jerry-built Army town, Sierra Vista, of some 15,000 people. At the southern end of the mountains is a small, isolated, attractive unit of the National Park system, the Coronado National Memorial. The park commemorates the fact or tradition that Francisco Vásquez de Coronado passed by the Huachucas in 1541, marching northward on his incredible journey of exploration and conquest. The memorial, directly on the Mexican border, occupies less than 3,000 acres in Montezuma Canyon, the most southerly canyon complex in the Huachucas. Between the park and the fort, most of the mountain land is owned by the U.S. Forest Service, is administered as a unit of the million-acre Coronado National Forest, which sprawls across southern Arizona in a series of noncontiguous tracts. Like all national forests, the Coronado is open to hikers, hunters, fishermen, campers, and increasingly recreationists are discovering and using the Huachucas. However, in general their activities are centered around Parker Lake, an artificial Forest Service impoundment and campground on the western side of the mountain. In most places, the Huachucas are so rugged and wild that casual visitors have no desire to bushwhack; they remain on a few cleared trails and leave the rest of the land and its inhabitants undisturbed.

The Huachucas are circled by a single public road. From Sierra Vista, the Army town, to the Coronado National Memorial, the national park, there is a twenty-mile section of paved highway, along which, in the canyon mouths, there is some residential development, mostly homes of civilian and military personnel. At the park, the road becomes rutted tortuous gravel, turns west, and at 7,000 feet crosses the range through Montezuma Pass. Thereafter it continues in a northerly direction following the western flank of the mountain and eventually, after forty rough miles, circles back to Sierra Vista. Between Montezuma Pass and Parker Lake, a twelve-mile stretch in which we did most of our chulo watching, there are only eight permanent residents.

Some of these facts of geography and natural history we knew before coming to the Huachucas or could deduce from looking at a map of the range itself. However, in general the Huachucas were *terra incognita* for us. Beyond the many facts we were ignorant of—where the trails ran, how the water flowed, what grew and lived where and why—we lacked the feel of the mountains, the confidence and familiarity that comes of living in and from a piece of land.

After what seemed like an interminable getting-ready, getting-there period, which stretched across the summer from Pennsylvania to Arizona, Ky, Terry, and I got to the Huachucas on the last day of August. (Ann and the girls remained in Tucson and commenced school.) We drove down from Tucson in the afternoon and, not knowing anywhere else to go, camped at the Forest Service recreation area that had been bulldozed clear above Parker Lake. It is a conventional public campground for out-of-cardoorsmen, a parking lot with bolted-down tables, grills, and toilets, but we were glad to get there. The rainy season was ending and after supper we sat with our tea mugs, staring at the western flank of the Huachucas which were draped in mist, occasionally illuminated by flashes of lightning. The dark empty mountains represented the end of a long, complicated trip and in them lay a year of our future. In different ways, to different degrees, we were apprehensive about how we would each cope with this place toward which we had been heading for so long, about which we had thought so much.

In anticipation and recognition of this mood which had been building for months, I had told the boys in various ways that we would explore the mountains as we had other wildernesses, *poco a poco*. What we found and learned one day would largely determine what we did the next. The chances were against our locating chulos in the first weeks, even months, and the success of our year, our pleasure, did not depend on doing so.

All of which was true, but does not completely satisfy you if you are seventeen, have improbably left school for a year, traveled 2,500 miles ostensibly to hunt for a small animal. Terry is the most direct, pragmatic of us all, has a kind of crunch-ahead, eye-on-the-main-chance personality. "Where," he asked after we had stared at the Huachucas for a time, "do you think those chulos are at?"

"Over there," I said, waving vaguely at the twenty-five-mile-long mass of dark brooding canyon, cliff, and forest— "someplace, maybe."

New Country

Even before we left the mountains late in the summer of 1971, we had begun to look back to the previous fall, our first two months in the Hauchucas, with a certain nostalgia. It was a pleasant, exciting time for many reasons, but we remember it now, enjoyed it then particularly, because we were as free in body, mind, time as we had ever been, perhaps as free as we will ever be. By conventional standards, we were of course conventionally free throughout the year, how or whether we studied chulos being a matter of absolute indifference to everyone else in the world. However, later, after we met and became preoccupied with the animals, they and our interest restricted our activities. We had the feeling that we should be where the chulos were, that it would be a great waste of luck if we missed seeing, learning what we could, because of sloth or insufficient discipline. The more time we spent with the chulos and the closer we came to the end of our time, the more we begrudged time spent away from them.

For example, in the spring and early summer of 1971, during the severe drought, there remained only one natural swimming place in the mountains. This was a six-foot-deep pothole eaten by Bear Creek out of the red rock in the floor of Bear Canyon. It was a very pleasant spot. The water was clear and cool, the rocks around it flat and warm, but shaded by sycamore and walnut foliage. As the drought, temperature, and dust increased, so did the attraction of this swimming hole. Living as we did, we could have driven over from Montezuma Canyon every afternoon, lounged in and around the pothole for as long as we wanted. However, though we talked a lot about it, we actually went there no more than once every ten days or so. Even when we did go, we went two at a time, the other two staying behind to—so to speak—watch the store, the chulos.

In the fall, there were no such self-imposed restraints. Since we needed to learn something about the character, the ecology of the country before we could make any judgments about chulos, anything we did or observed was of value. We entered the mountains during the last days of August with the simplest possible plan. We wanted to explore each of the major canyon complexes on the western slope of the Huachucas. If we found chulos, chulo signs, so much the better, but at first the principal purpose was to learn the land. We ruled out the eastern slope of the range, which is skirted by a paved road along which are clusters of small houses and trailers occupied by Fort Huachuca employees. We preferred the wilder country on the western side for essentially aesthetic reasons, and hoped that the chulos might also.

Since we could improve ourselves wherever we went, whatever we did, our ignorance gave us almost total freedom. It also made us hypersensitive, alert, as if we were camped in an emotional nettle patch. This is a sensation which unfamiliar country commonly stimulates in people who are curious about zoological, botanical, geological phenomena. There are, of course, enough natural wonders and mysteries within a hundred feet of everyone's doorstep to occupy the mind and senses for a lifetime. However, few of us are sufficiently imaginative, disciplined, or energetic to remain forever or even long contented in a raindrop ocean or grass-roots jungle. We need the grossly new and strange to get our juices flowing. This was the stimulation we found in the Huachucas, where everything we first saw, touched, smelled, felt raised the most obvious questions of what and why.

Related to the ignorance new country exposes, the curiosity it arouses, is another but deeper, perhaps almost instinctive sensation, the atavistic reaction of the out-of-territory animal. In the new mountains there did not appear to be (in fact, were not) greater risks than in the Blue Ridge. Yet the Huachucas felt, looked, and were so different from anything we knew that at first we had the vague notion that there were things which might jump at us; that we were likely to blunder into situations which would require immediate, extemporaneous evasive action. Fear is too sharp, too specific a word to describe this situation. It is rather a kind of generalized wariness which promotes sensitivity, alertness.

We had to learn the properties of the new rocks and ledges on which we were climbing, about the effects of eight and nine thousand feet of altitude, the high ultraviolet content of the unshaded sun beating down through the thin air, the logic and dependability of javelina trails which were often the only paths through the thick scrub. Though we did not like admitting it even to ourselves, we worried at first about rattlesnakes. While we did not have a special interest in herpetology, none of us were phobic about snakes, having collected and carried even venomous species when there was some reason to do so. Nevertheless we could not completely rid ourselves of the notion that we were heading into the heart of poison country. Partly this was because of tall snake stories, which are numerous in southern Arizona, and also partly because it is a fact that the Huachucas are good snake country, as they are good country for so many wild things. (Twelve species of rattlers live in or near these mountains, including several small high-altitude snakes which are found only in the mountain islands. Several venomous oddities—the Arizona coral snake, two rare, mildly poisonous back-fanged creatures—live in the vicinity. For good measure there are a lot of scorpions, and the Gila monster is occasionally found in the high desert at the eastern foot of the Huachucas.)

Once we got settled in the new country, we found that snakewise things were about the same in the Arizona mountains as elsewhere; i.e., we heard a great many more snake stories than we heard or saw snakes. According to our notes, we encountered thirty-two rattlesnakes during the year in which we were constantly poking about in the bush. This does not deny the fact that there are a large variety, perhaps a large number, of snakes in the Huachucas; it only confirms the obvious fact that rattlers and men occupy very different niches, meet each other less often than men, at least, fear they will. In Arizona, at the elevations at which we were working, the temperatures began to dip into the forties in November, and at that time snakes of all sorts began to hibernate in dens. They did not emerge until February or later, and thus for a third of the year there were for practical purposes no rattlers abroad. Even during the warmer weather there are phenomena serving to separate our two species. Being cold-blooded, a rattler cannot, for example, survive a ground temperature of over 110 degrees, a mark often recorded on the unshaded slopes and ledges. Therefore we seldom saw these snakes during midday when we and the chulos were most active. The rattlers came out to hunt and travel in the cool of the evening when the chulos had gone to their caves, we to our camp—an arrangement agreeable to all parties.

During the last month of our year, one of us—me—finally got poisoned but in a rather ignoble way. After a hard morning of sitting in back of the cabin, drinking tea, hobnobbing with the chulos, I decided to take a nap after lunch. Lying down against an oak tree, I brought my forearm to rest on a bark scorpion, who promptly stung it. It felt initially much like a bad bee sting, or a mild injection administered by a Navy corpsman. I went into the cabin, got a chunk of ice from the cooler, and put it on my arm. John was the only one about, and after it was apparent I was not going to collapse in a twitching heap, he suggested I go easy on the ice, as we had beer that would go warm, milk that would sour. In a half-hour or so, the arm was inflamed, had swelled up nicely, tingled somewhat.

"It is probably a good thing," John said, sympathizing. "I

mean everybody would think we spent the year in a bowling alley or something if some guy didn't shoot up one of us with his poison juice."

John had an ironic point. By then, we had met a good few people who seemed to believe or wanted to believe that we spent most of our time in the mountains battling sly and vicious beasts, if not snakes then bears, lions, javelinas, tribes of bloodthirsty chulos. Our credibility suffered because of the lack of such experiences. Certain of the vicarious thrill seekers seemed to feel that either we were, for purposes of our own, deliberately suppressing good adventure stories or else, as John suggested, we weren't really spending much time in the woods.

In point of fact, the American wilderness has always been (what is left of it still is) a benign one, inhabited by remarkably few creatures who could, much less would, dispute the territory with man. Historically the bees and wasps have accounted for more human deaths than any other species, with rattlesnakes in second place and psychotic, tormented, terrified bears a distant third. It is doubtful that in the last seventy-five years all other species combined have done in as many citizens as are scragged on a Labor Day weekend on a moderately busy interstate highway. In fact, the boondocks are now so safe, their inhabitants so timid and docile, that the remaining patches of wilderness currently serve as a kind of sanctuary in which it is possible to temporarily escape the risks and violence of the civilized regions.

After poking about the mountains for a year, we came to the conclusion that the most dangerous thing living in them was not an animal, real or imaginary, but a plant, the Huachuca agave. The agave is an aloe, a relative of the century plant. The unique Huachuca species stands up to five feet tall and from a distance is rather a pretty thing: a swirl of big, fleshy, rigid fronds, sea green in color, grow up from a thick root stalk. The fronds are six inches or so wide, and the end of each is tipped with a thorn the size of but much sharper than a tenpenny nail. These spikes can punch through the heaviest boot like an ice pick through butter. In what amounts to an ostentatious display of botanical over-kill, the edge of each agave frond is lined with smaller, curved thorns. These barbs were used for the purpose their shape suggests, as fishhooks by the Yaqui Indians, who also used the long terminal spikes of the agave as awls for working deer hide.

"*Muy bravo,*" a Mexican cowpuncher said one day of the Huachuca agave, as he sucked the blood off his gloved hand which he had carelessly brushed against one of the plants. This was not country hyperbole but a statement of fact. There are few living things more *bravo.* In the Mustang Mountains north of the Huachucas, a rockhound slipped in the scree, fell ten feet, landing on top of an agave. Before rescuers could hack him loose from the plant on which he was impaled, he was nearly dead from loss of blood, out of his head from pain. He was in a hospital operating room, so it was reported, for three hours while the broken spines were removed from his body, the holes they tore sewed shut.

Agave thrive in the full sun on rocky, slippery slopes where hundreds of plants will grow cheek by jowl, forming a murderous thicket. Walking on ledges and javelina trails above these colonies, we might at times consider rather casually what we would do if we met a rattler or a lion, but it was not good even to think about what would happen if we slipped, fell into, were pinned on the agave like a butterfly on a mounting board. The properties of the agave are such that familiarity breeds increasing caution, not contempt. After we had each been stabbed a few times, it became almost instinctive to look ahead for these *bravo* plants, to give them a wide and careful berth.

So far as real risk was concerned, Dain was in the most exposed position. He is a fine woods dog, an experienced naturalist's assistant-companion, has literally walked the Appalachians from one end to the other, having, when he was only two years old, trotted along with me while we walked the Appalachian Trail from Georgia to Maine. However, when he jumped out of the van into the Huachuca Mountains, he jumped into a totally foreign place where his previous experience was of little use, since he could not abstractively relate to it or determine the properties of agave, lions, javelinas, chulos, scorpions.

He suffered severely during the first weeks from thorns. In the brush, we could hear him yelp as he walked on, brushed against, nuzzled under a cactus, an acacia, an agave. At night he would lie by the fire, whining, licking his paws which were torn, filled with the tips of broken spines that we could not pull for him. The country was hard on him not only physically—the altitude, sun, aridity trouble a dog as much as or more than it does a man—but also psychologically. He was, it seemed, depressed by its strangeness, his ignorance. The scents, for example, that first came across his nose must have confused him in a way and to a degree that we can scarcely imagine. It was perhaps as if one of us had suddenly been put down in an absolutely unfamiliar place where in the distance we could see and hear exotic creatures, of whose existence we had previously been unaware, cavorting in ways and for purposes that were incomprehensible. Often we saw him stop along the trail, stand, sniff, look about indecisively as he apparently found a scent sign the making and meaning of which were beyond his learning and understanding. During the first weeks, he seldom strayed far away from us, limping along behind, subdued and cautious. There was little we could do except patch him up at night, praise him extravagantly to take his mind off the humiliation he was experiencing.

Though Dain had at first more difficulty in and with the new country than we did, he adjusted to it more rapidly and completely, the speed of his adjustment being related to the seriousness of his initial difficulty. For example, after a month in the mountains he could lope through a thicket without hesitation, without touching or snagging on the thorns. We, however, continued to pick our way, devoting conscious attention to avoiding the plants. Again I think this is a matter of superior acuity, observation. After being stabbed sufficiently by them, Dain developed what might objectively be called a feel for the presence of thorns. Considering how rapidly and unconcernedly he came through them, it seemed incredible that he could simply see the spines and adjust to shift his position in time. Probably other senses came into play. Perhaps there is a distinctive odor to thorns, a telltale sound of wind moving through thorn bushes, a special feel to the earth just outside the danger area. Whatever the reasons, Dain's "body knowledge" in this instance and many others served him better than our abstractive method.

Late in September, as Dain's confidence returned and after he had presumably classified some of the peculiar scents and signs of the new mountains, his spirits improved and he began to roam farther and farther from our heel, got back to the work he enjoyed most, turning up rabbits, squirrels, skunks, and such curiosities (for him and us) as javelinas and ring-tailed cats. Very likely he came across and learned to recognize chulo signs—perhaps even the animals—long before we did, but because of our slowness he had no way of passing along this information.

4

Chulo Hunters

When we came to the Huachucas in the fall, we were not only free to go where we chose, but could go or stay anywhere with equal ease, since at this time of year the country is, if not at its best, certainly at its most comfortable. The summer monsoons had stopped or were stopping; the ground, the trails were drying but the dust had not risen. All the springs were flowing and there was a clear stream running through every large canyon. Along the streams there were flat benches of loam, quilted with mats of new meadow grass, decorated with wildflower and butterfly mobiles. Since all the components of a good campsite—water, firewood, rocks for shelves and tables, level ground for sleeping, solitude, and scenery—recurred repeatedly throughout the mountains, we could spend a week or so in any spot as well and pleasantly as in another. Often we did not decide where we were going to set up camp until we reached the mountains on Monday morning. We would drive down from

Tucson through the lemon-yellow desert dawn, across the San Rafael Valley—also yellowish because of the light, the marigold and mustard bloom—toward the purplish Huachucas. We would see an eagle soaring over Cave Canyon, drive toward the bird, find Happy Spring, and live beside it for a week within the ruins of a stone corral—first built, according to local legend, by Spanish explorers. Or through glasses we would see a patch of bright fall foliage halfway up the side of Scotia Canyon, head toward it, see for the first time the cottonwoods and willows around the spring-fed pond on the abandoned Sylvania Ranch that four brothers from Nova Scotia, the Duncans, lungers and rustlers, had homesteaded in the 1870s.

While things were still in the early planning stage, I told Ky and Terry that a time I had been anticipating for some years had arrived. In consideration of their age and mine, I was commencing my retirement as a camper. Henceforth they would rustle the wood, fetch the water, try to drive tent pegs into rocks, organize the gear and grub, cook, and clean up while I sat around drinking tea, napping, and bitching about the service. Generally this is how things worked during the year, though after we had settled into our routine I started cooking breakfast. (Being an earlier riser, I found it easier to get started in the morning than to get the boys started.) Otherwise the boys were the domestics. Having been around camps since they were very young, they did not regard their new role as being a promotion or much of an honor. They understood, as many more romantic and less experienced souls do not, that the act of camping is in itself no fun, is simply housework without a house or attendant conveniences. Accepting the fact that camp living always involves—by contemporary standards, at least—some discomfort and inconvenience, the best approach is to do as little camping as possible: eat plainly, wash sparingly, sleep hard, so as to conserve one's energy, enthusiasm, temper for whatever work or pleasure one came to the woods for in the first place. Knowing all this, the boys accepted being the campers stoically, recognized their plight for what it was, another manifestation of the ancient tradition that rank hath its privileges.

So far as practical arrangements were concerned, Terry and Ky decided between themselves that they would rotate the work on a weekly basis; that one would do all the buying, organizing, cooking, cleaning, maintenance for five days, then have the next week free while the other camped. (One reason they warmly welcomed John when he arrived in October was that they could then work a one-on, two-off shift.)

Camp chores were less distasteful for Terry than the other two, and though he could not admit it for reasons of status, he may have found some of the work, particularly cooking, satisfying. In any event, all of us—even, to an extent, Terry—looked forward to Terry's week as the camper: Terry because it bothered him to watch Ky and John butcher the job; the rest of us because we were in various ways the victims of their butchery. On both sides of his family, Terry is Pennsylvania Dutch. These stubborn, matter-of-fact people may not actually carry a gene of orderliness and industry, but it amounts to much the same thing, since the virtues of and necessity for tidiness, frugality, hard work are drummed into them until such behavior becomes all but reflexive. Terry never said—never, I expect, thought —much about why when he was on camp duty there was one branch on which the pots must be hung; why if he said we would eat at six, we must eat at six; why he filled the gasoline lantern in the morning after breakfast rather than waiting, as the other two did, until evening when it was all but impossible to pour gas in a funnel without spilling it. It was simply the right way to do things.

Ky was easily the worst campman—not only disliked the work, as many do, but despised it. The boys changed shifts on Sundays, and as his time approached he grew noticeably more irritable as he brooded about what he was going to have to do. During the week, the rest of us could measure the depth of his distress by the raw noodles and burned rice we ate, by listening to him swearing to or at himself as he scrubbed sticky pans at the edge of a cold creek in the darkness.

At birth, Ky suffered an injury because of which he is an epileptic, suffering from occasional grand-mal seizures; he has about a 50 percent loss of normal hearing and a slight, almost imperceptible loss of muscular coordination. He has had to live with the knowledge that every so often, without warning, claps of thunder, bolts of lightning will rage through his head, knock him down, leave him writhing and senseless; that certain things that others do easily, unconsciously, he has to work at hard and consciously. However, there have been compensations; he has developed unique strengths and attitudes, chiefly a remarkable endurance, and a kind of I'll-never-be-a-victim toughness. Having had— chosen—to be a combatant, Ky is not notably patient or given to sweet resignation. His temper can be uncertain, his rages monumental. However, he has hit on a method of self-control which has helped him and those around him. His anger is invariably directed toward things, inanimate objects, rather than at people, fate, or—thankfully—himself. Because we have been together so much, often under trying circumstances, Terry and I know this better than anyone; Ky knows we know it. In fact, we can sometimes joke about Ky's rages as we can about Terry's sleepwalking or my increasing waistline. All of which made it obvious to all three of us that running a camp was the kind of work most calculated to frustrate and enrage Ky: small, messy, repetitious chores; trying to get a lot of things together in the right order at the same time.

In general, this is an account of a great many very good days, but mixed in there were inevitably a few bad ones for each of us. Unquestionably Ky's worst day, so spectacularly bad that it found a place in our private folklore, was his first one as the campman. Making out the grub list, shopping and reshopping as he discovered the list was incomplete, trying without order or plan to cram all the gear into the van, finding the ice chest that needed to be filled last had been packed first—a variety of similar aggravations occupied and ruined his entire Sunday in Tucson, put him in an ugly mood.

On Monday morning, we followed a jeep trail up Sunnyside Canyon, found a low, flat bench overlooking a good stream for a campsite. Terry and I helped unload, then, taking Dain, went off to work in the mountains, leaving Ky with a mound of gear and his misery. Terry and I did not have a bad day but it was a hard one. We followed a trail so faint, unused, that we often lost it, had to cast around for it. It crossed three largish canyons and thus six canyon rims. The elevation varied from 5,000 to 8,000 feet. The temperature was in the nineties and the September sun burned through the thin, dry air. In all, we bushwhacked thirteen miles, found no chulo signs, saw nothing spectacular except for a brief glimpse of the rear ends of a band of fleeing javelinas. We got back to camp late in the afternoon, stumbling with fatigue, with altitude headaches and throats full of cotton spit. Our immediate wants were simple: to stretch out on the grass, have somebody hand us a cold drink, smoke a couple of cigarettes, and then eat.

At the campsite, the two tents were raised after a fashion. The sagging ridges, slack ropes, and twisted pegs testified to the number and hardness of the rocks just under the topsoil. Amongst the litter of half-unpacked gear bags, the gasoline stove lay in several pieces. Ky was wearing a dirty, sloppy, blood-soaked bandage on his right hand and was hunched over the fire pit blowing on some feeble embers. (Alligator juniper and blackjack oak, which grew around the camp, make a fine big fire, but they are hell to split into kindling, to get started.) Obviously Ky had had a much tougher day than we had and was in worse shape. He acknowledged our entry into camp with a ferocious grunt.

As unobtrusively as possible, we located two cups in the debris, filled them with powdered orange juice and water, went to the chest for ice. There was a jagged rent in the metal cover of the box. Inside, the box was a quarter filled with rapidly warming, melted ice water, mixed with spilled milk. Later we found out that Ky, wanting a cold drink and figuring that we would, had taken out the block of ice, set it on the lid of the chest. Then he had attempted to chop off a few chunks of a size that would fit in a water bottle. In the process, the hatchet had glanced off the ice and cut through the metal box. Grabbing to keep the ice from slithering off onto the ground, Ky had raked his hand across the torn metal; thus the bloody bandage. Reduced to using one hand, he had decided to abandon the attempt to clean the stove, one jet of which was clogged—a job which had not been going well with two hands. After a time, he had coaxed some cedar twigs to burn, but then had spilled a pot of water over the embryonic fire.

"What in hell have you been doing?" my headache and wobbling legs asked through my sticky throat. It was a bad, unnecessary question.

"What the hell do you think I've been doing?" Ky screamed, standing up, whirling around toward us. "I'm cooking the fucking rice." So saying, he smartly kicked one end of a smoldering piece of cedar, which caused the pot to slip and slop some more water on the fire.

Later, much later, Ky dished up the food, a pasty conglomerate of Spanish rice and peaches, flavored with blood, coffee, and wood chips. We went to bed without much conversation. In the morning, while we were waiting around for the oatmeal to congeal, Terry tentatively asked Ky how his hand felt. He said it was all right and then, by way of letting us know the storm had passed, said, "Yesterday I wished it had been my throat."

"Bad day at black rock?"

"You don't know how bad."

"I got an idea," Terry said. "I ate that slop you cooked last night."

John, who became the fourth chulo hunter, joined us in mid-October, beat and bedraggled after having ridden a temperamental motorcycle across the continent from Delaware. We had reason to believe he was coming, having since September received a series of cryptic postcards: "Most of it is together, leaving soon." "Trouble, not leaving until next week." "Broke down in Tulsa but O.K.—stole a blanket," etc., etc. However, when he arrived we did not know how long he would stay, what he wanted to do, very little about him, since his involvement in our affairs had come about in a coincidental way.

John's father, Bill, is a sales executive, but more importantly he is one of a small, improbably obsessed group of which I am a member, men who coach girls' track clubs. One day the previous May, at Franklin Field in Philadelphia, Bill had said rather sourly and apologetically that he had a son (we had been friends for half a dozen years, but track, not family friends) who had nothing much but hair on his head, had heard about our Arizona plan, and wondered if there was any chance of being included in on it. I told Bill that the plan was hazy, that nothing like a genuine job was involved, but that if his son wanted to stop by to hear more about it, he would be welcome.

John showed up a week or so later. Whatever he really was, it was apparent why he made his father uneasy. He was tall, thin to the point of emaciation, walked with a kind of weary shamble. His black stringy hair hung to his shoulders and he dressed in the *Easy Rider* style, something loud, something country, something dirty. Though he actually spoke in the early Haight-Ashbury whisper which is once again popular amongst youth, his manner and appearance constituted in the code of these times a kind of shriek— dope, riot, hard rock, cop baiter, cop-out, communard, unisex, orgy, sloth, and heresy. Nevertheless he was painfully polite and shy, after the fashion of a business-administration major being interviewed by a Dow Chemical recruiter in 1952.

I told him what I had told his father: that if he wanted to show up with a sleeping bag and move into the mountains with us, there was nothing to stop him; that there would be no obligation on either side. If he didn't like the scene, he could split when he wanted, and if we didn't like him we would feel free to say so.

"I'd really like to make it. I really would."

"Why?"

"I've got to leave where I am, stop doing what I'm doing."

"Which is what?"

"Nothing. I work in this factory, a textile mill, which is so gross you could not believe it. Outside we make some sounds but mostly we hang around. There is one wall at the University of Delaware. What we really do is sit on it, watch each other. Every once in a while the cops chase us, which is exciting, but mostly we just sit and talk about leaving."

"Maybe you might not like what we're going to be doing, living outside, messing around with animals."

"I don't know. The only time I slept on the ground was at Woodstock, but I guess that doesn't count. It was just a bunch of inside people who happened to be out. I've never known any animals much. The only outdoor thing I was ever any good at was vandalism, and that was when I was a kid," John said judiciously.

At that point, John more or less came alive for me. Afterward I thought about his vandalism one-liner occasionally, but I do not think I understood what he meant or why he said it until much later, after we had lived together for some months. I think now this is how it came about. John could not explain why, but he wanted to go to Arizona as badly as any interviewee ever wanted a Dow Chemical job. He had the feeling his future depended on it. He was trying hard to tout himself, and wanted to offer something more impressive than working in a mill or playing a guitar. Suddenly he remembered starting fires with wood stolen from construction jobs, lurking in the bushes to hide from watchmen. It was not much but it was outdoorsish, and he threw it in as another might say, "and I can type thirty-five words a minute." Also, almost simultaneously, the absurdity of what he had said occurred to him. He was tickled by it and if I missed the joke so much the better, funnier. He let it stand as a kind of test, since we were both, after a fashion, trying to frisk each other's souls. If I was going to get uptight about a vandalism joke, then any scene I made was apt to be a bad one.

Since I knew so little about him, was uncertain about what he would do, John did not figure in our early plans. However, in retrospect it is hard to imagine what the year would have been like without him. Had John not escaped the wall, we might have done most, if not all, of the chulo work, but it seems certain that the general tone of the year would have been flatter, duller than it was. John is rare.

Among other things, John made the year much more fun than it otherwise would have been for the younger members of the party and also, in a curious way, more respectable. Any kid who had been to Woodstock, played a guitar in coffeehouses with a group called the Primeval Slime, wore stenciled T-shirts bearing that logo, wove macramé belts, and had ridden across the country alone on a motorcycle had passed the major coolness tests of contemporary teen-age society. That John, who had done these things, should want to join us, to become a full-time enthusiastic chulo watcher, gave the project a little class, put a kind of intergenerational seal of approval on it.

All of which was to become apparent in future happenings. When John arrived, he was mostly a teen-ager who had done a big thing, saved up his money from the textile mill, left home, ridden across the country on a sick bike, ended up on the doorstep of a group of people about whom he knew almost nothing. He was both exhilarated by what he had done and uneasy about what he had got into by doing it. Ky and Terry welcomed John cordially enough, helped him stow and clean up his gear, examined his bike with interest, and I suppose in private gave him a practical briefing on the forms and taboos of our tribe. At the same time, they sniffed at him, as was natural. In such situations, the behavior of men, particularly of young men, is in some ways comparable to that of dogs. Ky, Terry, and I were an established pack, the major questions of rank, responsibility, license having been settled long before. No matter how cool, how low a profile he kept, John was unavoidably an interloper, a threat to pack order, since his presence demanded that certain of our rules and traditions be openly explained, perhaps even changed.

We went to the mountains two days after John arrived, decided to camp in a place we had used before, in a sycamore and cedar grove at the edge of a small stream, a tributary of Bear Creek, which flows between the main mass of the Huachucas and an isolated, outlying ridge, appropriately called Lone Mountain. All of us helped unload the van and, as we did so, explained to John how and why we used the gear. I told him that he might as well get initiated early, to take the day, go over the equipment, set up the camp; that we would be back before dark and would like it if the fire was going and the tea water was boiling when we returned. The three of us took Dain and left immediately, fanned out, and spent the day working up Bear Creek to Bear Spring.

We came down the mountain late in the afternoon, stopped for a moment on the crest of the low ridge which divides the Bear Mountain and Lone Mountain canyons. Across the little valley we saw John coming down the side of Lone Mountain. We converged on camp at about the same time. The tents were up and the gear distributed around the clearing in some semblance of order. There had been a fire, but it had burned to ashes and there was no woodpile, no hot water.

"I climbed it," John said, nodding toward Lone Mountain. "That's the first mountain I have ever climbed all the way. It's cool up there."

"You're lucky it didn't get hot as hell down here. This country is damned dry; it's not a Delaware swamp. You go off and leave a fire, all you need is one of those little whirlwinds and you can touch off the whole canyon. On top of that, where in hell is the wood and water for supper?"

This was the final test, the last frisking between John and me. He shook his head and said more thoughtfully than defensively, "I'm a bungler. Everybody back home knows that. Why do you think they wanted me to come out here?"

It was, everything considered, not a bad—in fact, an almost necessary—way to begin. The incident served to reassure Ky and Terry that John was expected to shape up as they had, was not going to get a free ride because he was older, a stranger, less experienced. So far as John was concerned, nobody likes to be chewed on, but on the other hand being chewed on signifies among other things that you no longer have the immunity of a tourist or a guest. You are at least on the bus and can make a choice about whether or not you want to stay for the whole trip.

One of the better, more unusual things about the year was that while the four of us lived very close—physically, emotionally—to each other, there was little friction or unpleasantness. John and Terry almost came to blows one morning over a greasy skillet. Ky sulked one afternoon after both Terry and John had screamed at him for failing to be quick enough pulling the trigger string on a trap full of chulos. John blew up once, was moody for a day or two, after losing six dollars at poker dice and being needled unmercifully about it. I bitched at John and Ky a time or two for bungling, sloppiness, dereliction of camp duty. We had one, and only one, round about dope. All of these were minor flare-ups which left no blisters or scars. Otherwise there was nothing, no festering grudges, no offenses taken or intended. Our pack was a very peaceful, companionable, cool one.

5

Chulo Hunting

SEARCHING

During the first six weeks in the Huachucas, the pattern of one of our days was very much like that of another. The campman was more or less sedentary; in addition to dealing with his pots and pans, keeping his eyes open for anything that might happen in the immediate vicinity of camp, he had various supportive chores. For example, each evening we would set out a dozen or so mousetraps somewhere near camp (changing the microenvironment in which we trapped as often as possible). By doing this, we hoped to make a sampling of small rodents and insectivores, not only to satisfy our curiosity but also because it was possible that these animals might be chulo prey and, if so, it would be helpful to know who lived where in what abundance. The campman would check these traps each morning, take out any carcasses, identify them, add them to the mammalian check list we were compiling. (At the same time, and for the same reasons—general curiosity and possible association with chulos—we were making descriptive check lists of birds, amphibians, reptiles, invertebrates, fruiting plants and trees.) Also we habitually made impressions (with modeling compound) of any interesting tracks we came across, possible chulo spoor or otherwise, and once they were brought in it was the campman's job to clean up the molds and add them to our collection. During these first weeks when we were nomadic, we maintained a master topographic map on which the campman not only logged (using the field notes of the others) where we traveled each day but also especially significant observations, possible chulo signs, other biological, geographical information. The hope was that the map would provide not only a record, but a method of visually contemplating our records. (The hope was occasionally fulfilled. Thus later, when we had noted a good many observations of chulo signs—some secondhand reports of chulo sightings, some sightings of our own—the fact more or less jumped off the map at us that there were clusters of chulo activity in canyons where there was a lot of limestone and therefore a lot of small limestone caves and solution crevices.)

Leaving the campman to his chores, the other three of us (after John arrived) would put some water, modeling powder, a snakebite kit, a notebook, a few tortillas, a piece of cheese, an apple, and a can of snuff into a small pack, pick up a pair of binoculars, sometimes also a camera, and after breakfast go off into the mountains and spend the day walking slowly, stopping often to sit, look, and listen. It would be impressive to report that we quickly began to apply logic and woodcraft, developed a high-probability plan for locating chulos, confidently closed in on the animals. However, this would be untrue. As in most natural-history searches, we used our backs more than our brains during the first stages. We continued to walk and look, gradually increased our knowledge of the area, kept hoping to come across some major clue bearing on the question of where chulos might be found, how we could observe them. During the first weeks, there was always a possibility that we might blunder on a chulo, but initially this was not our principal objective. Rather we hoped to find chulo signs, or signs that might have been made by chulos, which would give us better information as to the activities of the animals than would an accidental encounter with one of them.

All terrestrial mammals, except the bat, move across the ground and all of them defecate. Thus the most common mammalian signs are footprints and scats. Quite obviously there are going to be more of these signs than there are individual mammals, and since the signs, if not permanent, are at least stationary, they will be easier to locate than the maker of the signs. Therefore if one wants to locate an animal, the obvious procedure is to look first for his signs and from them extract information indicating where the animal is, or at least where he is likely to be. However, in the Huachucas we shortly found out that there are peculiarities about the land and ecology which make it especially difficult to find signs. Another difficulty so far as the chulo is concerned is that since no one has paid much attention to the animals in southern Arizona there are few records, exhibits, authorities who can advise strangers where to look for chulo signs or, even worse, what sort of signs the animals make.

The border country is one of the worst possible places to look for tracks. It is rocky and, where not rocky, matted with tough, springy vegetation. It is dry and sun-baked. There are some dusty patches and places, but the steady wind erases marks from the dust almost as soon as they are made.

There were a few mud and sand bars beside certain ponds, streams, and seeps where the wettish earth would take and hold a footprint. We searched these carefully, reasoning that chulos would visit such places. They did, as it later turned out, but so did everything else that lived in the vicinity, open water being a kind of ecological pivot in such generally dry country. Javelinas, deer, antelope, coyotes, lion, bobcats, bear, skunks, chulos, other small mammals, and particularly cattle regularly come to these water holes. In consequence, there is a rich but usually hopelessly smudged, indecipherable conglomeration of signs on the banks.

Unfortunately for our purposes, raccoons also live in the Huachucas. Seen side by side, there are differences between a coon's track, which we knew well, and that of the closely related chulo. However, they are more similar than they are different, and the two animals are not in the habit of walking side by side. Working with guidebooks from isolated impressions, over which more often than not cows and wild pigs had walked, we were doubtful for some weeks about being able to distinguish chulo from coon prints. We remained so until we had made dozens of plaster-of-Paris study castings, watched chulos walking about, examined the feet of trapped animals.

Scats are perhaps the best of all signs, since they not only conclusively prove an animal was in a given spot, but tell something about him, specifically what he has recently eaten. With scats, abundance rather than scarcity, as was the case with tracks, often frustrated us. Creatures did not relieve themselves oftener in these mountains than elsewhere, but when they did their droppings hardened quickly and were effectively preserved. The same conditions—hot sun, wind, little precipitation—which made this poor tracking country promoted scatology. There was dung along every trail, in every draw and canyon bed, under ledges and in caves. Unfortunately much of it was deposited by medium-sized, more or less omnivorous mammals of which the chulo was only one.

The diet, gut size, and in consequence the scats of the fox, coyote, bobcat, skunk, raccoon, and chulo are more or less similar. Furthermore, scatology, if anything, is a less advanced science than tracking, more beset by variables, since size, age, health, as well as diet, influence the bowels of every animal. Scats from individuals of the same species, even those dropped by the same animal at different times, can vary greatly. On the other hand, under the proper conditions the droppings of animals of different species can be very much alike. The scats of a chulo who has been feeding on grasshoppers may more resemble those of a skunk who has been eating the same insects than they do those of another chulo who has stuffed himself with cactus fruits.

Olaus Murie, in his excellent guide to the tracks and scats of North American mammals, made a valiant effort to systematize what scatological information is available. However, his descriptions and drawings, particularly those of such relatively obscure creatures as the chulo, are more suggestive than definitive. (This is not intended as a criticism of Murie and his book. Dogmatic guides, which his is not, are usually bad ones, as the authors, in the interests of popularity and painless identification, tend to ignore exceptions, gloss over nagging similarities.) Thus when we disagreed on scatological matters, Terry claiming a dried-up piece of dung had been dropped by a skunk, Ky backing a chulo, and I a raccoon, each of us, like disputatious preachers, would go to the good book and find a passage in Murie which would support but seldom definitely prove our contention.

In such pursuits there comes a point beyond which authority and logic are useless; only observation and experience are of value. We came to know something about scats, as we did tracks, only after we had invaded a number of chulo dens, collected quantities of their droppings, pulled them apart, examined the contents and structure. A fixture in all our camps was a plastic bag full of slightly moist (to facilitate dissection) scats. When other entertainments failed, there was always the scat bag and records to occupy us.

Before going into the mountains, we knew from secondary sources, had guessed from looking at the foreclaws and snout of chulos, that they were rooters and diggers. We reasoned that such activity would yield useful signs. When we got out into the mountains, we found that diggings of a sort that might be made by chulos were indeed common. However, we also discovered by inquiry and observation that the country was infested by creatures who were both equipped and inclined to dig. The javelina, skunk, rock squirrel, Mearn's quail were persistent excavators while deer, coyotes, foxes would occasionally tear up a patch of ground. That so many animals should be rooters reflects the special nature of the habitat. Nothing moist can survive for long on the surface of the baked ground, under the fierce sun, unless it is somehow protected by a hard, horny, thorny shell. Therefore if you have a taste, as many creatures do, for juicy, tender edibles—tubers, grubs, beetles, snakes, lizards, mice—the best place to look for them is under in-sulating layers of rocks and topsoil. The only way to find them is to dig.

Foraging skunks, a band of javelinas, or a tribe of chulos will all work over a slope in much the same way. Initially we were unable to distinguish between the signs left by these diggers, but later, again after we were able to observe chulos, we found that their works were always marked in a distinctive way. Of all the mountain rooters, the chulo has the longest, most mobile snout. He often uses it in auger fashion, poking it into a hole he has dug with his claws, then pivoting around, his nose acting as a sort of bit, as he tries to probe deeper into the earth. Chulo diggings are therefore pockmarked with these small, conical nose holes.

Not until midwinter did we come to recognize the sign which most dependably indicated that an area was being used by a tribe of chulos. We missed it earlier because neither we nor anybody we had talked to knew that such a sign existed. A chulo tribe usually devotes an hour or two a day to resting and socializing (of which more later). Within the tribal territory there may be half a dozen spots favored for this purpose. They are usually located on a broad ledge, on the side of a cliff which is partly covered, protected by scrub. Invariably there is a dead or dying tree growing on or in front of the ledges used by resting chulos. The tribal youngsters swing on and chase each other about the branches of this tree, shred its bark, play tug of war with the shreds. The tree serves the youngsters as a piece of recreational equipment and is useful to the tribal elders in the same way that a swing set or slide is useful to a group of matrons who take their children to a playground. While the young chulos are helling around in the tree, the tribal matriarchs are free to gossip, groom each other, or nap without being mauled by their offspring.

After we had been in the mountains for two months, we found our first chulo tribe in the Cave-Oversight-Ida canyon complex. We found them there the hard way, by walking, watching, going over the ground again and again. Ten months later, when we were making some sentimental farewell walks through the Huachucas, Terry and I came down from the ridge one afternoon through Cave Canyon. There in reasonably plain sight we found, without really looking for them, two chulo resting ledges, the condition of which indicated they had been in use the previous fall. We had hiked this same trail half a dozen times in September and October without seeing these signs—or, more accurately, we had probably seen them but did not know what we had seen.

In our first months, we did not know that there were tribal rest ledges. However, we did at least assume that if there were chulos in the mountains there would be evidence of chulo activity which we could not then recognize—because of our ignorance about their behavior, could not even imagine existed. Therefore in addition to locating obvious signs—tracks, scats, diggings—we tried to look for, collect, and ponder over anything which might conceivably have something to do with chulos: shelters they might use, foods they might eat, creatures upon which they might prey or which might prey on them. Our reasoning was that, figuratively, all natural phenomena in an area are interconnected after the fashion of a spider web. The life style of a chulo can be thought of as one strand in this ecological web. It is touched, intersected by a great number of other strands, those of precipitation, temperature, juniper, the Yarrow's lizard, etc., etc., etc. Each of these strands in turn meets others, and therefore it is theoretically possible to pick up any strand in the web and follow it back to any other—to chulo, for example. In practice of course, this requires more patience and wit than most of us possess. However, we did as much of this web-following as we could. None of the energy so expended was wasted, since our eclectic wanderings and observations taught us something more about the country and, in a surprising number of cases, ultimately turned up information that helped us to better understand the chulos.

ADVISERS

If you are a stranger and are looking for something, an address, the men's room, a tribe of chulos, a reasonable thing to do is inquire of someone who is locally acquainted. Therefore during our first months we came out of the woods every now and then to talk to conservation, land-management, museum, school, country men and women, particularly to representatives of the Arizona Game Commission. (These later calls were obligatory. Except for migratory birds and a few special creatures such as eagles, which the feds have annexed, all wildlife in the United States, theoretically down to the last cockroach, is owned by the individual states. Therefore if you want to deal in any way with any species, it is necessary to have the permission of their legal guardians, the state game agencies. In this respect, our system is an uncommon one. Elsewhere beasts are usually owned either by private parties on whose land they live or by the central government. That other creatures must, presumably in the interests of orderly human society, be owned by somebody has been everywhere, throughout history, taken for granted by civilized peoples.)

Invariably those we called upon were polite, interested in our plans, wished us well with them, but were unable to contribute much specific chulo information, since their interests and expertise lay elsewhere. However, this socializing was not wasted effort so far as we were concerned. By midwinter, more or less everyone in the sparsely settled border country who might conceivably see or be interested in chulos had either met or heard about us, and a good many proved to be neighborly or curious enough to look us up when they came by a bit of chulo gossip or information. Also in this way we learned something about local society and history, made a number of good and interesting friends.

A man whom we met early in the fall and who was to become one of our best and most useful friends in the mountains was Henry Van Horn, a prospector who lives alone in a tight little cabin on the bank of a ravine which is a tributary of Bear Canyon. Van is seventy-seven years old, has lived in the Huachucas since 1925, and is altogether a remarkable man, though at first meeting a very prickly, gamy one. He was born in Colorado, worked in the mines there, became, I suspect, a Wobbly, quit the mines because the owners would not pay "a day's wages for a day's work," bummed across the country, worked in Detroit factories, tried to farm in New Hampshire; was drafted, kicking and screaming, into the Army and shipped to France, came close, he says, to starving to death there because the "officers kept all the grub for themselves," taught school in Paris; came West again to Bisbee in 1924, to the Huachucas a year later. He is an atheist, populist, pacifist, and by temperament an anarchist. However, he is above everything else a humanist, gentle, kind, concerned when it comes to dealing directly with other men. He therefore despises authority, on the ground that it dehumanizes, despises the agents of authority, from forest rangers to Army officers, because they are traitors to humanity.

"My arthritis is getting worse every year. People say I should go into town at least for the winter, but I don't drink beer or shoot pool, so what the hell would I do there? When you consider it, the ones that like towns the best are the rich, bosses, police, and politicians. If they had their way, they would herd everybody into a town where it is easier to keep an eye on us and where we are easily available when needed."

As it turned out, Van was the best and in fact the only reliable resident naturalist in the mountains, combining a quick, inquisitive intelligence, a lifetime of independent observation, considerable reading, and a wide acquaintance among geologists, botanists, zoologists, paleontologists. Through the years, these professionals have sought him out, or met him by accident as we did. Their high opinion of and indebtedness to him for local guidance and hospitality is acknowledged in half a dozen technical books and papers devoted to the natural history of the mountains.

We came to appreciate and depend on Van's local knowledge by degrees, but from the first we suspected he was reliable because he had two habits which invariably distinguish the careful observer, amateur or professional, from the dogmatic nature fakir. Van was a great qualifier, usually prefacing his remarks with "I only saw this once," "I had no way of checking on that," "I was not in a good position, so maybe I didn't get this quite right," or some other disclaimer. Secondly, he told stories about animals that tended to emphasize agreeable, pacific, orderly characteristics, which, unlike the bloody tales so often heard, usually indicates the reporter has actually observed what he describes, has had an opportunity and inclination to observe normal behavior, does not need to transfer his own fantasies and fears to other creatures. (For some reason, you almost never hear accounts in which the gentleness of animals is exaggerated; animal whoppers, like TV shows, concentrate on ferocity and violence.)

"I have great respect for blue jays and chulos," Van said on the first day we talked to him. "Neither will take food from another of its own kind. They will not rob another of the fruits of honest labor."

It is the kind of fey, doddering-old-man remark which is easily dismissed. Yet later we found out that it was not only true, at least so far as chulos were concerned, but also insightful. The first commandment of a chulo community is "Thou shall not take food from a member of the tribe." Only very young animals are excused from obeying this law. For the first six months or so after birth, juveniles can and do take food literally out of the mouths of the elders. When they are old and agile enough to forage efficiently, have learned what is edible and what is not, this privilege is abruptly withdrawn, and any adolescent who attempts to exercise it is swatted unmercifully by one of the matriarchs. Without this law, if stronger and more aggressive animals were permitted to rob weaker ones of the "fruits of their honest labor," much of the advantage of communal foraging and living would be lost, the tribal organization would quickly disintegrate.

"One day, just below the stock tank," Van Horn said another time, "I came across a chulo sitting in the base of a hollow sycamore. He looked pretty old to me but he was *bravo*. When I stopped to look, he came out, sat back, and waved his paws in the air like a boxer, as if to say, 'I'm not afraid of you.' I sort of laughed and said to him, 'Chulo, Chulo, we are a pair of old bastards. We've lived too long to fight with each other.' That chulo hung around here for a year or so. I'd feed him when I had extra grub and I'd talk to him. He was good company for an old fool. But do you know, I learned something curious from him, which I later came to believe is generally true with his kind. They like to be called chulos. When you meet them, always say 'chulo.' If you say 'coati' or 'George' or 'you son of a bitch,' something else, they become suspicious and uncomfortable. Isn't that the damnedest thing?"

It was. In fact, it seemed so odd and unlikely that we would not have believed it despite our respect for Van, except that later our experience tended to verify his. The word "chulo" did seem to have a peculiarly soothing effect on the animals. It was John with his good ear who may have hit on the explanation or at least the only explanation that occurred to us. Spoken in a certain throaty, snuffling way, the word "chulo" roughly approximates the sound tribal animals make when they are peaceably foraging together. The purpose seems to be to inform, in a sense reassure individuals as to the presence and position of others. Being themselves vocal and social, we found chulos were sensitive to human vocalizations. They seemed to react purposefully to tension or excitement in our voices and also, when there was a stranger with us, to the unfamiliar voice (though scent may have been the principal influence in this latter case). All of which made it at least possible that "chulo" is close enough to their own polite, friendly grunt of greeting to be accepted as such by the animals. Reasonably or not, it became our habit to do as Van Horn advised, to say "chulo" a few times when we met a chulo.

During the course of the year, we would stop by Van Horn's cabin once a month or oftener, bringing him extra grub and progress reports on our chulo study. One early spring afternoon, John and I stopped by Van's cabin and we got to talking about poisonous creatures. Van said he had been bitten by a small rattler, without much effect, had been stung often by scorpions.

"But so far as personal experience goes, the worst of the lot are those big centipedes. It isn't a very nice story but you boys won't be shocked. One night, it was hot as hell and I moved my mattress outside. I sleep raw in the summer, since there is nobody here to offend. I was just settling down when something grabbed hold of my privates and let me have it. It was one of those centipedes. I must have rolled on him. Now in that respect I am a very modest man; on a cold day I have trouble finding it. But the next morning it was swollen up half the size of a baseball bat and hurt like somebody was bearing down on it with a very stout vise."

On the way home, John and I laughed again about Van's centipede story. Then John said, "You know, he is the first really old person I have ever known. I've never really even looked at an old man before."

"Why not?"

"They frightened me; they're so freaky, all used up. The only thing I could ever think about them was that they were going to die."

"So will you, so will Van in a little bit."

"That's what I mean; I don't think that about him. It's like he's a good example. All those years are not just something he's dragging along behind like a crippled leg. There's something good he's got that we don't. It sort of makes you look forward to being old, instead of being frightened about it like I've always been."

I learned it from a one-legged Civil War veteran who sat in the shade of a big blueberry bush and told me stories about Libby prison. Ky and Terry, as well as John, learned it from Van Horn, who may have been the first admirable old man they ever knew. The lesson is that a tart old man who has kept his buttons, his brain, and eyes open gives hope and reassurance, promotes pride in mortality as no one else can. Most of us won't, for one reason or another, make it, but people like Van Horn testify that it is at least theoretically possible, suggest that it is worth trying.

The First Chulo

The narrow gravel and clay road which skirts the western side of the Huachucas is something like a pitted rollercoaster track with many sharp curves, ups and downs as it drops into, climbs out of canyons, washes, and creek beds. Between Montezuma Pass and Parker Lake, more than a hundred culverts have been laid under the roadbed to prevent it from washing out during the late summer rain and flash-flood season. We found that many mammals traveled through these artificial tunnels, foraged, drank, even denned in them, and left a record of their passage in the moist sediment which collected in the drains. Therefore, every week or so we would spend an afternoon driving slowly along the road, stopping and checking each of the culverts for signs or occupants. On September 28th while so engaged, we found our first live, wild chulo. Terry, Ky, Dain, and I were a quarter of a mile below the pass, coasting around a sharp bend toward a culvert when we more or less simultaneously saw the animal ambling along the berm side as placidly as and no more secretively than a browsing cow.

Since so much emotion and energy had been directed toward this moment, I remember my reactions well—in fact, recorded them that evening. My first feeling was not so much a sense of triumph as one of relief. Though we had been finding chulo signs, the longer we went without seeing one of the animals in person, the harder it was to put down the nagging doubt that maybe the local authorities were right, that there were so few chulos in the country and they were perhaps so elusive that we could not find them. If we did not, the whole year for which we all had such hopes would inevitably be tainted, transformed from an adventure into a kind of failure. Complicated plans would have to be altered, humiliating explanations made. One animal does not a study project make, but whatever else happened or did not happen, we had at least in a symbolic way done what we had set out to do—find a chulo. Thus the relief.

The animal himself was apparently far less concerned, far less interested in us than we were in him. As we sat motionless, very nearly breathless, in the van, he strolled toward us, tail held high, with the nonchalance of a boule-vardier who would not dream of being so gauche as to acknowledge the presence of, much less stare at strangers. Occasionally, almost absent-mindedly, he would flip over a rock, sniff at the ground. Later, after we had met other chulos—very possibly this same animal—in similar circumstances, we guessed when recalling this incident that his poise was something of a bluff, that his foraging had been pretense, a kind of displacement activity to cover up his inner confusion and curiosity.

In all, we watched the animal on the road for some five minutes. He continued slowly toward us and, when he came abreast of the van, finally glanced and sniffed in our direction. Then, still giving no sign of alarm, he coolly stepped over the side of the embankment and disappeared, apparently into a culvert, since there was nowhere else for him to hide. We eased out of the van, Ky going to the upper end of the culvert, Terry and I to the lower one. Peering inside, we found the chulo more or less lounging against the culvert wall, still unperturbed. Seeing or perhaps scenting us at both ends of the tunnel, the chulo grunted once in annoyance and then, suddenly exploding into action, dashed out of the pipe, running between Terry and me. He took refuge in a low oak growing twenty feet downhill and from there directed a series of grunts and coughs toward us. Mistakenly we thought these were sounds of fright and serious warning. In fact, they were, as we later learned, part of the animal's bluffing repertoire and could be roughly translated as "Take it easy down there or I'll get mad."

Thinking in terms of raccoons, hoping to scrutinize the animal further, photograph him, and perhaps record his vocalizations, I whistled for Dain, who on command had remained in the van, whimpering with excitement. Dain ran to the foot of the tree and began barking. The chulo, rather than climbing higher, bracing himself for defense like a coon and, as we had assumed he would, surprised us all.

First he sounded his true battle cry, a kind of snarling scream, and then he leaped, almost sailed out of the tree like a huge flying squirrel. Landing upright on the ground, ten feet beyond the trunk, he made a slashing pass at Dain, then fled down the mountainside. Before Dain could commence the chase, the chulo had a fifty-foot lead which he improved spectacularly. For a big dog, Dain moves well, but on the slippery, thorny slope it was no contest between him and the chulo, who ran jackrabbit-fashion in long bounds, sometimes leaping completely over boulders and low thickets. There being no point in testing the matter further, we whistled Dain back after a quarter of a mile of the hopeless pursuit.

MORE CHULOS

In retrospect, the first chulo was like a drought-breaking rain, or a home run that snaps a slump, for after him we began seeing the animals regularly. Two days later, I drove alone across Montezuma Pass, halfway down the east side of the mountain, to talk to Will Sparks at the State of Texas Mine. Will had grown up around the mine, living with a maiden aunt who owned it. However, after a hitch in the Army he had drifted off to Phoenix, married his wife, Deane, moved to and worked as a mechanic in Los Angeles. Eventually souring on city life, Will and Deane decided to return to Arizona and, in partnership with Deane's sister Dot and her husband Bob, reopen the old mine.

Will and Bob had come to the mountains first, at about the same time we did, and had been working hard all fall to make the abandoned mine compound livable. On the morning I stopped by, they had been struggling since breakfast with an ancient and balky water pump, were glad to take a break. I asked Will about chulos, and he said, "I think they are great animals," insuring during the first five minutes of our acquaintance that we would be what we became, close friends. "In fact, I tell people they are the perfect animal.

They take care of themselves, don't bother anybody, and aren't afraid of anything. They are smart and pretty and they are good to each other. Sometimes I think I wouldn't mind being a chulo. You want to see one?" asked Will, a large, handsome man who favors the *Cool Hand Luke* style.

"Sure I want to see one. We've been walking our asses off for six weeks looking for them. Whereabouts?"

"I think right now he is in the sycamore behind the tool shed. He comes down every morning to get Bob's biscuits, which is good, since nobody else can eat them."

"Any time you want, the stove's right in there," Bob offered.

"You'd better take a look at him now," Will went on, ignoring his brother-in-law. "There's no telling how long he'll last eating Bob's cooking."

As promised, the chulo was sitting on a limb, napping. When we approached, he woke up and without great enthusiasm accepted another biscuit from Will's hand. Though I did not know it at the time, I was meeting a prominent member of the Montezuma Canyon tribe, one with whom we would be much involved. In this case, there was no question later about the identity of the biscuit eater. He stayed around the State of Texas Mine, and Will and Bob kept an eye on him until we moved into the canyon permanently in December, marked and named the animal "the Supervisor," found out that he was the dominant tribal male.

During the next three weeks, we saw ten more chulos—a small band of four, and six singles—and had two good reports of other animals, one from a hiker who had encountered five animals on the top of the ridge, another from a rancher whose dogs had run and lost a solitary animal in Lyle Canyon. In the last week of October, we found our first tribe, which in some ways was almost as satisfying as seeing our first chulo. We had to meet tribes if we were to learn anything about chulo society, and we located this group by going to a place where we thought they might be and finding them there, an ego-inflating experience for hunters of anything.

Perhaps the most complex canyon system on the western side of the Huachucas is that of which Cave Canyon forms the core. Dropping into, intersecting Cave are three large tributaries, Ida, Oversight, and Bond canyons, and many smaller ravines and washes. The D'Albini ranch, founded by a pioneer Huachuca family, is located toward the mouth of Cave Canyon. There are still a few cattle and horses on the ranch, but the house itself is now used only on weekends by the family. The sole permanent resident is an old prospector, Carl Joerger, who lives in a cabin near the ranch house and acts as an unofficial but vigilant caretaker. He is another impressive representative of the prospector class, being an intelligent, well-read man who has a lot to say but unfortunately has great difficulty saying it because of a severe speech impediment which has locally earned him the nickname Squeaky. We had introduced ourselves to Carl shortly after coming to the mountains, but we never saw as much of him as we did of Van Horn, which was certainly our loss, not his. One difficulty was that Joerger is a fierce conservative in social and political matters. One of his pet peeves was restless, long-haired youth. "I see 'em," Carl squeaked (it is impossible to describe his manner of speaking, the agony which speech must cause him). "They come walking up the trails all dirt and hair. You can't tell the he's from the she's. Hippies," Carl pronounced, "are shit."

Since John's hair was already below his shoulders and the rest of us were growing shaggier of head and face by the day, it seemed neither diplomatic nor prudent to spend a lot of time with Carl. Though they did not put it as bluntly as Carl did, there were unquestionably a good few citizens along the border who felt as he did concerning these matters. Nevertheless, despite our hair and nomadic life style, we were generally received courteously, if curiously, as we were by Carl. Oddly, the more we came to look like The

Hippy of country-conservative nightmares, the less we seemed to bother people. Though our appearance was against us, we were apparently assigned a special niche. Everywhere around the mountains, we were known as the chulo chasers, regarded, I think, as harmless, nonrevolutionary eccentrics.

Whatever our differences, we remain indebted to Carl Joerger for a bit of information which led us to our first chulo tribe. Driving past the D'Albini ranch one afternoon, we were hailed by Carl, who told us that a young cowpuncher who had been hired to spot deer before the season opened for a group of city hunters had seen a large group of chulos in Oversight Canyon. "Schools and schools of them," Carl said. "Big ones, little ones, old ones."

We had camped in the Cave Canyon complex previously and, even before Carl's tip, had been thinking that we should try it once more. The canyon, of course, had not changed since we had camped in it three weeks earlier, but we had. Little by little, we had learned, or thought we had, more about what chulo country should look like, and all of us thought that Cave was one of the most promising canyons we had seen. Being well watered, it was heavily forested. In the thickets there were a good many madroñas, a red-barked, dogwood-sized tree, which at that time of year was bearing fruit we knew birds were eating and thought chulos might. Along the stream beds were long strips of mulch—soft, loose accumulations of sediment and decaying leaves—washed down from the upper elevations. In this regard, Van Horn had pointed out the obvious to us: "Chulos are not stupid and they are no more industrious than the rest of us. They like to dig in that soft ground in the canyons better than they do in the rocks and hardpan up on the sides."

We had not yet thought that there might be an association between chulos and limestone, nor did we know for certain that the animals used caves and crevices. However, we did know there was limestone in the canyon, a lot of good den sites available if they were interested in such things.

"It smells like chulos," Ky said on Monday morning when we moved in, set up camp in Cave Canyon inside the old Spanish corral at the edge of Happy Spring. He was speaking figuratively, of course, there being no odor of chulos or anything else except piñon. However, in addition to Carl Joerger's information, there was indeed a promising feel because of the good habitat. We had a sense that if we were chulos we would be in Cave Canyon. We decided that we would stay there until we found chulos or were reasonably certain there were none.

The Cave Canyon complex forms a large, irregularly oval indentation on the western side of the mountain, as if at this point a giant bite had been taken out of the Huachucas. The bite was a sharp one, for at the head of the canyons where they butt against the ridge there are almost perpendicular cliffs, sheer drops of 200 or 300 feet. On the first day in Cave, Ky and I put our sleeping bags and some dried soup and tea in a light pack and went off to circumvent the canyon head, to spend the night on top of the Huachucas. It was a hard walk up to and along the rimrock but an interesting one. In the course of the climb, we saw deer, a pair of eagles, a bobcat and a young bear, and many lion signs. That night, we camped at 9,000 feet, just below Miller Peak, the highest in the mountains. Though it was still October summer below, it was nearly winter on the ridge. The aspen were golden and we had to break ice from a spring for our soup and tea water. We saw no chulos but had not thought we would, having come to accept the fact that we were unlikely to encounter them while moving in the rough country. The purpose of our hike was to walk without any attempt at stealth around the rim of the canyon, in hopes that the noise and scent we and Dain made might move the chulos, if they were there, down into the canyon where Terry and John were waiting. Though we could not know whether this had the desired strategic effect, John and Terry did in fact both see chulos while we were tramping around on the rocks above. While sitting in Oversight Canyon, John had caught a brief glimpse of one large and three small chulos, presumably an adult and young of that year, foraging together. Terry had seen a single animal near Bond Spring.

On Wednesday, after we had returned, we spread out again. I took Dain and walked very slowly up Oversight Canyon, taking most of the day to travel three-quarters of a mile. Because of the other sightings and our mood of optimism, I had the feeling that I was in the middle of a puzzle picture, of the kind that used to be printed on the back of cereal boxes where you got a prize for locating all the raccoons, foxes, owls cleverly disguised as rocks, bushes, and clouds. I suspected there were chulos everywhere, hiding, peering out at me, lurking just beyond my sensory horizon. There was some evidence supporting this notion. There were many fresh diggings in the leaf litter on the canyon floor, a few piles of scats. I found new claw marks on a madroña tree, broken and chewed bits of madroña berries on the ground underneath. Dain, as always, caught and reflected my mood; he was hunting hard, seemed hypersensitive. Twice he picked up scent trails by the stream, followed them, led me back into the rocks to crevices and small caves which showed signs of recent mammalian use.

It was Dain in fact who saw, scented, and otherwise sensed our first chulo tribe. In midafternoon, we were sitting on the rocks, fifty feet back from the stream. Dain stiffened, whined softly. I looked in the direction he was looking, saw nothing, kept looking, and then saw chulos moving through the brush on the far side of the stream. There were, as best I could count, sixteen animals, nine of them juvenile, or at least much smaller than the others. They were foraging actively and, I thought at the time, were unaware of our presence. Then I heard a peculiar sharp grunt and they scattered, disappeared. Following them slowly came an adult whom I had not previously seen and who had apparently been hidden in a nearby windfall. As she stalked across the clearing, tail held high, this animal stopped for a moment and directed a hard look, or more likely a sniff, in our direction.

Later, recalling the scene, referring back to my recorded notes, I am confident that what I saw was a large foraging band or perhaps a full tribe, with young in the middle, adults surrounding them, and a mature female (the last animal) hanging back, keeping her eyes and nose on the others, the world in general. Though this was probably what was there to be seen, I saw little of it. In my notes, I said among other things that there was no apparent (the qualifier saved me) organization or interaction between the animals, no grouping of adults and young. Because I was looking for a conventional family unit, a female or a pair with their young, I did not see that there was a more subtle arrangement, a shifting communal organization which involved all young and all adults. Worst of all and, when I think of it now, for no better reasons than male chauvinism, I referred to the last chulo, the one who had followed the group and was almost certainly a female, as "he."

Ironically, after two months of searching, we located a chulo tribe at the worst possible time—two days before the opening of the deer season. The Huachucas in general, Cave Canyon in particular, are among the most popular shooting grounds in southern Arizona. The next morning, rather than trying to relocate the tribe, we were dodging hunters. They swarmed along the trails, looking for shooting stands and deer signs, and in the process driving all sensible wildlife up into the rimrocks. By late afternoon, the mouth of the canyon had become a kind of rural slum, with campers, tents, pickup trucks occupying every level space. Far into the night, we heard latecomers arriving, the pre-hunt festivities of the earlier campers.

Living as we had for years on an Appalachian ridge close to the Atlantic megalopolis, we had learned to fear and despise deer hunters, learned that deer season was a time when it was neither pleasant nor safe to be in the woods. Van Horn had warned us that things were no different in the Huachucas. "If you fellows are going to find any chulos, you had better do it before the hunters come in," he had advised the week before. "When they show up, anything in its right mind gets out. They aren't prepared for this country by temperament or condition. After a couple of hours of lugging their cannon and bottles around in the brush, their feet hurt, the booze is sweating out of them. They can't find any deer, but they are crazy to shoot something—anything from a lizard on up. That is when the chulos get it. They will blast a hole in a poor chulo and brag the rest of the year about their marksmanship and bravery."

All of which being true, and there being no way for us to protect the chulo tribe, we decided to get out of the mountains on the morning shooting commenced. While the boys were packing, I paid a visit to the nearest camp, where two hungover-looking gunners were drinking coffee outside a trailer of the size and décor of a portable Holiday Inn room. They said they had stayed awake all night and had started hunting at dawn, had already had two shots. I asked them at what. "At a buck, I guess," said one. "Anyway we could hear something pretty big moving around in the oaks."

Under these circumstances, we left, not elated as we should have been at having found a chulo tribe, but depressed, angry that we could not safely or profitably come back to the mountains for two weeks, that we might well be another six weeks finding whatever animals survived the gunners' invasion.

6

Kitt Peak

DESERT MUSEUM

While we hung about Tucson waiting out the deer season, we spent considerable time at the Arizona-Sonora Desert Museum, which is ten miles west of the city on the far side of the bare, burnt Tucson Mountains. A private institution which we joined as soon as we arrived in Arizona, the A.S.D.M. is both a tourist attraction and a local center of natural-history activity. Best known for its zoo and botanical gardens, it offers the only comprehensive collection of Southwestern plants and animals in the world. The museum proper and the museum library are both small but also regionally and thoughtfully specialized.

Chuck Hansen, the museum's energetic curator of mammals, was one of the first people we had met when we came to Tucson. "You people [we chulo watchers] embarrass me," had said Hansen, a large, bearded, cool young man who might play the intrepid scientist on a TV animal special and who does not give the impression of being frequently or easily embarrassed. "I should be able to tell you something, at least give you some leads, but I can't. We spend our time building exhibits, being handlers, keeping the animals and the tourists away from each other. We just don't get out in the field to do the research we should. When I pass our chulos, I say hello to them and that's about it. From an institutional standpoint, they are good mammals because they are hardy, don't make problems. That's no help to you, but if we can do anything just yell."

Hansen gave us more or less a free hand to watch, photograph, tape-record the vocalizations of the museum chulo colony when and as we chose. There were nine of the animals: an adult male and four adult females, as well as four juveniles who remained from eight born the previous summer. (The other four had been traded.) They were kept on what amounted to a dry-land island, a plot designed and landscaped to simulate natural conditions, surrounded by a deep concrete-lined moat. On the island were a tree, some rocks, and an artificial cave in which they slept, could escape the sun and attentions of the visitors.

Having nothing else to do in the chulo line, we spent some hours watching these captive animals. They seemed healthy and vigorous—in fact, if anything, hyperactive, being constantly on the move, pacing back and forth for no particular purpose, occasionally nipping, batting, squealing at each other. We were able to make little sense out of their behavior. Later, when we were able to compare the museum animals with wild tribes, we decided that there was in fact not much sense to be made of them. The pit at the Desert Museum was a kind of Bedlam. Though the facilities of the enclosure were excellent, captivity had driven the animals mad, as it might a man confined in a cell with a group of unsuitable strangers under circumstances in which it was impossible to establish law, order, friendship, or tradition. All of this was, of course, incomprehensible to us at that time, as it was to all other visitors who looked down into the pit and exclaimed at the odd, active, noisy animals. We saw only nine well-fed, apparently energetic chulos. We no more knew that they were demented than would an observer whose only field study of humans had been conducted through the window of a high-security psychiatric ward know that the inmates were eccentric specimens.

NATIONAL OBSERVATORY

One afternoon, I was reading in the library when Lew Walker dropped by the museum. Walker, who died a few months later, was one of the most prolific natural-history writers of the past several decades and had before his retirement served as the curator of birds and mammals at the museum. In the course of his return visit he came by to say hello, and it was a portentous meeting, so to speak, at least for us. Walker being as entertaining a conversationalist as he was a writer, we talked about a variety of things, creatures and people of mutual interest and acquaintance. Eventually we got around to chulos.

"Have you looked at that bunch at Kitt Peak?" Walker asked casually.

"No. I didn't know they kept any up there."

"They can't keep away from them. They're running around all over the top of the mountain. Every morning they come down and raid the observatory kitchen."

"We don't know anything about them. Apparently nobody else we talked to does either, the Game people or the Forest Service. In fact, I got the idea there wasn't much chance of finding them in the Baboquivaris."

"The chulos didn't read the same books you people did, I guess. I've seen them there a couple of times and they tell me they're around every day. I'd say fifteen, maybe more."

I went directly from the library to the museum office and called, at Walker's recommendation, Dick Doane, the supervisor of the Kitt Peak Observatory. He said that yes indeed, they had chulos—in fact, so many and so frequently that they were on the verge of being a nuisance. Under the momentary misapprehension that I was a collector or game warden, Dick asked if I had any suggestions about coping with them. I told him all I wanted to do was watch them and that I would be out early the next morning to tell him why. The lead seemed so promising that I was stunned, even a little suspicious. That evening, not wanting to raise false hopes, I told the boys I had heard that maybe there were some chulos around the observatory and that Ann and I would drive out the next morning to check the rumor.

Kitt Peak, which is some 7,000 feet tall, is at the northern end of the Baboquivari Mountains, fifty miles west of Tucson. The Baboquivaris themselves are the most westerly of the true mountain islands along the border. Beyond them, the Sonoran Desert begins in earnest. Much of the range, including Kitt Peak, lies within the reservation of the Papagos, a large but poor Indian tribe.

Some fifteen years ago, a number of Western mountain-tops had been examined; Kitt Peak, because of its elevation, conformation, surrounding clear skies, and then pure air, was selected as the best location for the National Observatory. It was then necessary to obtain permission of the Papagos to build a road up their mountain, erect the complex of astronomical facilities. In order to demonstrate to what purpose the mountain would be put, several tribal councilmen were invited to visit the small University of Arizona observatory in Tucson. Through the telescope they were shown the surface of the moon. Having studied the lunar landscape for a time, one of the Papago leaders turned to another and said, "It looks just like home. We should rent the mountain to these people." The story may be apocryphal but it is believable. The baked, cracked desert from which Kitt Peak juts and the dry, often bare mountain, its slopes tortured by a maze of ravines, washes, slides, make a very moon-like scene.

The observatory was established and is operated by a

consortium made up of the National Science Foundation and a number of large universities. It was built during a period when national interest in space and the heavens was intense, and when funds for even vaguely space-like projects were all but unlimited. Kitt Peak rising up out of the desert crowned by a dozen big observatories, a full complement of maintenance and administrative units, reeks of big aerospace money. However, it is also an attractive place, with a first-class look and feel about it. Rather than simply leveling the mountaintop and macadamizing it, the planners of the observatories and supportive facilities have scattered them unobtrusively (or as unobtrusively as a 150-inch telescope can be) among the ledges, outcroppings, pine and oak thickets. There are footpaths winding across the peak and outlooks through wild gardens. There is a sense about the place that somebody gave some thought to the pleasure and convenience of people as well as to the situation of machines.

Dick Doane was not only the supervisor of the institution but the unofficial mayor of the Kitt Peak community. (Some fifty scientific, administrative, maintenance employees live permanently on the Peak in attractive houses and apartments furnished by the observatory. An equal number of the staff, mostly Papagos, live elsewhere, are day workers.) Later, for reasons that had nothing much to do with his work or mine, Dick Doane and I became very good friends. However, we were first taken with him because he is a rare kind of civil servant, so relaxed and confident that he felt perfectly free to wander off in areas beyond bureaucratic precedent and regulation. Based on a fairly wide acquaintance with the type, I think it likely that seven out of ten public servants responsible for such an elaborate and expensive facility as Kitt Peak, if confronted with a credential-less stranger and three long-haired teen-age boys who wanted to prowl about his compound looking at small mammals, would have said no. Of the remaining three, approximately two and a half would have allowed as while they had no personal objection, any final decision would have to come, of course, from Regional Headquarters and/or the Washington office. The unexpected, the unprogrammed, tends to pain bureaucrats. It is much easier and professionally safer to abort freakish proposals than to decide whether they are harmless or useful.

Dick Doane said, in a way that implied that we were the ones doing the favor, that we were welcome to do whatever we wanted with the animals for as long as we wanted. If we needed anything while we were on the mountain, we should feel free to ask for it. There was only one restriction. Because ground lights of any sort could distort observers' experiments, we could not camp overnight on the peak. However, Dick told us where the key for the outer gate of the compound was hidden, told us to use it whenever we came before the place was officially open or after it had been locked.

On our first morning, Dick walked with us to the staff dining and recreation building and introduced us to the three cooks, Carolyn Rostek, Flossie Bucklew, Mary Rose, whom he recommended as the most frequent and knowledgeable chulo observers on the Peak. All three ladies proved to be classic aunt figures—ample, easygoing, laughing women, intent on stuffing people with fattening foods. As the four of us were to find out, the occupational hazard of chulo watching at Kitt Peak was foundering on whipped cream, pastry, large ice-cream sundaes. Anyone, but especially a teen-age boy, who did not have his mouth full seemed to make Carolyn, Flossie, and Mary uneasy.

Carolyn, who was more or less the leader of the kitchen crew, said the "cooties" had not been around that morning, but should shortly be appearing for a snack. ("Cooty" is Carolyn's version of "coati" and so the animals are generally called at Kitt Peak.) Carolyn then commenced filling a paper bag with sweet rolls for the chulos, a tray with coffee and éclairs for Ann and me. "You go out to those tables in back and wait," she directed. "The cooties will be around. If you run out of anything, just come back and ask. Maybe I'd better put in a couple more of those éclairs now. They're pretty good this morning, but if you don't like them the cooties will."

Behind the dining hall, facing south, looking toward the Santa Rita Mountains fifty miles across the desert, there is a small tiled patio, shaded by an arbor, furnished with wrought-iron tables and chairs. Just beyond the patio there is a corridor of natural thicket—oak, mountain mahogany, snowberry bush—which winds through the observatory grounds and down over the side of the mountain. After weeks of backpacking, bushwhacking, poring over frustrating signs, it was here in these resort-like circumstances, while sipping coffee, munching on fresh-baked goods, that we had our first intimate meeting with a chulo tribe.

Ann and I were on our second cup of coffee when the animals appeared, trotting through the oaks, having apparently come up over the west rim of the peak onto the observatory grounds. Shortly they were all around us, underfoot, on the chairs, squalling, grunting, gobbling up sweet rolls. Finding myself where I had thought I might never be, in the middle of a chulo tribe, I felt as perhaps a man does who comes upon a spring in the middle of the desert. I simply drank in chulos and was in no mood or condition to examine them critically, no more than a thirsty man would be inclined to measure the temperature or mineral content of his first drink of water. The tribe stayed around us for a half-hour, until they were convinced no more goodies were to be had. Then, in a leisurely way, they went back through the oaks in the direction they had come.

The following day, the boys and I were back shortly before sunup. For the next six weeks, we made the hundred-mile trip between Tuscon and the peak, through the desert at dawn and at dusk, every day except Sunday. We saw, had some dealings with, the Kitt Peak tribe on all but three of those days.

In addition to Carolyn, Flossie, and Mary, the other principal chulogist at Kitt Peak was Hondo, a Papago who had developed a special fondness for the animals. Together they had probably observed chulos more frequently than anyone else in Arizona, and from their recollections we were able to reconstruct the history of the tribe at Kitt Peak.

Hondo, who before coming to work at the observatory had cowboyed in the Baboquivaris, said he had sometimes but not often met chulos in the mountains to the south of the Peak. However, neither he nor any other of the Papagos we talked to had seen them in the desert west of the mountains. The first animal, probably a solitary male, showed up at the observatory in the winter of 1968. "He was such a strange-looking bugger," said Carolyn, "I didn't know whether to scream or laugh. We certainly didn't know what he was. We did know that he was hungry, so we fed him. He was around most of the time, but he must have slipped off and told his friends what good cooks we were."

In the spring of 1968, three other chulos appeared. They were nearly, if not completely, full grown, definitely were not "babies." They remained and were joined in the late fall by about ten others, including four little ones who were presumably juveniles born in the early summer. These animals, too, remained, and in the summer of 1969 the first chulos were born on or near Kitt Peak. "We knew when the old ones were due," Carolyn said. "They were so heavy they almost dragged on the ground and they were uncomfortable. They'd sit up and rub themselves," Carolyn explained, gesturing toward her own ample bosom. "They were bitchy. They'd snap at all the rest, couldn't even get along with each other. Then the pregnant ones disappeared. It must have been in June, because it was before I went on my vacation back to Illinois. We'd see them once in a while just before dark. Their udders were all stretched and they were scrawny, so we knew they'd had the babies and were nursing. They came back bringing their little ones in August. The little ones were about the size of rats. They weren't afraid at all, would come right up to us. Sometimes the babies would climb up and ride on one of the old ones' back."

As reconstructed by Carolyn, Hondo, and the others, filled in by our later observations, the growth of the Kitt Peak tribe is the only detailed history of chulos pioneering into a new area. First came an old male, wandering alone during the winter months, as is their custom. His scent trails may have guided the three animals who came the next spring. As a guess, they may have been yearlings or subadults, for at this time of year tribal organization is at its weakest and the younger animals tend to travel on their own, in small groups. Finally the principal members of the community arrived, the matriarchs and the young of that year, who in a sense settled the territory that the first animals had explored. So far as motive is concerned, Carolyn's explanation that the chulos found that she and the others were good cooks, generous people, is a reasonable one. The prime food source must have attracted the first animals and kept them and those who followed about the observatory grounds, which came to serve as a chulo sanctuary.

By the winter of 1969–70, there were approximately twenty animals. (They were numerous enough to make a casual count difficult.) The next summer, when we arrived in Arizona, was both a good and a bad one for the tribe. Nearly all the mature females must have bred and littered, for in late July there were between twenty and twenty-five cubs playing about the Peak. By this time, the tribe had settled in and become very bold about the good thing they had found—foraged through garbage cans, begged scraps from passersby, occasionally entered houses, cars, even the observatory buildings. They were at times a mild nuisance but in general were well liked, being friendly and entertaining animals, something of a curiosity. Eventually the good opinion that the Kitt Peak staffers had of them acted as a temporary control on the expansion of the tribe. When the large crop of 1970 cubs appeared, the urge to take pets was irresistible. As nearly as we could determine, at least fifteen of these infants were trapped, caught in nets, simply picked up and taken off the Peak by staff members for their families or friends. Five young chulos were trapped by a staff electrician and shipped off to a roadside zoo in New Mexico

By the time we arrived in November and were able to make an accurate census, there were twenty-four chulos in the Kitt Peak tribe: three adult males, who by that time had returned to their solitary status; two subadult males and probably three subadult females (their age being harder to determine), all born in the summer of 1968 or 1969; seven juveniles, born in 1970, survivors of the pet raids of the summer; nine adult females.

MEETING THE TRIBE

Kitt Peak proper, the more or less flat mountaintop, is a rough triangle of some hundred acres. The base of the triangle rests on the southwest rim of the mountain. A small canyon or large ravine, about two hundred yards wide, commences just below this rim and descends sharply to the desert, half a mile below. This canyon is littered with boulders, ledges, scree, some of which was pushed into it when the observatory facilities were being constructed. The canyon is also choked with low scrub, mostly oak and mountain mahogany. The upper quarter of this canyon, from the rim down, was the home base of the chulo tribe. At night the animals denned among the rocks and during the day, unless otherwise occupied, could usually be found there, sunning, napping, socializing, doing a little desultory foraging. Normally they would make two trips a day, either en masse (that is, all the animals except the solitary males) or in two groups, to the kitchen area. In doing so, they had beaten a path from the head of the canyon to the rear of the dining hall. The trail was circuitous, winding around the boulders, staying generally in the cover of the thickets, but it had been so frequently used that it took no woodcraft to find or tracking skill to follow.

There were two sources of open water. One was in effect an artificial spring, the overflow from the kitchen dry well which trickled out of a pipe, seventy-five yards southeast of the building, and flowed down a crevice in the rock for ten yards or so before being blotted up by the dry ground. The tribe regularly drank from this overflow. Directly opposite the chulo home canyon, across the observatory grounds, below the northeast rim of the Peak, there was a large open pond, a runoff and catch-basin reservoir which was a major water source for the observatory. Once a week or so, the tribe, perhaps feeling the need of a little exercise and excitement, would visit this pond, usually traveling just under the rim of the mountain and circling the observatory in a counterclockwise direction.

The chulos were not the only animals who had discovered the advantages of Kitt Peak and were living as, in a sense, clients of the astronomers. Large flocks of blue jays, ravens, sparrows, and juncos regularly scavenged on the grounds. Rock squirrels were numerous and there were a few skunks. A one-eared gray fox, boldly in the daytime, and a gaunt bobcat, furtively in the evening, visited the kitchen area looking for food. At least two mountain lions lived farther down the mountain. Sometimes they were seen crossing the access road, and they occasionally left their prints around the banks of the catch pond, but they were apparently too timid to visit the occupied mountaintop. All of these creatures (except perhaps the lions, about whom we had no evidence) deferred to the chulos. However, the jays were bold, if wary, competitors and would feed with them, keeping just barely out of their reach. The jays at times seemed to exasperate the chulos, who would rush at the birds, drive them off a few feet. But it was an unequal contest, like trying to bail out the ocean with a bucket. We never saw a chulo come close to catching a jay or, for that matter, permanently intimidate the brassy birds.

The Kitt Peak tribe exerted itself minimally for food, had no real competition, no enemies on the observatory grounds. That these easy circumstances influenced their behavior was an obvious assumption which occurred to us early in our acquaintance, but one which we could not verify until later when we had come to know something of "wild" tribes in the Huachucas. In comparison with the animals in the Huachucas, the Kitt Peak chulos spent far less time foraging, much more time lying around socializing, and initially they were less wary. In a certain sense, the Kitt Peak tribe might be thought of as a degraded one, but this is a simplified, not entirely accurate judgment. They were somewhat in the position of a hard-scrabble rancher or farmer upon whose property oil is discovered. The Kitt Peak tribe had accidentally come upon a very good thing, and they had wit and flexibility enough to modify their life style so as to enjoy their considerable unearned prosperity.

For our purposes, we badly needed, though we did not realize it at the time, just what we found at Kitt Peak, a chulo tribe living in relaxed circumstances whom we could observe easily and regularly. Had we known only the Kitt Peak animals, our information and conclusions about chulos would have been more distorted and incomplete than perhaps they are. On the other hand, had we not first become acquainted with these animals, learned something about basic chulo skills, behavior, traditions from them, we very probably would not have known how to introduce ourselves to the less tame animals in the Huachucas, would have had less understanding of how these tribes functioned.

In the Kitt Peak tribe, several of the animals had been or easily could be identified. Carolyn, Flossie, and Mary had made a particular pet out of a single male whom they called Charley. Charley was a large, heavy (very likely because of his status as the cooks' favorite) animal, scarred on one flank, who had lost both of his upper canine teeth. He would eat from the hand, pull at bootlaces or pants legs for food, and in general seemed more at ease with people than with his own kind. The cooks claimed that they had to give Charley preferential treatment because the rest of the tribe was mean to him, attacked and drove him away when they met. This probably was true, though we seldom saw such attacks since Charley went to great and obvious lengths to avoid any confrontation with the other animals.

A second solitary male was also easy to recognize, having lost most of his left ear in some previous skirmish. The largest of the females (as we later determined) was an exceptionally light, straw-colored animal whom we named Blondie. One of the juveniles became Kinky, because his tail had apparently been broken and the tip stood at right angles from the rest. We could also separate the juveniles from the adults because of their size, but otherwise we were unable to distinguish between the animals. In time, we might have been able to find something idiosyncratic about the appearance and behavior of each animal, as we were later able to do with the Huachuca tribe, but this would have been a long, slow process. (Individual animals are as distinctive in their features and behavior as are people. However, we are not accustomed to isolating, remembering the differences between members of other species.)

Without knowing who was who among the tribe, we found it difficult just to count the animals. Even while feeding in the open area behind the kitchen, the animals were in constant motion like so many water bugs, dashing back and forth, popping in and out of the bushes. Not knowing whom we were seeing, the four of us, all standing in the same area and concentrating on the animals, would often come up with a different count of those present. In a dense oak thicket, the chances of anyone not intimately familiar with the animals ending up with a good body count are very poor (thus the often exaggerated reports of very large tribes).

Not being able to distinguish between the animals also made it next to impossible to make any observations concerning who was doing what, the social behavior of individuals, the social dynamics of the tribe as a whole. Therefore, having found chulos we could observe, the first thing we had to do with them was rather clearly indicated. We needed to make a census of the tribe, determine the size, sex, and—if possible—age of each animal, then mark them in such a way that we could dependably re-identify them from a reasonable distance. To do any of these things, we obviously had to lay hands on the chulos. However, we wanted to do so in a way that would not injure, frighten, or drive them away. Just as important, we wanted to handle the animals in a manner that would reduce the chances of their mauling, frightening, or marking us.

Long before (in a sense, three years before when I had unintentionally killed a black bear with tranquilizers), I had ruled out the use of drugs as a technique of immobilizing and handling the chulos. There are exceptions, but as a rule tranquilizer guns, darts, baits work better on TV shows than in the field. Effective dosages vary from species to species, and in most cases, including the chulo, there is little data available on safe and unsafe practices. Having found a chulo tribe, we had no desire to decimate it with drug experiments. Also, once injected (which is a messy job in itself), an animal cannot be immediately released to wander about in a drugged state; he must be confined while he recovers. Everything considered, tranquilizing twenty-four animals would have been a dangerous, time-consuming, and expensive process.

Ten years ago, the late Harold Stabler, an extraordinary Quaker craftsman, naturalist, folklorist, and gentleman, designed, because I kept pestering him to do so, what I have always thought is the perfect live-animal trap. A Stabler trap

is an extremely simple device which can be built and repaired cheaply, quickly, by anyone, no matter how poor a
mechanic he may be. It is a rectangular box, the size and
materials of which are determined by what you want to
catch. (I have used Mr. Stabler's trap to take bears, shrews,
and a great variety of beasts of in-between size and character.) The box has two sliding doors. The first, when the trap
is set, is held open by tension provided by an engaged
mouse or rat trap. When the trigger is pulled, the door slams
shut. The trap can be operated automatically by attaching a
string from the mousetrap to bait inside the box, or can be
set off manually by a man standing some distance away
holding a string tied to the trigger. The second sliding door,
in the rear of the box, is fitted with a sleeve so that a holding
box or bag can be attached to it. Once the animal is trapped,
the first door having slammed shut behind him, the second
door is opened. The captive is prodded, cajoled, or often he
voluntarily seeks to escape into the holding container.

After watching the chulos, seeing no reason why they
could not be trapped in this way, Terry and I stayed in
Tucson one day and built a Stabler chulo trap. The box,
which was a frame covered with turkey mesh, was four feet
long, two and a half feet wide and deep, large enough to
hold at least seven (our record catch) chulos of assorted
sizes. We rigged the trap to be operated manually, since if
we caught chulos we wanted to get them out of the box,
release them as soon as possible. We made the sleeve so that
the mouth of an ordinary military-surplus duffle bag would
fit over it. We thought or hoped that, once a chulo was inside
it, we could draw the duffle bag around him straitjacket-
fashion and work with him without much danger to either
party.

The next day, we took the trap to the Peak and put it out,
unset but filled with scraps, behind the kitchen. As soon as
they arrived, the chulos found the box, entered it unhesitatingly. Thereafter, having learned that it was the principal

feeding station, they went directly to it when they came to the kitchen area.

Not knowing how the animals would react, we decided to experiment on Charley, the all but tame kitchen chulo. One morning, Charley obligingly wandered into the trap and Ky, who was the trigger man, pulled the door shut behind him. At first, Charley did not know or perhaps did not care that he was confined, went on gobbling scrambled eggs, bacon ends, cinnamon toast—the remains of the astronomers' breakfast. However, when the four of us approached, Charley tried to back out the door. Finding it closed, he began to tear frantically at the mesh and at the same time to grunt and snarl ferociously. Gingerly rapping on the wire, waving our hands, talking to him, we directed the chulo out through the back door and into the canvas bag, the neck of which I grabbed and hung on to tightly. Charley continued to thrash, but we were able to restrain him by compressing the bag. Once we got a good hold on his snout (the long muzzle of a chulo makes a particularly good handle), we were able to proceed with our measurements. When we finished, we dumped Charley out of the bag onto the ground. He galloped off through the bushes, tail held straight and indignantly over his back. However, fifty yards away, he stopped on a boulder. Panting (the experience must have been an exhausting one for such a stout, elderly animal), he stared back at us in a speculative rather than baleful manner. After having rested for a minute, he continued his retreat but at his customary gait, a dignified waddle.

Three hours later, Charley returned while we were eating lunch. After having begged as many sandwich scraps as we would give him, he walked over to the trap and without any particular hesitation entered it and began to feed.

So encouraged, we proceeded to trap the other members of the tribe, and found that Charley's behavior was more or less typical. Some animals struggled, seemed angrier than others, but once they were released, only two animals (about whom more later) showed any signs that the experience was traumatic or even a particularly memorable one. After being released, they might not come back the same day, but all the trapped chulos returned shortly and none seemed to bear any grudge against us or subsequently to avoid the trap. During the remainder of the year, we trapped forty-eight individual chulos and retrapped most of them half a dozen times without injuring or permanently frightening any of them.

Juvenile chulos both at Kitt Peak and later in the Huachucas were especially nonchalant about being trapped and, if they did not actually enjoy it, quickly learned how the operation worked, seemed to regard it as an easy way to earn a meal. Once they had been trapped a time or two, the youngsters would, as soon as the door fell, march directly to the rear of the cage, would jostle each other to leave through the rear door and climb into the bag, from whence they would be released. Often after they had been dumped out of the bag, rather than running they would circle around and try to re-enter the trap to continue their feeding.

That chulos, who in other situations learn rapidly and adjust their behavior on the basis of what they have learned, should have been so unconcerned about this experience was something of a puzzle. In retrospect, several factors may have contributed to their reaction or lack of it. Though we had to manhandle the animals, we did so very quickly. After a little practice, two of us working as a team could do everything we wanted with a chulo and release him within two minutes after he entered the trap. Though we held them tightly, for their safety and ours, we inflicted no pain. Finally it seems, because of the behavior not only of the chulos but also of other animals in similar circumstances, that truly extraordinary happenings often leave little impression on creatures. Being grabbed, popped into a duffle bag was simply beyond the experience and comprehension of the chulos, and thus perhaps was not, to be anthropomorphic, an experience upon which they were inclined to brood. I have a suspicion that had our capture technique required pursuit, involved any sharp pain, we might have quickly and thoroughly frightened them.

Whatever the reasons, the agreeable way in which the chulos tolerated trapping was an unexpected and fortunate phenomenon so far as we were concerned, and we were careful not to press our luck in this matter. For example, we did not take the linear measurements—length of ear, body, tail, rear foot—which are customarily made of mammals. To have made them accurately would have required greater and longer restraint, and while this information is of interest to taxonomists attempting to classify subspecies, it was not of prime importance to us.

We did weigh each animal each time it was trapped. This could be done easily while the animal was inside the bag, and weight, of all measurements, tends to reflect behavior, environmental circumstances. Thus we found that as a group the Kitt Peak tribe was heavier than the animals we later weighed in Montezuma Canyon. In December, the only month in which we weighed a number of animals from each group, the average weight of the Kitt Peak juveniles was 3.6 pounds, adult females 9.4, and adult males 14.5. The corresponding weights in Montezuma Canyon were 3.2, 8.9, 13.6. All of which was simply statistical substantiation of the obvious fact that the Kitt Peak tribe ate better and more regularly than the animals in Montezuma Canyon, or perhaps than any other chulos in Arizona. (Of all the animals weighed during the year, old Charley, the pet of the Kitt Peak kitchen staff, was the heaviest, weighing in November 21.4 pounds.)

Among both the Kitt Peak and the Montezuma tribes there was a seasonal fluctuation of the weights of the individual animals. The chulos, at least during 1970–71, were at their heaviest in November and early December, reflecting, it seemed, the fact that in southern Arizona the long warm fall, after the summer rains, is the most benign and, from the standpoint of a creature like the chulo, most bountiful season of the year. By mid-December the animals had stopped gaining weight, and in Montezuma Canyon three-quarters of the animals lost weight—up to a pound—during January and February. In the spring of the year, the juveniles, perhaps responding to easier and better foraging conditions, showed a spurt of growth, gaining on an average about two pounds between April and June. The females also showed weight gain but this was at least in part because of their pregnancy. The adult males, however, did not gain or lose weight during the spring, which may have been because of the stresses of the mating season, in some cases the serious debilitating wounds which they received in conflicts with other males.

All chulos, even the juveniles, can be sexed accurately by a quick external examination. (This is not always so with small mammals.) Determining the age of a chulo was more difficult. Size alone was sufficient to identify juveniles, who do not achieve their full growth until they are eighteen months old. From July to May, any chulo weighing less than six pounds can safely be assumed to have been born during that year. After they are a year old, the sexual characteristics of the males serve to indicate their age, since the testes do not descend until they are twenty-four or twenty-five months old. Thus a full-grown male, an animal of ten pounds or so, whose testes have not descended is regarded as a subadult, somewhere between a year and two years old. Subadult females could not be so accurately identified by sexual characteristics. However, weight and, as we later found out, behavior within the tribe gave some clues. After they have reached physical and sexual maturity, determining the age of chulos is a matter of guesswork. Roughness of the skull, scar tissue, the condition of the teeth give some hints but they are not definitive. Again we felt that if one were to follow a chulo tribe for a decade or so, it would probably be possible to determine age by behavior, by the function which an animal performed within the tribe, by her or his relationships to other animals. (The general consensus based largely on records of captive animals is that the "natural" life span of a chulo is between twelve and fifteen years.)

In addition to weighing, sexing, and trying to estimate the age of the animals we trapped, we examined them quickly for deformities, injuries, obvious signs of illness, external parasites. When we could, we tried to pick up each member of the tribe once a month, repeat and record the results of this examination.

Though trapping and handling the chulos proved to be surprisingly easy, marking them, which was a principal purpose of the whole operation, was not. Many people working in the field with mammals have had the same need as we did—some method of quickly, painlessly marking captives so that they can be easily re-identified. Many techniques have been tried and few are entirely satisfactory. Ear tags, which are affixed staple-fashion, can be inserted quickly and are relatively permanent, but they are necessarily so small that the animal must be retrapped in order to be re-identified by the tag number. Streamers of color-coded plastic are sometimes used with ear tags or collars. They are visible from a distance but tend to encumber, distract an animal, particularly one such as the chulo, who operates in dense, scrubby thickets. Also we had the feeling that strong and dexterous as they are with their forepaws, chulos would very probably rip off such markers almost as fast as we could apply them. There are several methods of hot and cold branding or tattooing animals but all take time, are painful, and the marks are not highly visible. Collars in which small radio transmitting units are mounted are sometimes used. Animals so equipped can be identified, tracked with a radio receiver from a considerable distance. However, bio-tele-metric collars take considerable time to fasten onto the animals, and the radio equipment is very expensive and fragile. Those who use it run the risk of becoming slaves to machinery.

In talking about our marking problems, Lyle Sowls, the University of Arizona javelina specialist, said that he and his students had bleached and dyed the wild pigs. They used commercial hair dyes and in consequence there were Sultry Red and Summer Blond javelinas roaming about the Arizona mountains. We tried bleach but found that it was messy to apply. (The principal result of our bleach period was that all of us lost the outer skin of our fingertips.) Furthermore it is hard with chulos to bleach spots large enough to be seen from a distance and yet small enough to allow for a twenty-four-animal position code. After abandoning bleaches, we began experimenting with a variety of dyes, paints, and cattle waxes which we daubed, sprayed, or rubbed on the chulos' tails—an obvious place to try to mark these animals. The results were gaudy, and while we were trying this method tourists came regularly to Dick Doane's office to ask about the animals they had seen, or thought they had seen, with brilliant red, blue, yellow, or green tails. However, none of the dyes, which could be quickly applied, would last more than a week or so. As soon as the last of the animals had been colored, the marks on the first ones had begun to fade and we would have to commence retrapping.

Finally we hit upon a marking technique which so far as we knew had not been used previously but which worked well, or at least better than anything else with the chulos. As anyone who potters about outdoors knows, one of the most important technological breakthroughs of our time has been the invention of good, waterproof tape. With it you can mend a tent, canoe, sleeping bag, camera, lash together a lean-to, blaze a trail, make a pair of snowshoes, bind an ankle. As it turned out, you can also mark a chulo's tail. A two-inch band of tape, wrapped lightly around the tail, was visible for about as far as we could see through glasses, did not bother the chulos in the least, and could be applied in a matter of seconds. Six rolls of colored tape gave us more than enough combinations to code all the animals. Best of all, the tape was surprisingly durable, would stay in place for from three to six months.

SPECTATOR SPORTS

At one time or another, most of the Kitt Peak staff came by the dining hall to talk to us about or watch us trapping and handling chulos. We especially seemed to entertain the Papagos. Several of the younger men such as Hondo took a technical interest in our ambitions and problems, would often slip away from wherever they were supposed to be working and sit with us in back of the kitchen, drinking coffee, sunbathing, telling stories, and, when necessary, giving us a hand with the chulos. There were also two older men of great dignity and silence who often stopped by— more, it seemed, to study us than the chulos. They were both carpenters at the Peak, but Hondo told us they were in real life tribal officials. I often had the suspicion that our activities may have given them hope that the fall of white civilization was imminent.

As a tribe, the Papagos are especially jovial and courteous people. The two elders, though they did not or would not speak much English, were no exceptions. They would stand at the side of the dining hall, smiling politely but watching us intently, in a sociological manner. Every now and then, when we were wrestling around in the dirt with a bagged chulo, our paint cans, and tape, they would step behind the building and, out of sight, we could hear them giggling.

One morning, when John and I were putting an orange and blue marking on Chulo No. 7 (after being trapped, each animal was assigned a permanent field number), the two men came up quietly behind us, and after a time the more prominent of them asked, "What color you like best?"

"It doesn't make much difference. I mean it's just to mark them."

"One color's good as another," the Papago suggested helpfully.

"Yeh, except each one has a color of his own. I mean this one is blue and orange."

"Mmm," said the old Indian thoughtfully. Then he and his companion walked away, giggling as they went.

Unfortunately from my standpoint—but, I am sure, fortunately from theirs—the two carpenters, Hondo, and it seemed like the majority of the Kitt Peak Papagos were with us on the morning of my most humiliating chulo-trapping experience. Our technique for handling chulos was not elegant but it was generally effective. Once the animals were in the duffle, we would weigh them on spring scales. Then we would put the bag on the ground. One of us would feel around through the canvas until we got the captive's head, and turn him around so that the tail faced the mouth of the bag. The bagman would then hold the animal's hindquarters with his hands, straddle the bag, sit lightly on it to keep the chulo from wriggling his head and foreshoulders. The marker could then roll back the mouth of the bag and examine, paint, or tape the animal. On this particular morning, we had finally been able to trap the last of the three solitary males. He was, as we later discovered, the dominant one of the three, a large sixteen-pound animal, wary and extremely strong. He struggled desperately in the bag and, as the holder, it was all I could do to restrain him while Terry examined and marked him. In the struggle, my hat had fallen off, my dark glasses had dropped to the ground and been pulverized, and I was sweating profusely. Then suddenly I felt a stabbing pain in my left buttocks. I hollered and leaped straight in the air, still holding on to the neck of the bag, the bottom of which remained attached to my rear by means of a large canine tooth which the chulo had driven through the canvas, my pants, and half an inch of me. It was, for the rest of the party, a great moment. For a time, it seemed that it might be too much of a happening for the two elderly Papagos. Dignity and diplomacy were forgotten. They stood heaving and choking with laughter, beat each other on the back, even did a little shuffling dance step. They continued to gasp and chortle as I went back, so to speak, to the mat with the bagged chulo. When we finished and finally released the animal, the two turned abruptly, without looking at me, and walked away, their shoulders shaking. They never mentioned the incident directly to us again, but I have the feeling that it may have earned me a small niche in Papago folklore. In some ways, it is nice to think that in years to come little Papagos may be entertained with the story of the damn-fool white man who tried to sit on a chulo's head and got bit in the ass. It is the kind of tale that lends itself to pantomime.

In general, we had few scars to show for our experience as chulo trappers. Occasionally the marker, reaching in the bag for the tail, would come too close to a chulo's head which was too loosely held and get his hand slashed. One day after we had moved back to the Huachucas, where we used the same technique, a chulo which Ky was holding for John to mark wriggled free, leaped out of the bag. As Ky and John each tried to grab it, the frightened animal escaped over Ky's shoulder, ripping his shirt with his claws and raking furrows across Ky's back. Such accidents resulted from our carelessness or clumsiness, and as a rule handling chulos was painless for all parties.

Young chulos do not cut their permanent canine teeth until they are almost a year old. The milk teeth are sharp but small. They can nip with them like a puppy, even crunch a lizard, but cannot do much harm to a man. Therefore we handled the juveniles casually. Not only could they not bite effectively, but they seldom tried to do so (the docility perhaps being related to the incapacity). After we came to know more about them, we often dispensed with the bag, simply reached inside the trap, picked the juveniles up, held them in our hands while we worked with them. They struggled very little and even at times seemed to enjoy the fondling.

The Kitt Peak period amounted to a kind of introductory course, Chulology I. There, under almost ideal, laboratory-like circumstances, with the Kitt Peak tribe acting as obliging and patient tutors, we learned something about the basic characteristics and faculties of the animals, not enough to answer many questions but enough to raise questions about them, to give us some notion about what we wanted, what we should and could learn. In this introductory way, we were immediately struck by three properties of the chulos at Kitt Peak: their apparently exceptional sense of smell, their communicativeness, and their communality. To a considerable degree, much of the rest of our year was spent trying to collect more information about these characteristics. The longer we were with the animals, the more it seemed to us that these were critical phenomena, shaping, to an extent explaining, the life style of the chulo.

THE SCENT WORLD

Smell is perhaps the most extraordinary of all mammalian senses. Good olfactory apparatus enables its owner to form a kind of three-dimensional impression of the world. Thus, approaching a thicket from a considerable distance, a chulo knows, because of his ability to read scents, a good bit about the condition of that patch of brush—if, for an obvious example, there is a bobcat lurking within it. He also knows something about its history; if there has been a cat in the thicket during the past several days, does a cat frequently pass by the place. Finally, because of scent, he will have some notions about the immediate future of that thicket: is a bobcat approaching it.

Man's sense of smell was, it appears, never of the first rank and has apparently degenerated from lack of use. Our feebleness in this respect is a major reason why we have so little understanding of the life styles of keen-scented bloods. Being barred from the scent world, which is such an important one for them, we find it extremely difficult even to remember that it exists, let alone to develop techniques or instruments which would enable us to measure, analyze the influence of scent perception on the behavior of other creatures.

What little information we receive through our noses is of a crude sweet, sour-acrid, rose-skunk sort. Lacking facts, it remains a matter of speculation but it seems likely from external evidence that the scent impressions of some animals are quite different; are as rich, subtle, and detailed as the visual ones we receive. A chulo, for example, may, because of scent, have rather complete knowledge about whatever there is to eat or drink within a quarter-mile radius. It seems probable that each member of a band of chulos foraging through heavy thickets knows by scent impressions not only who is in the group but their relative position, something about their activities.

There seems a good possibility that some species may use a rather complex system of scent communication. We know that dogs and beavers, for example, deliberately mark the boundaries of their territories with urine or glandular secretions and that these scent posts convey information to others of their kind. Certain emotions change body odors. Sexual excitement gives rise to a distinctive odor and serves to pass information between members of many species of insects, fish, mammals. Fear, we think, has its own smell, which is recognized and reacted to by certain animals. I have always thought it likely that we recognize and understand only the most obvious of these scent signs, that there are many others about which we know nothing. For example, among social animals like the chulos, it is not impossible that certain scents express moods of sociability, amity, challenge, surrender, alarm, curiosity. We assume, largely because the converse boggles our imagination, that such communication, if it exists, must be reflective, involuntary, that the glandular change and thus the scent change occur as an automatic reaction to a specific stimulus. However, it might be a more willful matter, and some creatures may have developed the ability to control scent releases, just as they or we can control the gestures and sounds we make. Thus if a female chulo bringing up the rear of a group is surprised, she has a variety of vocal signs she can give to inform the other animals as to the whereabouts of the danger, its nature, to command specific responses from the others. I do not discount the possibility that in such a situation the chulo may be sending scent as well as sound messages.

We were no more able than most—less able than the few physiologists who have begun to investigate the olfactory ability of other species—to measure the keenness of the chulos' sense of smell, to penetrate their scent world. However, there was considerable circumstantial evidence that they make use of this sense frequently, perhaps constantly, and depend heavily upon it.

A chulo will frequently stop whatever she is doing—foraging, traveling, playing, napping—sit back on her haunches in a bear-like position, raise her long slim nose, and move it about slowly like a rotating radar antenna. Until some better explanation is advanced, it seems likely that she is doing what she appears to be doing—sniffing the air. She assumes this characteristic position because it allows scent-bearing air to pass more freely across her olfactory membranes. It seemed to us more likely that they rose up in this manner to sniff than to look about their surroundings. Chulos, we thought, were relatively shortsighted, as are many creatures of rough, brushy, forested country who have no need for the keen far-sighted vision of an eagle, a hunting dog, or even a man. Vision, it seemed to us, was the chulos' second or third sense. (Our impression was that their hearing was approximately comparable to our own.) Certainly in the terrain in which we found them, a good nose would seem to be more useful than good eyes and, evolution being a pragmatic process, species tend to develop and refine the most useful, most used faculties.

In an olfactory way, the parking lot behind the Kitt Peak kitchen where we often met and fed the chulos must have had much the same impact on a nose as, say, a jetport would have on hearing. There were so many mingled smells—men, chulos, food, gas, oil—that the scent messages must have been confused, cacophonous, so to speak. In any event, while they were scurrying about the parking lot, noses down looking for food, chulos would often literally bump into us, apparently to their surprise and embarrassment.

In moving away from real or imagined danger, simply traveling from place to place, a chulo tribe proceeds in an orderly formation. An adult female leads the march and she is closely followed by all the tribal juveniles, occasionally by another adult. Behind this first group come other adults and subadults. The last animal is invariably another adult and dominant female. All the animals—except, of course, the leader—follow *exactly* in the footsteps of those who have preceded them. At Kitt Peak, the tribe normally followed the same path between their home ravine and the kitchen feeding area. However, it was fairly easy to demonstrate that it was scent, not visual or tactile impression, which kept them on this trail. If not being pressed or harassed, the adults and subadults whose position was between the leading juvenile group and the rear-guard female tended to mosey along slowly, singly or in pairs. Often they were out of sight of one another, strung out two or three minutes apart on the path. If we intercepted one of these animals, made her leave the path, she would begin, nose to the ground, to cast about like a hunting dog, trying to recover the scent of the animal who had gone ahead. She would do this even though the worn chulo trail itself was plainly visible. Even more significantly, the animals who followed behind the one who had been driven from the path would leave it exactly where she had, make the same unnecessary detour before regaining it. Even though the trail was familiar to them from daily use and must have reeked of chulo scents, they obviously wanted to follow the most recent scent, that of the animal who had gone just before them.

Juvenile chulos, who reacted so docilely to being trapped and handled, displayed some signs of panic if they carelessly strayed or were driven only a few feet from the tribal scent trail. They would dash about frantically, trying to reorientate themselves, and if they were not able to do so in a very short time they would squeal for help or to let the other animals know where they were. Without being able to document or measure the phenomenon, reduce it to graph paper, we believed that scent was a kind of binder which kept the tribe together, contributed greatly not only to the physical but to the psychic security of the animals.

Indisputably, chulos have a sweet tooth. They are fond of wild grapes, figs, plums, cactus drupes, and, once they discover them, have an insatiable greed for man-made goodies. As a standard chulo-watching aid, the four of us carried marshmallows, the small, thumb-sized variety, which made a cheap and convenient bribe. After the tribe learned about us and marshmallows, we found that we could hide a single candy in a small pocket or cuff and the bolder animals would immediately find it, even though it had been hidden secretly. If we met the animals when only one of us was carrying marshmallows, the tribe would unhesitatingly rush to the candy bearer.

For us, the scent world of the chulos was like a distant mountain range, protected by impassable barriers. We could dimly perceive its outlines, but the details remained hidden. However, we at least knew it was there. Often during the course of the year when we were mystified by individual or collective activities, we would conclude that it was impossible even to attempt an explanation, since the behavior was probably rooted in the sensual dimension of scent, into which we could not follow the animals.

COMMUNICATION

Social animals are invariably more demonstrative than solitary ones. A bear, weasel, or cat, who spends much of his adult life alone, tends to be deadpan, uncommunicative, seldom having reason to describe his state of body, mind, emotions, or to declare what he will or will not do. On the other hand, wolves, baboons, and porpoises are more demonstrative because they live in continual association with others of their kind, must cooperate, must coordinate their activities and desires with those of other members of the community. All creatures communicate, but the more complex their social organization the more sophisticated their system of communications tends to be.

Knowing that they were social, we were not surprised when we first met a chulo tribe at Kitt Peak to find the animals squealing, chirping, grunting—apparently exchanging information by these vocal signs. At first the chulos, from our standpoint, were simply noisy, the vocalizations meaningless to us. However, we assumed that they had meaning and that if we were to learn something about the chulos' life style we would at least partially have to master their language. We commenced the study of Chulo at Kitt Peak, continued it when we moved back to the Huachucas. After six months, we thought we could understand Chulo reasonably well and even learned to speak a few words of it.

Whether or not the system of communication used by the chulos and other "lesser" animals should be called language is a matter of dispute. In essence, those who disapprove of the use of the word "language" to describe the communication system of, say, the chulos do so on the grounds that only human communication, which is especially abstractive and intellectual, should be so dignified. While it may be an interesting problem for semanticists, it is inconsequential when it comes to dealing intimately with a community of other bloods, trying to understand what communicative creatures are doing, are going to do. We found that there was a considerable exchange of information between chulos accomplished by the use of discrete vocal, visual, and perhaps scent signs. Some of the signs seemed to be reactive; that is, direct, involuntary, very likely inherited responses to specific stimuli. Other signs seemed to be learned, were selected for use by the animal as being the most appropriate sign in the particular circumstances, and served to transmit relatively abstract information. It seemed to us that the regular, elaborate information-exchange system could, as easily and meaningfully as anything else, be described as language.

There being no Chulo grammars or dictionaries, it being a matter of complete indifference to the natives whether we understood their language or not, we learned what we did of Chulo by spying and eavesdropping. When we heard a new sound or saw a new gesture, we tried to remember or, better yet, record it on tape or film, to make some notes about the circumstances in which it was used, the response of other animals to the sign. When we reached the point that we could predict the reaction of one animal to a sign made by another, we felt we had more or less made it our own.

Vocally, Chulo is a deceptively complicated language. At its root are three sounds, or rather families of sound, the squeal, the chirp, and the grunt. However, these basic sounds are modified, inflected in a bewildering variety of ways, many of which were unquestionably too subtle for us to distinguish and identify. Also the position of a sound in what might be thought of as a Chulo sentence modified meaning. Thus a squeal-grunt might mean, "I was surprised but pay no attention, it was a false alarm." If the sequence was reversed—that is, the grunt preceded the squeal—the meaning would be entirely different: "There is something curious—look out, it is dangerous."

The squeal is used principally by juveniles but also by adults when they need to express what are essentially juvenile emotions. In June, we were able to watch the birth and then follow the development of four chulo cubs. These blind, immobile, helpless infants were able to and did squeal lustily as soon as they were born. During their first month, the squeal was their only form of communication, and it was almost entirely a reactive sign, like the cry of a human baby. Young chulos squeal if they are hungry, cold, are being jostled by their litter mates, or become separated from them. The infant squeal is high and piercing, and draws an immediate response from adults of both sexes. The litter we watched was born on the back porch of our cabin in Montezuma Canyon to a female, Mona, whom we had taken, after she was impregnated, from Kitt Peak. During her confinement, Mona became tame and trusting, and even when the cubs were only a day old she permitted us to handle, weigh, measure them. She showed no concern so long as they did not squeal. As soon as they did, she would attack us, and the attack was a genuine, not a *pro forma* one. Also, when Mona's cubs would squeal and adult members of the Montezuma Canyon tribe happened to be within earshot, they would react violently, come running toward the porch and claw at the screen, trying to reach the bawling babies. In such circumstances, they were in an exceptionally aggressive, pugnacious mood and we stayed well away from them. (It was in this way, during our last months in the mountains, that we discovered that the surest way of attracting a chulo is to play the recorded sound of an infant squeal.)

Neither we nor apparently the adults could determine whether when he squealed a newborn cub was or was not in serious difficulties. Since during their first six months chulos are great crybabies and squeal at the slightest provocation, the adults would have little time for anything else if they felt compelled to answer every squeal. However, this situation naturally corrects itself. After about their third week, the cubs began to develop a repertoire of squeals—in a sense learn their first meaningful words. From this point on, the adults began to discriminate in their reactions to squeals and adjust their behavior in accordance to the information which they received from the youngsters. Among the distinctive variations of the juvenile squeal, we were able to identify the following:

"Help—I am in terrible trouble!"

This is the first squeal juveniles make after birth. It is loud and sustained. Young animals who are anything but stoics tend to overuse it. Adults always respond to it, come quickly to investigate. As they grow older, the cubs use it less and less often, more and more legitimately. This squeal remains in the vocabulary of adult chulos but among adults is used only *in extremis.* Several times an adult squealed in this fashion when we were manhandling it in the marking bag. A single male, wounded, pinned to the ground by Dain, squealed like a newborn cub.

"Come—I may need help."

This is a somewhat less intense or panicky version of the preceding squeal but, so far as we observed, was not used by the cubs until they were out of the den traveling with the tribe. In general, it indicated surprise and fear. We heard it used by a cub who had come across a garter snake; by one who, to the consternation of both animals, came face to face with a single male who had escaped the vigilance of the females. Occasionally a cub being handled or marked would squeal in this fashion. Females would respond, come to investigate, but in general seemed less concerned than when they heard the all-out "Help" squeal.

"Let me alone."

While competing for a nipple, later for bits of food, while playing, cubs would often pile on each other, push, shove, wrestle (though seldom nip). The cub who was or thought he was getting the worst of such encounters would often squeal piteously. If the squealing continued, an adult might amble over, nuzzle the cubs, distract them, but there was no urgency in the response. This squeal usually served to break up the roughhouse; the other cubs would draw back, pause momentarily.

"I want it."

Another squeal that functioned as a kind of juvenile challenge. Two cubs foraging in the same place, competing for the same piece of food, might begin to squeal at each other. Often the one who squealed longest and loudest was successful, the other backing off. Adults never responded to this squeal, apparently feeling that it signified a situation which the youngsters should work out by themselves.

"Please."

This seemed to be another version of the "I want it" squeal, but was directed by cubs toward adults, represented a kind of begging for a bit of food, which the adult usually surrendered to the cub. Occasionally when a cub was imploring an adult to groom him, or to continue grooming him, he would use a softer version of this squeal.

"Don't beat me."

Cubs were raised, educated permissively. Occasionally however, an adult, usually the female who brought up the rear, would become thoroughly exasperated with a dawdling or straying cub and would cuff it gently. When she did so, the cub would crouch, squeal briefly, then take his proper place in the tribe. There was a suggestion of surrender in this behavior, a certain sense that the cub was acknowledging the justice of the cuffing by his lack of resistance. Several times we saw a subadult animal either refuse to give up food to a cub or actually try to take food from the cub and cuff at the younger animal. The cub immediately squealed, using the "Come—I may need help" signal rather than the "Don't beat me" response. In each case, an adult female came at once and forced the subadult, who had broken the tribal "cubs are inviolate," to retreat.

"*Wait.*"

Occasionally a cub would become separated from the tribe, lose the scent trail. If so, he would squeal insistently but softly, which was a reasonable reaction, since it would be risky to advertise his plight any more than was necessary. Upon hearing the call, one or several of the adults would halt, grunt, and do as the cub requested: wait until he had found his way back.

The squeal remained part of the adult vocabulary but was seldom used and then only in very special circumstances.

"*I surrender*" (male to male).

In the spring, the tribal males who had been solitary throughout the fall and winter began to edge closer to the tribe to court and eventually copulate with the females. Often two or more of these males would meet in the vicinity of the tribe, and they would battle in a way to be described later. In the majority of cases, no blood was shed in these confrontations. After a period of ritual maneuvering, posturing, and cursing, one of the males would surrender. The surrender signal was always the same. The defeated male would flatten himself on the ground, raise his head, and begin squealing in a way that was very similar to the infant "Help" call. He would remain fixed in this position and continue to squeal while the victor circled contemptuously. Once the dominant male moved away, the inferior animal was free to get to his feet and run.

Curious as it may seem, this is logical and useful behavior. By squealing—in fact, acting for a moment like a juvenile—the vanquished chulo is plainly communicating the information "I'm a poor sniveling little coward—no threat to you, boss." Also by squealing, the loser is invoking the tribal taboo against molesting juveniles. Properly performed, we never saw this ritual fail in its function of preventing physical violence. Once squealing his surrender, the defeated animal was immune to further attack.

"*I surrender*" (male to female).

During the fall and winter, the adult females invariably drove off any males who came too close to the tribe. Normally the males would move off before any direct confrontation took place, but occasionally a particularly wrathful female and a stubborn male would meet. When they did, the female would attack the male, would nip and cuff him. The males never retaliated, but would begin to squeal, and when this surrender signal was given, the female would release the male, permit him to retreat unmolested. The attacks were not serious, but they may have been at some time in the development of chulo social customs. Therefore the surrender squeal served again to prevent real violence, which would have been risky for the individuals, disadvantageous for the tribe as a whole.

The majority of vocal signs—in a sense, words—used commonly by adult chulos are based on the grunt, a snuffling, snorting, guttural, very pig-like sound. Changes of the frequency, pitch, or volume change the meaning. The subtle variations in sound must be heard to be understood, cannot be described in words. However, some of the grunt words and phrases which the chulos use and we learned include:

"*All is well.*"

Foraging together, at their ease, chulos will grunt softly, almost as if talking absent-mindedly to themselves. The sound seems to serve the purpose of letting tribal members know the general location in which other animals are working, gives reassurance that all is well. If several animals suddenly stop grunting, this constitutes a kind of negative signal, indicating something curious, perhaps threatening, has caught their attention. Cessation of the "All is well" grunting alerts the animals for some new type of comment.

"*I have found————.*"

The frequency and what might be called the excitement content of the "All is well" grunt will change when a chulo comes across a good food source. There were distinctive grunt patterns which informed us, and therefore presumably the other chulos, when an animal had found fruit, a large colony of insects, a lizard, a snake, carrion, very likely other edibles. The grunting seemed to indicate the quantity as well as kind of food. If the chulo discovered what amounted to only a few mouthfuls, the other animals seldom responded, but if she had come upon a quantity of food, other animals would join her. The effect was cumulative. For example, to draw the tribe to a good observation area or simply to see what they would do, we would occasionally hide a pound or so of dog food, wait for them to find it. The first animal to come upon the cache would begin to grunt, "I have found carrion [which is how the chulos spoke of dog food] in some quantity." The nearest animals would immediately amble over to investigate. If there was enough food for them and others, they in turn would grunt, and this would call in animals who had been foraging even farther away. Considering the circumstances in which chulos forage, it was a very practical cooperative response. It let the tribe know who was eating what, and also if there was enough food to warrant other animals interrupting their own foraging to share in the find.

"*Greetings.*"

This was another soft grunt, used when chulos who were scattered about a foraging area met, or when members of two tribal foraging bands which had been separated convened. This was the grunt which sounded somewhat like the word "chulo," and the one we used when meeting chulos. By the end of the year, much to our pleasure, some of the chulos would greet us with this grunt when we met. We thought it indicated that we had been accepted as a curious kind of tribal auxiliary.

There was a large and important group of grunt words and phrases which expressed varying degrees of curiosity and alarm. Particularly when used by the matriarchal females, these signs identified the object which caused the grunt, indicated the state of mind of the grunter, her assessment of the situation, and finally served in a sense as action commands directed toward other tribal members.

"*Attention.*"

"There is something curious—degree of threat unknown but probably slight." The "Attention" grunts would continue until the female had further information. If she went back to the "All is well" grunting, this indicated a false alarm. Or she might investigate, find that the thing she was curious about presented foraging opportunities, and if so, she might change to the "I have found———" signal. There was also a series of signs used to identify and alert the other animals to various categories of threat.

"*Caution.*"

"There is potential danger, but it is a long way off."

"*More caution.*"

"There is danger but it is easily avoided, not a cause for panic."

"*Extreme caution.*"

"There is danger—be ready for defensive or evasive action."

"*Danger.*"

"There is danger but not extreme. Retreat. I will challenge and investigate."

"*Extreme danger.*"

"Run or fight."

Closely related to the alarm and warning grunts was a series of challenging grunts used by the adults in actual confrontation with a threat or potential threat. Again, these signs identified the cause of the commotion and indicated what action the adult was taking, suggested action for the other animals. Also, there was a high degree of bluff in much of this challenging behavior, the object of the chulo seeming to be to make herself appear so formidable that whatever she was confronting would back down, retreat.

"Challenge" (to a harmless but inedible non-chulo).

We were often challenged with this grunt, which was a low cautionary one. It was used to indicate "I see you" (to us). "It's them again, stay alert but I have them under surveillance" (to the other chulos).

"Challenge" (to a possibly dangerous non-chulo).

In the beginning, this was the way in which we were challenged. We also heard it directed toward Dain and to strange humans. It declared, "Come a step closer and I'll attack" (to the intruder), "Be ready for trouble, but I think I can handle it" (to the chulos).

"Challenge" (to a possibly competitive non-chulo).

We heard this when a small foraging band in Copper Canyon came upon a coyote and drove it away from a deer carcass. We heard variations of it when, for example, we were feeding chulos and, after having given them what we thought was enough food but they did not, we would take away the dog food or marshmallow bag. The meaning of this challenge grunt was simply "I intend to take what is mine. If you resist, we will gang up and attack you." In our case at least, this was mostly bluff, since the chulos never carried out their threat. The coyote, however, accepted the ultimatum and retreated without attempting to test the temper of the chulos.

"True challenge."

This is the chulo battle cry, the equivalent of a carnival man yelling, "Hey, Rube!" The grunt becomes so sharp and staccato as to be a snarl. A grunting-snarling chulo will attack. The sign perhaps serves not only as the ultimate challenge to the intruder but also as a call for assistance. We heard it most often when we were marking trapped animals and an adult would become thoroughly enraged or a juvenile would give the *in extremis* "Help" squeal. Several adults might advance on us (while the other animals fled) giving the true battle cry. If only two of us were so challenged, we retreated, dropped the chulo we were working with, feeling that discretion was the better part of valor. If all four of us were present, two would distract the angry adults while the other two would finish what they were doing.

There was also a series of warning and challenge grunts used between chulos under special circumstances. Juveniles, for example, had a peculiar kind of buzzing grunt which they would use to challenge each other in play. They would respond in much the same way if they were startled by some strange happening—say, a rock kicked loose by another member of the tribe, rolling past them on a slope. On the only occasion when we saw members of two tribes meet, some of this buzzing-grunting took place, followed by welcome grunts. (The buzzing-grunting, which is normally a juvenile expression, might be appropriate in these circumstances, being used to express a nonhostile, almost playful challenge.)

Females had several challenge-warning grunts which they would direct toward interloping males, but these were perfunctory, since in dealing with the males the matriarchs tended toward action rather than argument. During the spring breeding season, competing males used a large repertoire of challenge-warning bluff words and phrases, the meaning of which will be described later.

There was a curious group of vocal signals which perhaps deserved to be regarded as a separate category, but which were vaguely related to the grunts. We called them the "ha-ha" sounds. A chulo calling ha-ha not only sounded like a laughing man, but in certain ways appeared to be expressing the same mood and emotions. The ha-ha seemed to indicate a kind of amusement and excitement mingled with a certain taunting contempt. In the fall and winter, we heard only the adult males ha-ha. The Bungler, a male who became the pre-eminent cabin chulo, was an inveterate user of ha-ha. He used the sound not so much as a greeting but as an announcement of his presence. He would arrive, climb up in the oak tree by the back door and begin to ha-ha, the sign obviously being directed toward us, somewhat in the same spirit as an agile boy might yell down, "Ha-ha-ha, you can't catch me." There was a tinge of hostility in the sound but more playfulness. There was an element of challenge, but mock challenge, as if he were announcing, "You come up here and I'll knock your block off," knowing full well that we would not or could not.

There was another male, a much more sedate animal than the Bungler, whom we called "the Old Man." A corner of his regular winter territory also butted on the cabin yard, and he would often appear in the late afternoon. (The Bungler was a midday animal, being a late riser and an early retirer.) At this time, we would let Dain, who was usually on tight heel or shut in the cabin during the day, go for a run while we were fixing supper. Often he would pick up the trail of the Old Man, find him and chase him up a tree. As nearly as the interior feelings of another creature can be assessed, it seemed that Dain looked forward to these runs and did not regard them as a serious hunt but as a form of recreation. The chulo probably did not find them so entertaining, may have regarded them as a mild nuisance. However, after they had been through the routine several times, the Old Man gave no indication that he felt he was in mortal danger. When Dain approached, he would climb up a tree, hang over a low branch, and ha-ha loudly at the barking dog.

A certain amount of ha-ha usually preceded the courtship battles between the males. More surprisingly, so far as we were concerned, the adult females began to ha-ha in the spring. As their glandular condition changed preparatory to breeding, they became more tolerant of the opposite sex; the females, rather than challenging and attacking an approaching male, might ha-ha at him. Later, when the males and females had begun to pair off, there was considerable mutual ha-ha as a prelude to copulation. One afternoon in late April, when feelings of romance were strong and general, the ravine behind the cabin sounded like a hysteric ward in an asylum as two males and four females, in various combinations, called ha-ha back and forth in maniacal fashion. When the tribal elders began to ha-ha, it seemed to alarm the cubs mildly, make them restless, like children in the presence of drunk, disorderly, or impassioned adults.

The chirps—soft, trilling, often bird-like sounds—were signs used almost exclusively between chulos who were at peace and ease with one another. Juveniles would chirp when they were playing pacifically together. Close chulo acquaintances would chirp to one another when they met or as they walked along or rested together. There was a good bit of chirping on the rest ledges during mutual grooming sessions, and on the few occasions when we could successfully eavesdrop, the chulos chirped in their den caves at night. Since the chirps were used for private, domestic discourse, we knew less about them than we did about squeals and grunts. Even after we had been more or less accepted by the tribe, our presence created a certain tension, and as we approached close enough to hear them, the chulos usually stopped chirping. However, in general we felt that chirping was the chulos' language of affection, and perhaps of gossip, or something close to it.

Chulos, like many other creatures, use a variety of nonvocal signs for communicative purposes. For example, their long, highly visible tails served at times as a kind of semaphore (and may have evolved in their present form partly to function as a communication device). Any quick tail movement, raising it suddenly when it was down, lowering it when it was up, served as an attention getter and was often followed by some vocal exclamation or comment. During foraging or traveling, chulos' tails, waving above the low scrub, were fairly good indicators (to us and therefore probably to other animals) of not only where a particular animal was but what she was doing. When an animal found food or when her curiosity was aroused, the tail would begin to vibrate, and the faster it did so, the more excitement was indicated. Another characteristic chulo gesture is tail lashing. This was normally used in accompaniment with and to emphasize and punctuate warning and challenge grunts. Males in courtship confrontations also lashed their tails.

Another frequent chulo gesture is one which we called the "defiant posture." In this position, a chulo plants herself firmly, spreads, bows her forelegs, raises her tail straight over her back, lowers and turns her head to one side, opening her mouth, exposing her teeth. She will assume this posture in warning-threat-challenge situations. A chulo in this position looks formidable, which is probably exactly the impression she is trying to create. After we got to know them well, a tribal matriarch on encountering us would assume the defiant posture casually, as one might wave one's hand to a passerby, hold it for a few seconds, then go on about her business. She was not really in a defiant mood, but indicated that she could become defiant if we tried any funny business.

Among the adults (males also used the defiant posture in their courtship skirmishes), the lower the head was held, the more serious was their hostility. There was a functional—as well as perhaps a symbolic—reason for this. Before a chulo can deliver one of its slashing attacks, it must, because of the elongated shark-like jaw, turn its head to the side. Two males posturing defiantly for each other's benefit would sometimes almost stand on their heads in an attempt to look as ferocious as possible and, by doing so, cow their opponent through psychological rather than physical warfare.

In moments of affection and sociability, chulos will often

rub noses, nuzzle, pat each other with their paws. However, again these were private gestures which we therefore did not often observe and whose precise meaning and significance we did not understand.

Given the chulos' keen noses, dependency on scent, it seemed to us, as noted, that it was not only possible but probable that odor was an important, perhaps a major factor in their communicative behavior. However, we were able to observe, identify the use of only one such scent sign. Male chulos will mount a log, less frequently a boulder, urinate a few drops, and smear the urine by rubbing their bellies back and forth across the surface. We presumed that they did this to leave a scent sign, as a dog or beaver will, indicating that they had been in the spot, and perhaps something about their mood and intentions.

Chulos, as do so many animals, use a combination of visual and vocal signs (and this combination may well be multiplied by the X factor of scent) to express themselves. Thus an animal might first drop her tail, then grunt while assuming the defiant posture, and finally lash her tail to indicate different degrees of challenge or warning. In all, we thought we could identify and roughly understand about a hundred chulo signs and sign combinations. We suspected that the animals used at least as many other signs which we did not recognize, could not translate, or simply did not observe. Whether or not this complex communicative system can properly be called a language, we had no feeling that we were dealing or associating with dumb animals. Even though we could contribute only feebly to it, eavesdropping on chulo conversations was exciting, entertaining, invariably instructive.

COMMUNALITY

On the morning when we first met the Kitt Peak tribe, as the animals loped through the brush toward the dining hall, our strongest impression was that we were looking at a community of animals. There was an overwhelming sense of what might be called the responsiveness of one animal to another, that the group represented a kind of container within which, and oddly because of which, the individuals operated. Subsequent months of observation enabled us to define this social responsiveness more precisely. We came to feel that one chulo is not a comprehensible unit, any more than is one finger of a hand. A chulo is an extension, a component of his tribe, and his or her behavior reflects the tribal connection.

There are many mammals who are regarded as social. (Because of reproductive habits, there is no mammal who is not somewhat social, who does not at times live in association with and is dependent upon others of its kind.) Deer, buffalo, bats, prairie dogs, voles, for example, often congregate in large groups and are commonly said to be social. However, many of these congregations are better understood or defined as collections rather than as communities. Often the animals seem to congregate principally because of terrain, climate, good food sources, and to be motivated largely by self rather than group interests. Within the collection, the behavior of these animals is, in fact, frequently and profoundly antisocial. Many of the activities of individuals and family groups are devoted to defending a particular territory; finding food, shelter, mates within the herd or colony; and in rather fierce competition against its other members.

Predatory communes are as a rule much smaller than the collections of herbivores or rodents, seldom numbering more than a hundred individuals. Also, security is of less obvious importance to communal predators than to collections of prey species. A wolf, a lion, even a chulo is quite capable of protecting himself effectively even when separated from the group. On the other hand, the organization of predatory communities tends to be more complex than that of any other mammalian societies except those of the primates and man. Within them, there is considerable cooperative behavior. Communal hunting is an obvious example: wolves pursuing deer in relays, the ambush of a zebra by a pride of lions, a chulo tribe beating the bushes for lizards. However, there are many and more subtle displays of cooperation: the collective education of the young, group play, mutual grooming, the care of group members who are ill or injured. Predatory communes are usually tightly structured, characterized by ritualized social behavior, taboos, hierarchical organization. Since individual predators are formidable creatures, potentially dangerous to their own kind as well as to their prey, the function of many of these traditions, which can be called laws as well as anything else, is to prevent or reduce intercommunity competition and violence.

The advantages of cooperative hunting, education, security may be prime reasons for the evolution of predatory communities, and these advantages certainly contribute to the maintenance of the groups. However, there seems to come a point when, "practical" benefits aside, the community itself becomes a possession of infinite worth to the individual communard, and defending, maintaining the community is one of the principal motivations of individual behavior. It appears as if communal predators could live (as they sometimes are forced to) without the commune, but, having acquired communal tastes, living without the commune is so unsatisfactory that animals will subordinate, jeopardize individual interests in favor of those of the group.

Female raccoons, bears, deer, and most other female creatures will vigorously defend their young against threats. Yet once the maternal bonds are broken, the female is not inclined to risk her own safety in an effort to protect another of her kind. On the other hand, a female chulo bringing up the rear of a tribal procession will, under threat, challenge the intruder, give a warning call, and if necessary do battle while the other animals (none of whom may be her immediate offspring) retreat. At the other end, the forward-leading female will wait with the tribe until it is joined by the rear guard. At the proper signal, the forward leader and other tribal adults may turn back, *toward danger,* to assist the rear guard. From the standpoint of individual survival, the behavior of the deer, raccoon, bear appears to be more advantageous. The action of the chulo, who does not save her own skin when she easily could, makes biological, evolutionary sense only in terms of the tribe and the great value which the chulos have apparently come to place on maintaining their community.

After a year of observing chulos, our strongest, final impression was the same as our first of their communality. Nearly all chulo behavior, even that of the adult males who are alone for part of the year, is comprehensible only in terms of their communality, of their responsibilities to and relationships within the tribe, which in a sense is a kind of superorganism created by the chulos.

7

Montezuma Canyon

RETURN TO THE HUACHUCAS

A tenet of faith among classical economists is that the wants of man are insatiable. Depressing as it is, there is nevertheless much to be said for the validity of this claim. While we were planning the year, even during the first months while bushwhacking about the Huachucas, the prospect of having six weeks to observe chulos as intimately as we did at Kitt Peak was much more than we hoped for, even at our most optimistic. Yet after we had been at the Peak for a month, despite the hospitality of the observatory staff and the cooperativeness of the chulo tribe, we began to feel restless, discontented, that we should be trying to improve our circumstances.

The chief practical disadvantage of working at Kitt Peak was the daily hundred-mile round-trip drive between Tucson and the observatory. Each morning we left the house at dawn, returned twelve or fourteen hours later, after dark. The life style was more that of a commuter than an outdoorsman. Sleeping in bags in the tiny living room of the Tucson house, which was never intended to accommodate all of us at the same time; driving two and a half hours a day; following chulos about garden paths; watching them from a patio while we stuffed ourselves with fresh pastries —this wasn't how we thought we would spend or should be spending our year in the Wild West. Finally, though we had nothing to compare them with, we had the suspicion that the Kitt Peak chulos, moving leisurely from their protected ravine to the free-lunch stand behind the kitchen, were not a typical tribe. Nevertheless we stayed on because, having found chulos, having become accustomed to harvesting a daily crop of information about them, we could not bear to start looking for them again, going days on end without seeing the animals or catching only brief glimpses of them.

By this time, however, our luck was running strong, and in early December we were given a choice other than Kitt Peak chulos. Harry Busch, a young ranger at the Coronado Memorial, the small National Park unit in Montezuma Canyon at the southern end of the Huachucas, called to say that they were seeing large groups of chulos, sometimes as many as thirty at a time. The animals were often around the ranger station and seemed to be moving throughout the lower canyon.

In October, we had camped for a week in and carefully combed Montezuma Canyon without seeing chulos, except for the male who hung around the State of Texas Mine cadging biscuits. Before and after that time, the park rangers and Will and Bob at the mine had been keeping a special lookout for chulos and had not seen any until November. Therefore from where and why this tribe suddenly appeared was a mystery. (It remains a mystery, though by the next summer we had collected enough circumstantial evidence to support one explanatory theory.) However, the chulos were indisputably in the canyon. Not only were the rangers and the miners reliable observers, but on a hurried one-day reconnaissance back to the Huachucas, John and Ky located a band of ten in the canyon. Finally, in mid-December, we decided to take a chance, to leave Kitt Peak and the chulo tribe that we more or less had in hand there, and go back to the Huachucas to look for new animals in the bushes of Montezuma Canyon.

Montezuma is the most southerly major canyon in the Huachucas. It runs more or less parallel to, a half a mile north of, the Mexican border. The canyon proper is about three miles long, heading up at Montezuma Pass, where the crest of the Huachucas is 7,000 feet above sea level. At its mouth, at an altitude of 4,500 feet, the canyon empties into the flat, burnt, almost treeless San Pedro Valley. A century ago, by report, the San Pedro was a lush, verdant place. There were even beaver in the San Pedro River, which is now a feeble, muddy, silt-filled stream. Today the valley—because of overgrazing, settlement, the lowering of the water table, hard and thoughtless use in general—has become a high desert.

Montezuma Canyon, as most of the big Huachuca canyons do, follows a twisted, tortured course, just as the flood waters which cut it did. The canyon walls are steep and in places there are almost sheer limestone faces. The sides of the canyon are cut, gashed by many tributary canyons, ravines, and washes. The slopes are littered with cliffs, outcroppings, boulders, loose slides of rock. In the upper elevations there is some piñon, ponderosa pine, fir. Juniper grows throughout the canyon, but the principal cover is provided by half a dozen species of oak, manzanita (a red-barked laurel-sized bush), mountain mahogany, wait-a-bit acacia, cholla cactus, agave, yucca; these together make up a thick, thorny, and in many places ferocious chaparral. Montezuma is not as wet a canyon as Bear or Cave. There was no permanent stream when we were there and only half a dozen year-round springs or seeps. All in all, it was dry, exceedingly rough, and not the most scenic spot in the

Huachucas. However, after we had walked many times over most of it, lived in it for a few months, we came to admire it, which is usually the case when one comes to know a bit of wild land, no matter how harsh and homely.

Off and on during the last century, prospectors have poked about in Montezuma Canyon, encouraged by the rich strikes which were made near Tombstone and Bisbee, just across the San Pedro Valley. There are the remains of half a dozen mining ventures in the canyon, test holes, a few shafts that were worked, waste piles—all long since abandoned. (Eventually, Will Sparks gave up the idea of reopening the State of Texas Mine and put his mechanical talents, enormous ambition, and energy into a heavy-construction equipment service.) There are patches of short and bunch grass in the canyon, and grazing rights are theoretically owned by several valley ranchers. However, the canyon provides dry, sparse pasture, and while we were there no cattle were run in it. In addition to the State of Texas Mine compound about halfway up the canyon, the Coronado Memorial toward the canyon mouth was the only enterprise, so to speak, and the rangers and their families the only other residents of Montezuma.

The facilities of the memorial are minimal. At the mouth of the canyon there is a picnic area, a small administration-exhibition building, a maintenance shed, four ranger residences. This compound is rather grandly called Park Headquarters. The trans-Huachuca road runs past the headquarters, but after it passes the picnic grounds it is unpaved, rough enough in many places to rip mufflers and oil pans off low-slung cars, steep and winding enough to frighten flatland tourists. The road leads to Montezuma Pass, where there is a tiny shelter and a magnificent outlook from which on a good day one can see fifty miles to the east or west across both the San Rafael and the San Pedro valleys to the distant Santa Rita and Chiricahua mountains. In addition to the road, there is an excellent footpath, Joe's

Canyon Trail, which winds three miles down the side of the mountain from Montezuma Pass to the Park Headquarters.

Because of its lack of formal attractions and its isolation, the memorial is not a busy place, to put it charitably. In the winter, when the road is bad and the wind cold, and during the summer rains and heat, days, even most of a week, may pass without a bona-fide tourist. Our first impression of the mini-park was that it was an unnecessary installation representing a kind of bureaucratic conceit or bungle. However, the longer we were there the better we thought of it. The dubious historical association aside, the small border tract contains some of the best wildlife habitat in southern Arizona, the most typical mountain-island terrain. Now it seems to me that if anyone wanted to see and get the feel of this rough, exotic country but had only a limited amount of time, perhaps the best thing he could do would be to spend an afternoon walking down Joe's Canyon Trail, through the empty, scrubby Montezuma Canyon.

Joe's Canyon Trail is the handiwork of George Brown, a thin, leathery San Pedro Valley rancher who also has doubled for years as the memorial maintenance man. George commuted daily to the park, but the other members of the staff—Hugo Huntzinger, the superintendent; two rangers, Harry Busch and Gil Withers—lived permanently in the headquarters compound with their families. After we settled in, there were few days when we did not see some or all of the ranger community. We potlucked (though the trade was considerably balanced in our favor), played cards, drank, partied together, shopped for and borrowed from each other, became exceptionally close friends. So far as the chulos were concerned, the rangers became as interested as we were in the animals, loaned us all manner of equipment, let us make free use of their radio communication system, darkroom, reference library, washing machines, showers, central plumbing. Most important, Hugo, Harry, Gil, and later a temporary ranger-historian named Walt Chavez spent many more hours than duty or even conventional politeness demanded, watching chulos, recording their observations. Their work in effect all but doubled the territory we could keep under surveillance, the observation power at our disposal. After a time, it became difficult to determine whether the Coronado Memorial was operating as a park or as a chulo-watching station. To say that the Coronado rangers and their wives assisted with the study of the Montezuma tribe badly understates the situation. In many respects, the study was as much theirs as ours.

GRUB STAKE CABIN

We had left the Huachucas in mid-fall, the best or at least the most comfortable season in those parts. When we returned, it was winter, not the kind of winter we knew in the Northeast but still a season which presented certain problems, influenced our activities. From December until April, we could always see snow on the peaks, above 8,500 feet. Below that elevation, snow occasionally fell but did not, at least did not that winter, lie long on the ground. On the whole, the days were invariably bright, clear, and dry, and at noon in the full sun we could often work without shirts. However, there was always a sharp, skinning, dust-laden wind, and at night the temperatures dropped spectacularly, invariably falling below the freezing mark. During our first two weeks back in the mountains, we struck some unusually ferocious weather, a bit of cold rain, snow flurries, and nighttime temperatures only a few degrees above zero.

Terry, Ky, and I had lived outside in worse, more uncomfortable weather and could have dealt with a Huachuca winter without exceptional hardship. However, cold- and bad-weather camping is a job in itself, which requires so many adjustments, so much extra work, and consumes so much energy that it leaves little time or enthusiasm for anything else. It is one thing to spend a winter day moving about in the mountains, coming back, eating quickly, and crawling into a sleeping bag. It is something else again to sit all day in one place in a cutting wind watching for chulos, then do the camp work, and after that spend an hour or so by flaring lantern light writing up notes, trying to think about what you have seen rather than about your sleeping bag. Having been told by George Brown and others that the weather we were having in January was more or less what we could expect to have until March, I decided that we would have to make some arrangement other than open camping if the chulo study was not to degenerate into a pointless survival exercise.

On the northeast side of Montezuma Canyon, about 6,000 feet up, there was an empty stone cabin and a dilapidated barn which we had walked past several times but had not investigated. However, shivering around an open fire, we remembered two important things about the cabin: its windows were intact and it had a chimney, therefore presumably a fireplace.

On a Friday before we left for a weekend in Tucson, I asked George Brown about the place. He said that the cabin sat on a patented mining claim that had been part of the Grub Stake Mine property. Mining having been long halted, the claim and cabin now belonged to a rancher in the San Rafael Valley who George said was hoping to trade the hundred and fifty acres to the Forest Service for a piece of valley property near his ranch. "The last time I was in it, it was a pretty snug place," George said of the cabin. "It might suit you boys fine."

That weekend, from Tucson, I called the rancher. There was some back and forth necessary to convince him that we were not dope dealers (not an unreasonable assumption, since dope running had become a profitable and common occupation along the border). Deciding that we were, if a bit peculiar, at least what we claimed to be, the rancher said that since he and his partners had no immediate plans for the property we could have the use of the cabin and the hundred and fifty acres of land for as long as we wanted for twenty-five dollars a month. He volunteered that there were a lot of odds and ends of furniture in the old barn, which we were free to borrow if we wanted. All in all, it was the best real-estate transaction I have ever made and very likely ever will make. Domestically, zoologically, aesthetically, acquiring the Grub Stake cabin turned our lives around and to a certain extent those of the Montezuma chulo tribe. Now, for any of us involved in the Arizona year, the cabin and cabin life is the first thing we recall, talk about, and such recollections, because we are no longer there, are always a little painful.

The cabin was a quarter of a mile in from and above the main Huachuca mountain road. The narrow, rutted, pocked public road was itself bad, but the lane or trail leading up to the Grub Stake claim was terrible. It ran along a ledge of the mountain, crossed through two sharp ravines and a field of boulders. To get the van up to the cabin yard, we had to spend two or three hours a week working on this road, filling in the pot and spin holes. However, the forbidding track did have the advantage of insuring privacy, since only we and the rangers, with our special knowledge of the intricate terrain, could or would even try to negotiate it.

Grub Stake cabin itself sat on a kind of mini-plateau in a grove of oaks and junipers at the edge of a deep ravine which we called Clark's, after one of the previous owners. Clark's Ravine split into two smaller ravines which we named, without much imagination, the West and East ravines. These two washes were separated by a great dike of limestone, the prow of which pointed down toward the cabin. This formation, which we named the Wedge, was in fact a sharp bony shoulder of the mountain and sloped sharply back up to the canyon rim. It became prominent in the affairs of the chulos and therefore in ours.

On moonlit nights, the white limestone of the Wedge shone almost incandescently, and from it we were often serenaded by a caterwauling mountain lion who hunted the vicinity and eventually bore her kittens somewhere up in the rocks. A pair of red-tailed hawks nested on the Wedge within sight of the cabin porch. A band of seven javelinas, a dozen deer, a pair of bobcats, an assortment of skunks, foxes, ring-tailed cats, squirrels, lizards, snakes, and scorpions lived on the Wedge and in the vicinity of the cabin. There was a small seep spring around which had formed a half-acre of bog at the head of the West Ravine. At the foot of the Wedge there was a good all-weather spring which flowed into a then unused stock tank from which we drew water and in which we bathed.

The cabin itself was almost too substantial to be called that. It was a hexagonal building, apparently having been built in this odd shape so that it might be squeezed between two large oaks that grew immediately in front of and behind it—a touch which gave us a good feeling about the unknown builder. The fieldstone walls were two feet thick and the four windows along the front, which faced Montezuma Pass, were deeply recessed. A single long room, in which we ate, worked, read, entertained, ran across the front of the cabin. On the inner wall of this room there was a big and efficient fireplace. Filled with mountain oak, which was tough to cut but would burn down to a handful of light ash, the fireplace would heat the entire cabin when the outside temperature was well below freezing. There were two other rooms: a kitchen, with a long counter, a drain, a bank of cupboards; and a bunk room. A screened porch ran across the rear of the cabin, looked directly down into Clark's Ravine, and in the distance overlooked lower Montezuma Canyon and beyond it the San Pedro Valley and Mexico, to the south and east.

The repressed domestic instincts of the three boys were released in a torrent when we moved into the cabin. For most of the first week, they played house while I did what chulo watching was done. Terry's first move was predictable.

He borrowed mops, brooms, brushes, cleaning compounds from the rangers, swept out the dead mice, scrubbed everything fore and aft. Then he sorted through the furniture in the barn and salvaged, after a little carpentry, a long table, six chairs, and the remains of a sofa. Finally he went shopping in Sierra Vista, came back with a checkered tablecloth, pots, pans, and some more cleaning supplies. When Terry finished, the cabin would have done credit to a Lancaster, Pennsylvania, housewife. John took over the interior decorating, contributing a bizarre collection of posters, candles, ropework wall hangings, and exotic mobiles made out of skulls, twisted logs, bits of old mining equipment. When Terry and John got through, the cabin had a curious but pleasing appearance, part Sausalito houseboat, part gallery of found art, and part Pennsylvania-Dutch parlor. In the meantime, Ky turned to the outside, rescreening the porch, carting away accumulated litter from the cabin yard, rejuvenating the outdoor john.

Like all new homemakers, the boys wanted to show off their nest and, as they worked, began to make plans for a cabin-warming. The details of other people's parties seldom being of interest to those who did not attend, it is enough to say that Grub Stake cabin was warmed and the affair was generally conceded to be the highlight of the Huachuca social season. Unquestionably the weather contributed to its success. Saturday noon before the night of the bash, it began to snow hard, and kept on snowing the rest of the day. By party time, only Harry Busch and Chuck Shipp, the Patagonia forest ranger, both of whom were driving jeeps, were able to get through the drifts. They ran a guest shuttle between the Coronado Park Headquarters and the cabin until the snow became too deep even for them, at which point we were all satisfactorily snowbound. Somewhere there may be forty people who would not find it memorable to be crammed together in a warm cabin on a lonely, blizzard-swept mountain with fifty pounds of steak, a washtub full of potatoes, ten cases of beer, and two guitars (John played rock, Will Sparks played country Western). However, if there are such people, none of them were at the Grub Stake cabin-warming.

EUPHORIA

After we moved into the cabin, Ann, the three girls, and Mary Jane (a long-time friend who had quit her job in Washington and joined the chulo commune in January) began weekending with us in the mountains. One Sunday afternoon as she was getting ready to go back to Tucson, Ann asked John to round up the week's dirty clothes so she could bring them back clean the next Saturday. It took John some time, finding a sock here, a T-shirt there, a pair of pants in the kindling box.

"You should really get a laundry bag," Ann suggested. "You could throw everything in there when you took it off, keep it together."

"I guess we should," John said, but then added with no impertinence intended, simply as a matter of fact, "except out here we live like we want to."

John spoke the literal truth. For seven months in the Grub Stake cabin, the four of us were probably as content as it is possible to be. Perhaps it is best simply to note, without much explanation or defense, some of the phenomena which contributed to our exhilaration and euphoria.

Embedded within the imagination of most American males is a vision of a kind of Western Shangri-la. It is a wild and scenic place chock-full of sun, wind, solitude, sweet water, piñon-scented air, smokeless cookfires, rank but comfortable bedrolls. It is a place where everything is and anyone can be straight, cool, and natural. It may be a phony legend, fed, shaped by Kit Carson, John Wayne, and the Marlboro man, but it is a potent one. All of a sudden, we found ourselves living in a place and a way that exactly duplicated the legend, in a prospector's cabin high up on a

Western mountain with a mountain lion to sing to us. This was of course as satisfying and exciting as watching a pumpkin turn into a carriage would be.

We lived almost entirely in the present, spent very little time paying off yesterday's debts, seldom had to mortgage today in the interest of tomorrow. We had no deadlines, no marking or accounting periods; no one, no institution to whom we would ultimately have to justify ourselves. We were not forever saving up, making plans, getting ready to do something. There was a rare harmony between what we wanted to do, could do, thought best to do, and what we did do.

We had very few outstanding wants. We had enough food, comfort, tools, work, recreation, companionship, time, and money to do whatever we wanted to do. We had no feeling that we should be doing something else, would be enjoying ourselves more if we were in a different place, differently occupied, with different people. We could not conceive of being better situated, no matter what our resources.

Every day we had real work to do, something that exercised our bodies and minds and that we thought worth doing. I think this was particularly important for the boys, who because of their age had always before had to make do with hand-me-down work, jobs that adults had outgrown or found tedious and distasteful. One morning, for example, when there was ice on the water, John and I got up before dawn, ate quickly, went down the canyon and set up our cameras in front of a cave where we knew the chulo tribe had denned during the night. When the animals emerged, we photographed them, then followed them up and down the canyon slopes until dark. By the time we got back to the cabin and finished our notes, we had been working for fourteen hours. Sitting in front of the fire, groggy from fatigue, I mumbled to John that it had been a long, long day.

"It's been a cool day," John said. "Wouldn't it be great if people could work like they wanted to all the time? But I guess that wouldn't be right, or at least it wouldn't be work."

There were good vibes between the four of us. There was sufficient mutual trust, respect, and affection so that we seldom felt the necessity of being secretive or defensive. We ordered, organized our own tribe according to the most obvious natural laws—codified formally into the cool-uncool rules of etiquette. It was cool enough to wear the same pair of socks for a week, but uncool after the second day to take your boots off and steam your socks in front of the fire. It was uncool while cooking to steal food out of the pot, but once the food was on the table, it was not uncool to grab the last pancake. If John wanted to go back to Tucson for a few days, it was uncool of Ky to insist that it was technically his turn, but on the other hand it was uncool of John to ask the favor for trivial reasons. It was cool to mock, tease in the normal course of things, but extremely uncool not to stop before the needle hit a nerve. It was cool to show chulos to visitors, but uncool to break faith with the animals, show them off to others, force visitors on them. Dope was uncool, because buying dope was likely to be dangerous for our tribe. In general, anything you wanted to do was cool unless it had an uncool effect on one of the other three.

We had a lot of good days, one after another, and what is perhaps even rarer, we knew we were having them as we had them. After a time, when it became obvious that the whole scene was not going to dissolve, disappear, we got to feeling like a gang of thieves who had pulled off the perfect crime, could joke about our luck. One night, we were all sitting in the front room clustered around the gas lantern on the long table. The fire had been fed for the last time, was burning nicely, the wind was howling outside, blowing a few flurries of snow down the canyon. We had finished our work, had played a few rounds of poker dice, and had turned to private amusements. John was enmeshed in a web of string which he was tying into an elaborate macramé wall hanging. Terry was dissecting scats. Ky was reading about

Pueblo Indians. I was plunking away on a miniature harp, trying to learn how to play "Home on the Range." Dain was on his back in front of the fire, twitching and yipping softly as he chased something, perhaps his old chulo friend, through his dreams. John looked up from his knots for a moment and said thoughtfully, "This is the freakiest place I've ever seen. It's like a therapy ward in a loony bin."

OBSERVATION

Despite the agreeable circumstances, our mood was still ultimately dependent on our relations with the chulos. If things had gone bad with them, frustration, the sense of failure would probably have soured our life style. Fortunately we did not have to test this hypothesis. After we moved back to Montezuma Canyon, we had a feeling of steady progress in our work, could see signs that we were beginning to establish some rapport with the animals, winning, if not their affection, at least their tolerance. In consequence, we were able to make almost daily additions to our information about the tribe. Nothing—not good scenery, good companionship, good living—promotes contentment, psychic certainty as success does.

Our first job in Montezuma Canyon was the same as it had been at Kitt Peak—to trap, examine, mark each member of the tribe, assign her or him a field number. At Kitt Peak, the chulos had been thoroughly accustomed to people, had operated in an artificially restricted area. However, in Montezuma Canyon the animals were reasonably wary, scattered about in six or seven square miles of very difficult brush and cliff country. Therefore it took us nearly six weeks—many long, slow, cold days—of sitting to get our hands on all the Montezuma animals. To speed up the process, we used two traps, one set halfway up the canyon, the second in the vicinity of the park picnic area which the chulos visited with fair frequency. Each trap had to be manned, which was simply a matter of sitting and waiting, fighting off the blue jays from our bait, pulling a string at the proper time. However, if animals were taken, then the trapper had to have help, since removing a chulo from the trap was at the very least a two-man job. For this reason, the use of the park radio system was of great assistance. While two of us watched the traps, the other two would take up observation stations elsewhere in the canyon. When the trap-man needed help, he would call in on a walkie-talkie to the park office and the message would be relayed to a "free" man via the central transmitter.

The walkie-talkies were also very helpful when it came to observing the animals elsewhere than around the traps. We shortly learned that unless they chose to let us, it was next to impossible to follow or surprise a band of chulos. Because of their keen scent, they knew where we were long before we knew where they were. Also the brush was so thick, the canyon sides so rough, and we were so clumsy that pursuit or even surreptitious stalking was out of the question. While becoming acquainted with the tribe, we found the only dependable method of observing the animals was to sit down in a likely spot and hope that they would come within range. The radios enabled us to improve this technique somewhat by developing a kind of relay system of observation. When one of us would spot the chulos, he would let the others know what they were doing and in which direction they were moving. If we were properly positioned, it was some-times possible for one of us to make a circuit, take up an observation post ahead of the tribe, pick them up when they had passed out of the view of the first spotter. However, the system was far from perfect. There were many times when we guessed wrong, did not execute the maneuver properly, and lost the tribe in the brush.

After a month or so, things began to improve. The chulos had seen us often, began to lose some of their suspicion. We had handed out a lot of marshmallows, had begun to learn something about chulo etiquette, the idiosyncrasies of individual tribal members. Increasingly we were permitted to accompany the animals at a respectful distance. Also we were freer to try to do so. Having marked all the members of the tribe, two of us no longer had to remain in one spot tending the traps. In March (for reasons to be described later), the tribe shifted its operations up the canyon into the immediate vicinity of the cabin. Therefore we put one trap in the cabin yard, baited it each day, but did not set it except when we wanted to pick up some of the animals to determine weight loss or gain, some special change in condition. The open trap became a chulo feeding station which most of the tribal members visited once every day or two, usually in the morning. As a rule, several of us would simply wait around the cabin until the animals appeared, and when they left we would go along with them, would sometimes be able to stay with them for most of the day.

Finally, as we became better acquainted with the canyon and with the chulos, we were able to make better guesses as to what the animals might do, where they might be. For example, when we learned where the tribal resting ledges and denning caves were located and which animals were likely to use them when, we would often go directly to these spots, find a good vantage point, and wait for the tribe to appear.

In general, our observations of the Montezuma Canyon chulos did not involve much high strategy or ingenious equipment. Each day, we tried by whatever method seemed best to see as much of the chulos as we could, observe them as accurately as possible. Everything we observed contributed to our learning, and in most cases the significance of a given phenomenon was not apparent until we had repeatedly observed it, were able to relate it to other observations. For example, we might see two particular chulos together one day. The fact was duly noted, but not until we saw the same animals together many times—or failed to see them together often—were we able to see and analyze behavior patterns. In such work there are few Eureka moments, not very many days we could look back on and say this is when we discovered something or the other. (Exceptional events are exciting, curious, but they ultimately are not so satisfying or important as are repetitious happenings.) Our understanding improved as a result of the slow accretion of observations, but gradual as the process was, we were aware of and pleased with it.

Any such study is next to worthless unless considerable time and effort is given to making and keeping records. Observations are as fragile as memory and spoil quickly if not preserved. Furthermore each bit of information is like a piece in an unassembled jigsaw puzzle. Unless you have the pieces in some permanent form where they can be moved about, tried here, fitted against another piece there, any attempt to solve the puzzle, to create a large picture is doomed.

In our case, after we began to see chulos, when the flow of information became considerable, it was not unusual for us to spend two hours a night with our field notes. At first the boys were not enthusiastic about this duty, which is moderately dull and smacks of school homework. However, in time, as with so many other things, they came to see the point, which was that the only real trophy, the useful product of our work, was our collection of information. By the end of the year, everyone was able to take some pride in the size and quality of this collection, one's individual contribution to it.

Our most important chulo record was something we called an association chart. This was a daily log in which we noted which chulos we saw when and where and the members of the tribe with which each was associated. Physically we used 2′ × 3′ sheets of graph paper for this log, each sheet being large enough to accommodate thirty days' worth of

Date	Sex	Field Sex Number	F-16	F-17	F-19	F-21	F-22	F-23	M-1	M-2	M-3	M-4	M
Daily Total			12	12	12	9	2	13	18	9	12	1	
Singles			2	2	2	1	2	1	0	2	1		
Band Sighting No. 1			4-6 1:45	4-6 2:30	4-6 11:00	2-6 10:30		5-7	4-6 8:30	3-6 4:30	2-8 7:45		
Band Sighting No. 2									2-6 11:00				
Band Sighting No. 3									4:30				
JUVENILES	F	1	B 1	B 1	B 1 B 1			B 1	B 1 B 3	B 1	B 1		
	M	2	B 1	B 1	B 1			B 1	B 1 B 3	B 1	B 1		
	F	3	B 1	B 1	B 1			B 1	B 1 B 3	B 1	B 1		
	F	5				B 1			B 2				
	M	6				B 1		B 1	B 2	B 1	B 1		
	F	9				B 1			B 2				
	F	13	B 1	B 1	B 1			B 1	B 1 B 3	B 1	B 1		
	M	14	B 1	B 1	B 1			B 1	B 1 B 3	B 1	B 1		
	F	15				B 1			B 2				
	F	16				B 1			B 2				
	F	18	B 1	B 1	B 1			B 1	B 2		B 1		
	F	22				B 1			B 1 B 3		B 1		
ADULT FEMALES		7	B 1	B 1	B 1			B 1	B 1 B 3				
		8				B 1		B 1	B 2				
		11				B 1			B 2	B 1			
		12	B 1	B 1				B 1	B 1 B 3	B 1	B 1		
		17	B 1	B 1	B 1			B 1	B 1		B 1		
ADULT MALES		4	S-12:00 S-4:00	S-11:00 S-3:00		S-2:30	S-10:30				S-4:00	S-9:00	S-12
		19			S-5:30						S-2:00		
		23											
		25	S-5:00	S-10:00	S-10:30		S-7:10 a.m.	S-9:00 S-4:00					
		26	B 1	B 1	B 1			B 1	B 1	B 1			
		27											

Our method of recording daily observations of chulos, associations between animals, was nei[ther] formidable to compile nor as difficult to decipher as it may appear to be.

A vertical column was used to enter each day's observation. The horizontal columns were as[signed] to particular chulos, designated by her or his field number.

The sighting of a single animal–i.e., an adult male–was designated by the letter S, follow[ed by] the time at which the first observation was made. If a band was observed, the time of observati[on and] number in the band were noted at the head of the daily column. The number of adults was give[n...] A 4-6 entry indicates that of the ten animals observed, four were adults and six were juveniles[...] sightings might refer to two different groups observed during the same day or might refer to th[e same] group observed several times during the same day. If we saw a band at 10:00 in the morning, temporarily in the brush, and relocated it a half an hour or so later in the same vicinity, both [obser-] vations would be included in one band sighting. However, if we lost contact with the group [for an] appreciable time, we would record the first sighting as B1 and the second as B2. Bands were re[corded] according to their appearance during the day. For example, if we saw one band at 8:00 a.m., me[mbers] of this group would be designated as B1. If we saw the same group at noon, a second note, B2, be made for each animal. If at 5:00 p.m., we saw a band of a different composition, these a[nimals] would be designated as B3. The next day we might see the B3 animals first, and therefore in tha[t day's] entry they would be designated as B1.

April 5th was a good and somewhat complicated day. It serves on the sample chart as an exam[ple of] how our recording system operated. On that day we observed twenty members of the tribe. Th[...]

	M-10	M-11	M-12	M-14	M-15	M-16	M-23	M-24	M-26	M-27	M-28	M-29	M-30	M-31	A-1	A-4	A-5
9	13	1	17	8	20	11	9	1	10	7	14	20	20	9	8	15	20
	2	1	0	0	1	3	0	1	1	0	2	2	1	1	0	2	1
0	4–7 2:00		5–12 8:30	3–5 8:30	3–6 9:00	2–6 10:00	3–6 12:00		3–4 2:30	3–4 4:00	4–8 10:30	6–12 8:30	4–6 8:30	2–6 6:30	2–6 9:00	5–8 11:00	4–5 2:00
0					4–6 1:00				2–0 4:30				3–6 10:00				2–0 2:30
																	3–7 5:00
	B 1		B 1	B 1	B 1		B 1				B 1	B 1	B 1			B 1	B 1
	B 1		B 1	B 1	B 1		B 1				B 1	B 1	B 1			B 1	B 3
	B 1		B 1	B 1	B 2	B 1	B 1				B 1	B 1	B 1			B 1	B 3
			B 1		B 2	B 1					B 1	B 1	B 2	B 1	B 1		B 1
	B 1		B 1		B 1				B 1	B 1	B 1	B 2	B 1	B 1	B 1	B 1	B 3
			B 1	B 1	B 1				B 1	B 1	B 1	B 2	B 1	B 1	B 1	B 1	B 3
	B 1		B 1	B 1	B 1		B 1				B 1	B 1	B 1			B 1	B 3
	B 1		B 1		B 2	B 1	B 1				B 1	B 1	B 1			B 1	B 3
			B 1		B 2	B 1			B 1	B 1	B 1	B 2	B 1	B 1			B 1
			B 1		B 2	B 1					B 1	B 1	B 2	B 1	B 1		B 1
	B 1		B 1		B 2	B 1	B 1				B 1	B 1	B 2	B 1	B 1	B 1	B 1
			B 1		B 1				B 1	B 1	B 1	B 1					B 3
	B 1		B 1		B 2		B 1		B 2		B 1	B 1	B 1				B 1
			B 1		B 2	B 1					B 1	B 1	B 2	B 1	B 1		B 1
			B 1		B 2	B 1			B 1	B 1			B 2	B 1	B 1	B 1	B 1
	B 1		B 1	B 1	B 1		B 1		B 1 I 8				B 1			B 1	B 3
	B 1		B 1	B 1	B 1		B 1				B 1	B 1	B 1			B 1	B 3
	S–9:00	S–3:00			B 2	S–9:00 S–3:30	S–4:00		B 2		B 1	B 1	B 1			B 1	B 3
									S–12:00			S–7:30					
						S–8:00											
											S–7:30A					S–4:00	
	S–5:30				B 1					B 1	S–5:00	S–1:00	B 2	S–5:00		B 1	B 2 B 1
	B 1			B 1													
					S–5:30	S–4:30			B 1				S–5:00			S–5:00	B 2

ng (B1) was of a band of four adults and five juveniles who came to the cabin yard to feed at
p.m. The band fed for about fifteen minutes and then left. Ky and Terry (John was in a cave
ting chulo scats) followed this band toward the cliffs behind the cabin. When the band left, the
ᴧer, an adult male (No. 25) remained behind. Shortly another male, Twenty-Seven, appeared, and
and I witnessed the battle between the two animals which is described on page 235. (Together
ungler and Twenty-Seven were designated as B2.) About two hours after both males had departed,
ᴧond foraging band of three adults and seven juveniles appeared. They were designated as B3.
fed for a half-hour and then also departed, traveling in the direction of the cliffs. I followed
until it became obvious that they were heading toward the place where Terry and Ky were
ᴧdy stationed. I called the boys on the walkie-talkie and told them what was happening. By this
the B1 group was high on the ridge and, while the boys watched, the B3 group did not join with
If we had observed longer, we might have seen such a union take place, since the next day all of
ᴧnimals were observed together. However, we were having steak that night, and so Terry and Ky
ᴧbly came back to the cabin about 6:30.

he association charts gave us a format for accurately recording our daily sightings and com-
ᴧions of animals. From the charts, we could refer quickly to our tape-recorded notes on which the
ᴧls of what we observed were given. Since we could record a month or more of daily reports on a
ᴧe chart, this provided a method of collating our observations. Shifts in associations between
ᴧals and the continuation or disintegration of social patterns were documented by the daily entries.
ᴧE: *No sightings were made on February 18, 20, March 7 and 13.*

entries. Laying the sheets side by side, we were able almost at a glance to note stable patterns of association within a tribe, changes in associations.

We stored our more general observations, kept a diary on magnetic tapes. After we had finished the written records, while we were having our second or third cup of tea, we would turn on a tape recorder and talk about what individually and collectively we had done during the day. These recording sessions were a relatively painless way of storing away a lot of information. After a time, they came to be partly adversary proceedings in which we forced one another to clarify observations, challenged each other's methods, conclusions, interpretations.

In all, we took out of Arizona at the end of the year six notebooks of written records, 70 hours' worth of magnetic tape, in the neighborhood of 1,500 still negatives, 2,000 feet of exposed movie film (from which John and I eventually put together an hour-long narrative). A year later, we were still studying these records, culling over, trying to collate them. They represent, in a sense, the raw ore we extracted from the Arizona mountains, which we hope can be refined and fashioned into useful commodities.

THE CHULO CYCLE

By mid-January, we had taped, identified, marked all the members of the Montezuma tribe: four adult and two sub-adult females, six adult males, twelve juveniles (eight females and four males) born the previous summer. From then until we left them in August, the tribe was stable. There were two fatalities, but none of the remaining animals left Montezuma Canyon, and no new ones (with two brief, insignificant exceptions) entered it. Nevertheless the behavior of the individual animals, their function within the tribe and its organization, changed greatly—in fact, was always changing.

Chulos are emphatically cyclical mammals; that is, there is a rhythmic pattern to their lives as they regularly respond to recurring external and internal stimuli. It is often difficult for us to properly appreciate such a life style, since man appears to be one of the least cyclical of mammals. In part, this is because of our physiology; for example, our constant state of sexual receptivity. In part, it is a matter of conscious design, our history-long effort to isolate, immunize ourselves against seasonal and environmental change. We have had some success in making ourselves a creature for all seasons, eating the same foods, living in the same place, working in the same way throughout the year. In the process, we have developed a uniquely linear, birth-to-grave existence.

Chulos, on the other hand, are so cyclical that it is pointless, impossible to describe "normal" behavior, either social or individual, except in seasonal terms. The same chulo is a much different animal functionally in June from what she was or will be in January, is engaged in different activities, has a different influence on her environment, different relationships with other members of her tribe. Furthermore each June and January she will be much the same animal that she was in previous Junes and Januarys.

Changing external stimuli, temperature, precipitation, light affect the individual animal directly, and indirectly the kind and amount of food and shelter required. In the late spring and summer, for example, the tribes tend to avoid the hot, baked canyon floors and flats, to forage on higher, cooler slopes and ridges for lizards, snakes, insects, small mammals and birds. In the fall after the rains, when the country is green, full of new, sweet, tender vegetation, the animals grow less carnivorous. In the winter when the peaks are snowbound, windswept, inhospitable, when the small prey species have migrated or hibernated, the chulos seek the sheltered canyons and valleys, dig through the litter for overwintering plants and animals. The chulo cycle also reflects, is created by, physiological changes (sexual changes being the most obvious) which occur at more or less the same time for all the animals.

The cycles—economic, sexual, social—are interrelated and interdependent; they support, modify each other, blend together so subtly that they cannot be truly isolated without distortion. However, it seemed to us that in an abstract way (all rational analysis is a compromise; phenomena are arbitrarily distorted for the sake of easier understanding) the year of the chulo in southern Arizona could be divided into four major periods, each of which was characterized by distinctive patterns of individual and group behavior.

From September until March, the adult females, sub-adults, juveniles are never apart. (There must be accidental separations, but we at least never saw one of these animals alone.) They live, sleep, forage together in cohesive, tightly organized groups in which the influence and authority of the adult females seems to be paramount. In addition to simple, individual survival, which is always a concern, the tribe during this period is preoccupied with the protection, education of the juveniles. During these months, the adult females do not permit the adult males to associate with the tribe, and therefore the males are solitary, each keeping more or less to himself, having his own territory within the larger tribal territory.

The sexual segregation begins to break down in March, when courtship occurs. All males make attempts and some of them succeed in rejoining the tribe, becoming themselves communal animals. Copulation occurs in April.

From mid-April until late June, the females are pregnant. The change in their condition changes their social behavior. They begin to relinquish their tribal functions and responsibilities. The juveniles are therefore forced to depend increasingly on their own skills and experience, are socially, psychologically weaned at this time. Even though overt sexual activity has ceased, the adult males, on a rotating basis, remain with the tribe, and it is during this period that they make their most obvious contribution to tribal welfare. Being at this time the only adult tribal members whose vigor is unimpaired, the presence of the males provides some security for the heavy, gravid females, the half-grown, inexperienced juveniles.

During the latter part of June, the pregnant females leave the tribe, seek out small caves or dens in which the cubs are born. For the next six to eight weeks, each female is preoccupied with her own cubs, rarely meets and shows little desire to associate with other tribal members. In August, the females lead their cubs out of the birth dens, and for a time each female forages alone with her own young. However, there are more and more contacts between the family groups, and by September they have merged. Quite rapidly, maternal family bonds disappear, are again replaced by tribal ones.

MEMBERS OF THE MONTEZUMA CANYON TRIBE
A STATISTICAL AND SUBJECTIVE SUMMARY PROFILE

Adult or Subadult Females. Females may breed at two years of age and after that time are considered adult. Between the first and second years, they are subadults.

Field Code Number	Date of Birth	Winter (1970–71) Weight in Pounds	Number of *Times* Observed
7	Probably 1969	9.2	72

No. 7 was a subadult animal. We assumed she was a year and a half old when we first met her, late in 1970. In tribal affairs, she was a mid-band animal of limited authority and responsibility.

8	Before 1969	11.2	62

No. 8, "Calamity" (after the Jane of the same name), was a large, handsome, aggressive animal—somewhat more impetuous and unstable than the other females. She was a forward leader of one of the two winter foraging bands.

10	Probably 1969	9.0	61

No. 10, another subadult, was killed by a truck near the State of Texas Mine in December, 1970. She appeared during the brief period of observation to be a mid-band animal.

11	Probably before 1969	9.6	5

No. 11 was relatively wary, a rear leader of one of the two foraging bands.

12   Before 1969   10.2   85

No. 12, "Queenie," was a responsible, stable adult of placid and, to us, agreeable disposition. She was the forward leader of one of the two foraging bands, and retained this position when the tribe foraged together as a single group.

17   Before 1969   7.9   87

No. 17, "the Witch," was a small, old, toothless, partially blind animal of superior intelligence, experience. Her sense of smell was remarkable and her personality was subtle. She was the principal female of the matriarchy, a rear leader of one of the foraging bands who retained this position when the tribe foraged together.

The Juveniles.   Juvenile animals were born late in the spring and early in the summer of 1970. During their first year, juveniles are, so far as behavior is concerned, sexless, their personalities as yet undifferentiated, unformed. They have few social responsibilities except to respond to adult females. They are educated beautifully, though permissively, protected carefully.

Field Code Number	Sex	Winter (1970–71) Weight in Pounds	Number of Times Observed
1	Female	3.0	76
2	Male	3.2	75
3	Female	4.7	72
5	Female	4.2	66
6	Male	4.2	36

On May 5, 1971, after the matriarchal order had begun to disintegrate, No. 6 strayed from the band and was not thereafter observed. Presumably he was killed by a predator.

9	Female	4.0	64
13	Female	5.2	69
14	Male	5.4	66
15	Female	4.2	60
16	Female	5.8	58
18	Female	3.2	66
22	Female	3.3	74

The Males. Males become mature, the testes descend, at the end of their second year. Between their first and second years, they are subadult. For inexplicable reasons, there were no subadult males in the Montezuma Canyon tribe, though there were two among the animals at Kitt Peak. Since the males become sexually mature after breeding season has been completed, there may be a third category. A physiologically mature but socially immature male—i.e., a 2- to 3-year old animal—is capable of breeding but is a virgin. One of the tribal animals, No. 26, listed below may be an example.

Field Code Number	Date of Birth	Winter (1970–71) Weight in Pounds	Number of Times Observed
4	Before 1968	16.8	78

No. 4, "the Supervisor," was among the males the dominant animal. During the winter period, he remained physically, psychologically closer to the tribe than any of the other fully mature males. In the spring, he copulated with most, if not all, of the females. An animal of great boldness and dignity.

19   1968 or before   15.8   8

No. 19, for a male, was exceptionally timid. He was present but did not choose to compete with the other males during breeding season. It is possible that he was attached to the small tribe in the adjacent Copper Canyon, sometimes strayed occasionally, hopefully into Montezuma Canyon.

23   1968 or before   13.8   20

No. 23, "the Old Man," from dental evidence and that of general condition, appeared to be an old animal. Of the five males who competed during breeding season, he appeared to be 4th in rank. Was wounded during the battles and probably did not breed.

25   1968 or before   17.2   64

No. 25, "the Bungler," was an intelligent, inquisitive, but self-indulgent animal. For a considerable period, he was pre-eminently the "cabin chulo." He and No. 27 (below) were the 2nd- and 3rd-ranking males during the violent, competitive breeding season. They were peers and their positions would change from time to time. Several times, the Bungler attempted to challenge No. 4, the ranking male, but in each case surrendered ritually before violence occurred. He may have copulated with one of the mature females. However, though his intentions and desires were obvious, he was generally not enough of a warrior to become a lover.

26   Probably 1968   14.8   37

No. 26, "Nancy," held the anomalous position within the tribe mentioned above. Though sexually mature in the winter, he remained with the tribe, the only mature male permitted to do so. His presence was tolerated, though his status was that of a second-class citizen, and he was often treated roughly by the females. He may well, because of age (less likely because of personal idiosyncrasy), have been a sexually inexperienced, virgin animal. At the opening of the breeding season, he was driven forcibly from the band by No. 4, the ranking male. Nancy remained solitary during the spring and summer of 1971, the period in which the other males associated with the tribe. During this period, he was shy and furtive, stayed well away from the tribe.

| 27 | 1968 or before | 13.4 | 39 |

No. 27 lacked the rank and confidence of No. 4, the style and adaptability of No. 25. However, though the smallest of the males, he was a persistent, durable animal. He repeatedly challenged No. 25, and these challenges often resulted in violent passages in which both were wounded. No. 25 would often outface No. 27 in ritual encounters, but the latter would invariably triumph if physical contact was made. Among the males, he was most often with the juveniles after the pregnant females had relinquished their authority.

8

The Matriarchy
(Fall and Winter)

THE TRIBAL ARRANGEMENT

Since we first became acquainted with the chulos in the fall,
we tended—still do—to treat this as the beginning of their
year. So long as the obvious is kept in mind, that a circle has
no beginning or end, this time serves as well as any other as
a point of entry into their lives. In fact, as far as field study
is concerned, picking up the chulos when we did had some
practical advantages. The matriarchal period lasts for six
months and is the longest and most stable in the annual
chulo cycle. During this time, the daily routine remains
much the same for months on end and thus allows for a
rather leisurely accumulation of data regarding the basic
skills, adaptations of the individual animals, their social
organization, the species' position within and influence on its
habitat. Had we met the chulos during spring or early
summer—when their behavior is somewhat frenetic, their
society in a state of flux—we would have had far more
trouble making sense out of their activities than we did in

the fall. Also, in the fall and winter the tribe is, in general, less secretive than in other periods. Security, the protection of the juveniles, is a major preoccupation. However, the security is provided for more or less by strong-arm methods, the tribe being more inclined to outface—in a sense, out-muscle—any potential threat than hide from it. Further-more there always seems to be some advantage in introducing oneself to a well-organized group which has a chain of command, acknowledged leaders. Just as all that is needed to be tolerated by a bureaucrat Indian in the field is to have a letter from a bureau chief in Washington, so once we were able to convince the principal females that we were harmless, the other chulos quickly accepted us. It was an "If the boss says it's O.K., it's O.K. with me" situation. Things would not have been so easy in the spring and summer. Then the animals tend to be more secretive, involved in private sexual, domestic activity. Tribal organization is looser and, to a larger extent, individual animals must make independent decisions.

A peculiarity of the fall-winter period is that though the ani-mals, except for the old males, are at their most social and the society of the chulos most tightly organized during this time, the tribe seldom functions as a single unit. Rather it divides, to travel and forage in smaller bands. During the winter months we watched them, we saw the entire Monte-zuma Canyon tribe together during the day on only five occasions. In each of these instances, the animals seemed to convene more by accident than design, the foraging bands meeting, mingling for a time, then separating. The Kitt Peak animals were more often together at full tribal strength than the Montezuma Canyon tribe. Perhaps their smaller terri-tory and the central, artificially provided source of food increased the chances of foraging bands meeting, permitted the animals to remain together for longer periods. However, even the Kitt Peak tribe was more often encountered in separate bands than as a whole.

Both tribes tended to divide into only two groups, rarely into more and smaller units. This may have reflected the fact that the two tribes were almost exactly the same size. A larger tribe of, say, forty animals (as the Kitt Peakers would have been had they not lost so many young to pet hunters in summer) might well have formed more foraging bands. We were casually acquainted with a small tribe—probably less than ten animals—who lived in Copper Canyon in the Huachucas. Admittedly we did not have many observations of these animals, but when we saw them they were always together in one group, did not divide into bands.

The most obvious explanation of why the tribe should regularly subdivide in this fashion was that a band of eight or ten animals was a more efficient unit for foraging and traveling than a tribe of eighteen or twenty animals. In the winter, when food was scarcer, harder to find, the two Montezuma bands sometimes foraged as much as a mile apart. By doing so, they presumably could separately investigate more varied food sources, and thus competition between tribal members was reduced. That the tribe was much oftener—in fact, usually—together after April when food was more abundant may in part bear out this theory, but does not conclusively prove it. In the spring and summer, the sexual condition of the adults, the maturing of the juveniles had a strong influence on intertribal relationships. As with all behavioral phenomena, the foraging-band system was unquestionably the result of a variety of interlocking needs and pressures of which we could recognize only the most obvious, or perhaps none.

Usually there were ten animals in the first of the Montezuma tribe's foraging bands, eight in the second. (At Kitt Peak, twelve and nine was the most common division.) The first Montezuma band generally consisted of two adult females, whom we called Queenie and the Witch; a subadult female who never distinguished herself in our eyes sufficiently to earn any name but Seven, her field number; the odd-man-out male, Nancy, who remained with the tribe throughout the winter; and six juveniles. The second band was made up of two females, Calamity and Eleven, and six juveniles.

The somewhat complicated but invaluable association charts, on which we daily recorded whom we had seen with whom, showed that the group of adults was relatively stable during the winter. For example, from December to March, Queenie of the first band was with the Witch 70 percent of the time; we observed her with Seven 60 percent and Nancy 65 percent. On the other hand, she was with Calamity only 30 percent of the time and Eleven only 25 percent. Records of the association between other adults were similar. However, the pattern was not rigid. No two adults were always together, and each of them at times traveled or foraged with each of her tribe mates.

The juveniles were less regular in their association. They showed no strong loyalties to any one group or individual. They would remain for a few days, seldom for a week, in one combination; then a new one would be formed. The shifting pattern of juvenile association underscored one of the important features of chulo society. From October on—and perhaps earlier, since we did not have good records of September—whatever maternal bonds had existed between a mother and her cubs apparently became weak or disappeared, were replaced by tribal ones. In addition to the evidence provided by our association charts, we had the strong impression, based on many observations that could not be summarized statistically, that the allegiance of a juvenile chulo is to *an* adult, not to a particular adult, and that adult females react to and in a sense care equally for all cubs. A cub was free to take food from any adult. If a cub was in trouble, real or imaginary, the nearest adult would answer his call for help. In times of threat or alarm, the females obviously were concerned about the situation of the tribe or band, not of any particular cubs within it. The adults never appeared to resent or try to prevent the cubs switching from one band to another, following another adult. The tribe seemed to serve as a communal nursery, a kind of nomadic kibbutz.

Since the composition of the foraging bands changed often, since the juveniles and females were never alone during this period, and since we never saw these changes occur, it seemed reasonable that the transfer of animals between bands must occur at night when the bands would frequently join and den together in a cave.

In Montezuma Canyon, we knew of four caves, all in limestone, which the chulos regularly used at night. Only two of these dens were large enough for us to enter, and both were tight squeezes even for John and Ky, who are configured like snakes. However, we never knowingly entered even these two caves when they were occupied by chulos. (Twice, when crawling through the passages to collect scats, we surprised a male who was catching a midday nap.) Since there was no chance of entering a cave which they were using without the chulos knowing we were there, it seemed to us that no purpose except harassing the animals would be served by trying to do so. Therefore the best we could or were willing to do was to watch them go into the caves at night, come out in the morning. (So far as we knew, once having entered a cave in the evening, none of the animals emerged until daylight.) Occasionally we risked sitting near the cave entrance to eavesdrop and would hear considerable soft, chirpy conversation.

In general, I think that our ignorance about what went on at night in the caves, where the animals spent nearly half of each day, was the most important gap in our understanding of the chulos. It would be surprising, would set them apart from most other mammals, except possibly men, if they went underground and simply slept for ten or twelve hours. The chances are strong that they were awake and active during part of the period, and very likely were at their most communicative and convivial.

The nighttime activities of a chulo tribe remain not only a mystery to us but a general one. John Kaufmann, in Panama, had the same difficulties we did (but for different reasons) observing the animals during this period. Throughout much of their tropical range, including Panama, chulos sleep in trees on large platforms of branches, twigs, leaves, vines, which they construct. It is no easier to spy on these retreats without disturbing the animals than it was for us to penetrate the caves of the Arizona tribes.

The matter of where and why the chulo changes from a tree to a cave sleeper would make an instructive study in itself, might answer some questions concerning the ecological impact of the species, factors restricting its range. Though we continually looked for signs of chulos building and using tree platforms, we found only one example of this behavior, and it was a curious one. Hondo, our Papago friend from Kitt Peak, had taken a cub, a juvenile male, from the Peak in the summer of 1970 as a pet. The cub was removed to Sells, the Papago town in the desert where Hondo lived. He was not caged, was allowed to roam freely, and, centering his activities around Hondo's pigpen, took up with the shoats, apparently for companionship. In November, when the cub was a little over four months old, he began to build nests in a low paloverde tree that shaded the pen. When we visited Hondo's place, we found the nests were fairly substantial, constructed of paloverde branches and pieces of string that the cub had pulled out of an old mop. Whether loneliness, boredom, or individual genius motivated this animal, we of course did not and do not know. However, he was the only tree-nesting chulo we saw or heard about in Arizona.

So far as use of the four caves in Montezuma Canyon was

concerned, there did not appear to be any regular pattern or rotation. A band, the entire tribe, or a single male might use a cave for a single night, then move on to another, or might continue to sleep in the same cave for several weeks at a time. It seemed to us that which caves were used when by what animals was largely a matter of convenience, depended more on the availability of food than on any special properties of the cave or territorial behavior on the part of the animals. Late in the afternoon, chulos would simply and sensibly head for the cave nearest to them. As long as they foraged in that area, they would use the same den; if they wandered farther away, they would bed down in another cave.

In addition to the four communal caves, adult males had a number of smaller crevices and overhangs which they used as dens. So far as we observed, the males never shared one of the large caves with the females and young during the fall and winter. Otherwise the animals were not possessive about their dens. There was, for example, no sense or evidence that certain caves "belonged" to one or the other of the foraging bands. We thought that the two bands met and denned together in the same cave two or three times a week. Since we did not follow each band each day to a den cave (often the animals would not permit us to do so, and we did not want to push our luck, give them a sense of being harassed), this was partly a matter of deduction. We assumed that since switches between the bands never seemed to occur during the day, they must occur at night. Therefore, when the composition of the bands did change, we assumed that the animals had met and shared the same cave the night before. Exactly how and why these transfers occurred we did not know. It may have been a very casual process. After the tribe had denned together at night, the principal females of one band or the other might simply leave the cave in the morning, and the juveniles, subadults nearest to them, those ready to get up and go to work, might join them.

One of the most striking phenomena concerning the foraging bands was that while their composition, particularly among the juveniles, changed frequently, the number of animals in each band was often the same. Between mid-December and the first of June, when the matriarchal organization had all but disintegrated, we saw the Montezuma tribe divided into two foraging bands on seventy-six days. On twenty-nine of these days, or about 40 percent of the time, there were ten animals in one band, eight in the other. The next most frequent combinations were eleven-seven and nine-nine. The most extreme division (excluding several exceptional situations—a male and female pairing off during breeding season) was thirteen-five, which we saw only three times. Considering the eighteen normally "communal" animals—i.e., the adult females, juveniles, and the odd male, Nancy—there were eight possible combinations for the two foraging bands. Therefore it would seem that the eight-ten division occurred far too often to be a chance matter.

All of which raises an intriguing question having to do with the mind of the chulo. If, for example, the strong tendency of the Montezuma tribe to divide into bands of ten and eight was not accidental, as it did not seem to be according to our records, then it must to a certain extent be a matter of choice. The animals had to have some—presumably nonabstractive—mathematical sense, an awareness of the difference between ten and eight or twelve and six; had to do something, cooperate, communicate, in such a way that the magic number was maintained. Being unable as we are to understand the inner processes of other animals, any explanation is sheer guesswork. However, it may have been that being divided into bands of ten and eight gave the Montezuma animals a certain sense of security, fitness, propriety, that this sense was so refined they would feel somewhat less at ease if they were divided into groups of eleven and seven, even more uneasy if they were foraging in groups of twelve and six. To repeat, it is also sheer speculation, but it is possible that this sense of social propriety is so keenly developed as to serve the chulos—at least in this situation—in much the same fashion as the ability to do sums serves us.

FORAGING

All the foraging bands we watched at Kitt Peak and in Montezuma Canyon were organized and operated in similar fashion. As they moved about, one female, always the same one, brought up the rear. Between the forward and rear leaders were the other adults, subadults, juveniles. The most obvious function of this order was to provide for the security of the younger, smaller, weaker, less experienced animals, whom it was all but impossible to approach without first encountering one of the matriarchs.

How rigidly this formation was maintained depended upon circumstances. When the animals were actually foraging in a promising spot, the tribe or band tended to fan out somewhat, each animal investigating nooks and crannies which might contain food. When traveling between foraging areas in more or less relaxed fashion, the line of advancing chulos might be strung out for fifty yards or so. However, if they—particularly the matriarchs—had any feeling that they were being pressed (for example, if we were following them), the line of march would be tightened up smartly. The young would move to the front, just behind the forward leader, gaps in the line would be eliminated, and the rear leader would move along alertly, often stopping to assess the situation, challenge us, give warnings.

While actually foraging, the chulos did not practice grand predatory strategy, as packs of wolves and prides of lions are said to do. However, there were some obvious benefits to the individuals because of their communal method of hunting.

An advancing party of digging, rooting, probing chulos stirred and kept stirred up a variety of small reptiles, insects, other invertebrates. In their efforts to escape one chulo, these creatures would often scurry directly into the paws or jaws of another. In effect, the band functioned as a kind of living net, which swept through thickets enmeshing all manner of edibles that one animal alone might not have found or captured.

The frequency and relative ease with which chulos were able to prey on Clark's and Yarrow's spiny lizards provided evidence of the efficiency of this cooperative, if haphazard, method of hunting. The Clark's and Yarrow's are both largish, 5- to 8-inch (including tail) lizards of the iguana family. As we found out when we were trying to catch them as food for Mona, the chulo who bore a litter of cubs on the back porch of the cabin, they are extremely swift and wary creatures. Though both species are common, it would often take the four of us most of a morning to capture a pair of these lizards.

Because of both their habits and those of the lizards, the chulos were more successful. The Clark's and Yarrow's are essentially rock and boulder creatures, but on warm days these big lizards would climb into trees to sunbathe and to hunt for insects. If disturbed, they invariably ran down the tree, even jumping from a limb to the ground, seeking to escape under the cover of rocks. This tactic often turned them into chulo meat. Juvenile chulos, who are more active and restless than their elders, love to play in trees and would sometimes swarm up one which held a lizard or two. The lizard would start down the tree, often eluding the cubs, but sometimes landing directly in front of an adult chulo snuffling about on the ground underneath. Particularly in the spring, when lizard hunting was good, adults often seemed to work their way purposefully toward trees where the juveniles were playing and unintentionally flushing lizards.

Chulos are quick, cat-like, when it comes to pouncing on small prey. Normally they try to grab and hold down their victim with their forepaws, then dispatch it with a few well-placed nips. With a creature the size of a garter snake, Clark's, or Yarrow's lizard, they would first bite off the head, then nibble away at the rest of the carcass at their leisure. Sometimes after killing a large lizard or a small snake, a chulo would carry the remains a considerable distance before finding a comfortable spot in which to finish the meal. Not infrequently, when the band was traveling between foraging areas, several of the animals would march along with limp, deceased lizards dangling from their jaws. This behavior would of course have been impossible, or at least unprofitable, except for the tribal taboo against stealing food from one another.

Whether innate or learned, one foraging technique of the chulos is especially valuable to them in southern Arizona. Spininess is a notable characteristic of many living things, vegetable and animal, in the dry border country. For example, the fruit of the cholla cactus and the body of the tarantula—both items of chulo diet—are covered with penetrating bristles. Having obtained either this fruit or spider, a chulo circumvents the protective spines quickly and easily by rolling the object back and forth between her or his forepaws. Presumably the process rubs off the bristles that would penetrate the chulo's mouth or tongue but cannot penetrate the tough, leathery pads of the forepaws. Habitually chulos fondle many potential food items briefly before putting them in their mouths, very likely to cleanse them of foreign matter such as bits of sand or gravel. However, when the situation calls for it they will work at this chore persistently and diligently. I once watched the Supervisor, one of the Montezuma males, spend almost five minutes rolling, rubbing, dressing out, so to speak, a largish tarantula. Reportedly the same technique is used by other omnivorous animals of the region. Coyotes, for example, have been observed batting cholla fruits through the dust with, it is thought, the intent of removing the spines.

PREDATION AND DIET

How and if chulos dealt with game larger than reptiles and invertebrates we could only conjecture, since during the course of the year we were unable to observe one of them preying on a bird or a mammal. The nearest we came was an incident again involving the Supervisor. One afternoon, I had worked my way up a narrow draw that feeds into the main canyon from the north and that we called Blue Water Ravine because of a small seep, heavily impregnated with copper compound, which has stained the rocks a brilliant aquamarine. I settled myself on a ledge overlooking this ravine, and after a half-hour or so I heard a commotion in the brush below. At first, I had no idea what was creating the disturbance, but then I caught a glimpse of the Supervisor. Since we treated the singles less diplomatically than the foraging bands, I edged down the slope to see what he was doing, found him crouched against a log, holding the headless body of a rock squirrel. As I came closer, the Supervisor picked up the squirrel and with difficulty retreated slowly through the brush, trying as he did so to grunt menacingly at me through a mouthful of squirrel. The body was still limp and the blood was fresh, but since I did not actually see the chulo take the squirrel, there remained the possibility that another predator—say, a hawk—might have done the killing and been robbed by the Supervisor.

This observation was supplemented by another, which occurred three days later. At that time, the Supervisor was spending most of his nights in a small cave about a hundred yards below the Blue Water Ravine. Outside this cave there was a large oak in which he often napped on warm afternoons. Ky and I came past this tree about three o'clock and saw the chulo in it. Normally he curled up in one of the higher crotches. However, this afternoon he was draped over the lowest limb, six or eight feet above the ground. The change in position did not seem significant to us, and, we stopped to watch him for a bit, because it seemed to be a good time and place for us to stop for a break. The Supervisor remained motionless for five minutes or so, giving no indication that he was doing anything but resting. Then, to our amazement, he exploded into action, leaped off the limb, and set off in hot pursuit of a rock squirrel, whom he had either driven into or found under a pile of boulders at the foot of the tree. The chase was short and, in this case, unsatisfactory from the Supervisor's standpoint, since the squirrel succeeded in reaching another rockpile sanctuary twenty feet away. However, there did not seem much question that the chulo was trying to catch the squirrel and that lying in wait, like a cat before a mousehole, was a hunting technique sometimes used.

We had the feeling, based on circumstantial evidence, that chulos preyed on skunks. Often when we trapped and were handling the chulos, they smelled strongly of skunk, and we sometimes found skunk remains in their scats, though again this was not conclusive as far as predation goes, since they may have been feeding on skunk carrion. Also the Kitt Peak garbage-disposal crew, a group who took a vocational interest in a variety of small mammals who raided the trash cans, told us that after the chulos moved onto the Peak the skunks all but disappeared. Finally, skunks are largely nocturnal hunters and den up during the day in rockpiles and windfalls, exactly the sort of places which foraging chulos investigate. It seemed most probable that chulos encountered skunks and, being larger, stronger, more agile animals, were physically capable of preying upon them. There is also the possibility that the presence of the band might distract a skunk, tend to protect the individual chulo by making it difficult for the skunk to direct his protective scent spray against any one of his attackers.

One of the persistent rumors concerning the chulos was

that they fed largely on birds' eggs in the spring, particularly those of the turkey and quail, which were, of course, coveted by human hunters. Again we had no direct evidence either confirming or denying this assumption. A crissal thrasher, a big curved-bill brush bird, built a nest and laid eggs in a stand of cholla cactus near the stock tank above the cabin. John kept a close watch on this nest, wanting to photograph it when the eggs had hatched and the cactus was in full magenta bloom. However, he never got to do so, since one morning he found the nest ripped apart, the eggs gone. The chulos used this area extensively and were adept enough to have reached it through the protecting spines, but that they did so was conjectural. In general, it seemed to us that if a foraging band were to come across birds' eggs or nestlings, they would eat them, but there was no evidence that they went out of their way searching for nests as some hunters claimed they did. We did some experimentation with chulos and chicken eggs. They would eat raw (or, for that matter, cooked) eggs if cracked, put in a pan, but when we offered them eggs in the shell they showed little interest, either did not know how—or did not want to bother—to crack the shells.

From direct observation, pulling apart hundreds of scats, and from what we considered good reports, it became apparent that the chulos were exceptionally omnivorous animals, being willing to feed on virtually anything edible that they could find. So far as wild animal food was concerned, we found they had eaten (though not necessarily killed) squirrels, skunks, mice, pack rats, small snakes, lizards of all kinds, and a great variety of insects and invertebrates, including scorpions. (Chulos apparently have some knowledge of and respect for the properties of a scorpion. They treat it as a cat will, batting at the creature, avoiding the stinging tail, until they have stunned or crushed the scorpion. Then they eat it directly, with no ill effects.) Chulos are indisputably carrion feeders. We found them worrying deer carcasses, road-killed snakes; and George Brown, the rancher, said he had seen them feeding on cattle carcasses.

The chulos' taste in vegetables is also catholic; they feed on, among other things, acorns, piñon nuts, manzanita berries, plums, peaches, wild grapes, cactus fruits, the tender fruiting stalks and later seeds of agave, a variety of roots, tubers, and wild grains. In southern Mexico, where Ann and I lived during the early 1950s, the chulos had a poor reputation because of their fondness for new corn. Anyone who has seen what one family of raccoons can do to a cornfield when the ears are in milk can perhaps sympathize with a farmer who has been raided by an entire tribe of chulos. So far as man-prepared food was concerned, bait we put out or garbage, there was little edible that they would not eat.

Though they are completely omnivorous, we found that the chulos are fairly discriminating in their taste, show considerable preference for certain foods, a characteristic which may have something to do with their keen sense of smell. At our feeding stations, they would carefully pick through the scraps, eating what they liked best first, then, if they were still hungry, finish off the less desirable food. Sweets of any sort were clearly their first choice, followed by fats. The staple at our feeding stations was dried dog food, which was cheap, easy to pack in, and, we reasoned, harmless, if not healthful, for the chulos. They would always eat this if nothing else was available but seemed to regard it as dull, bland fare. Also we noticed that they became bored if we offered them the same kind for too long a time, and therefore we changed brands and flavors at regular intervals.

Strangely, one of the few foods chulos would not eat, so far as we observed, was fish. During the period when we were trying to find fresh food for Mona, who was nursing her cubs on our back porch, we netted some small dace-like minnows out of the pools in Bear Canyon. Though we offered them to her (and later to other chulos) both alive and dead, neither she nor other members of the Montezuma tribe would have anything to do with them. There may have been other factors involved (a fish out of water is not a fish, so far as a chulo is concerned), but this lack of interest was in harmony with another observation we made, which was that chulos did not seem particularly fond of aquatic habitats. They would sometimes show up along streams or ponds, but not so often as we had thought they would, considering what a rich variety of food such places offer and the near relationship of the chulo to the raccoon. It may be that in the Huachucas, competition with the raccoon, who is very much a water-directed animal, tends to influence the chulos and that water is an important ecological boundary dividing the niches of these two closely related mammals. Chulos, of course, drink but it seemed to us that they were much less dependent upon open water than are many mammals in this dry country. As a general but not hard and fast routine, the tribe seemed to wander toward a water source in the late afternoon and the animals usually had a drink before retiring. (Because of the long muzzle, a chulo drinks much like a bird, lapping up water, then tilting his head back to let it run down his throat.) However, several times it seemed to us that they went more than twenty-four hours without drinking. In July, when the sun was at its hottest and the drought at its height, the chulos, not surprisingly, became more interested in water, and we began to put out a dishpanful along with the food at our feeder. They used it regularly, not only drinking but often, accidentally or intentionally, tipping it over and lying down to cool themselves in the puddle.

Despite the wide variety of creatures the chulo does in fact feed on, the list of animals on which border residents imagine the chulos prey upon is far more extensive. We heard many—always second- or third-hand—accounts of chulo bands running, dragging down deer. Under certain very special circumstances—meeting with an animal dying of gunshot wounds or disease; coming across a newborn fawn—chulos might and would be capable of killing a live deer. However, from their standpoint it would make little economic sense wasting their energy in any sort of pursuit so unlikely to yield results. Furthermore there is nothing in the tribal organization which suggests it is or ever was adapted to this sort of hunting. Another persistent story was that chulos were confirmed cannibals. This tale, which we heard from half a dozen people, always took much the same form. There was a certain time of year (variously reported as fall or spring) in which the old males battled ferociously for the leadership of the tribe. The loser was invariably set upon by all the other animals and eaten, presumably in a sort of ritual celebration. This was, of course, nonsense of the usual "Animals are more violent and savage than we are" sort. However, fantastic as this story is, it is possible to see, given a good imagination, how it may have started. The males will fight amongst themselves during the spring, not for tribal leadership but to determine who will be admitted to the tribe. They will sometimes slash each other seriously, and though we did not see such a case it is possible that an occasional animal may be killed in these precourtship fights or wounded so severely that he later dies.

So far as other chulos feeding on chulo carrion, it is again possible and, if it occurred, would hardly indicate depravity, only a certain frugality. We had heard this so often that when a subadult female of the Montezuma tribe was killed on the road in December, we let her carcass remain in a roadside ravine for several months. The chulos regularly foraged in, traveled past this place. However, neither they nor anything else except maggots touched the body—or even, so far as we could tell, investigated it.

The gaudiest chulo attack story was told to us by an Arizona State Police trooper. This cop was in the habit of stopping by the Coronado Park Headquarters about once a week to drink some of Gil's coffee, chew the fat, and malinger for an hour or so. Now and then, we would happen to meet him there. At first, he had some obvious suspicions about our presence and motives but, after a time, came to accept us as one of the peculiarities of this backwoods federal canyon. One afternoon when we were sitting around the ranger room, the cop said, "It sure is funny how things change. Way back, my daddy and I used to hunt those chulos, figured they were varmints. Now you have come all the way across the country to study them." The officer was in fact a man in his mid-thirties, but there is a subparagraph in the code of the modern West which calls for countrymen, particularly when talking to Easterners, to imply that they are ancient, suggest that they were contemporaries of Wyatt Earp and the Clantons.

"How come you used to hunt them?"

"Hell, we had to. I grew up on a poor old ranch over by the Chiricahuas. We were trying to protect our stock."

"From chulos?"

"Sure. Those rascals—they'll jump on the back of a little calf, sometimes a couple of them, and ride along there until they chew her head off. You never heard of that?"

"No."

Occasionally in one of the den caves, we would find a scrap of food, a bit of bone or hide which we thought had been brought in by the chulos. However, so far as we knew, this was a casual thing, a chulo perhaps having a tidbit in his mouth when he came into the cave, carrying it back into the passage to snack on, as a man will take a sandwich to bed. We had no evidence that they made a practice of storing food. Nor did chulos grow fat in the fall as raccoons will, enabling them if necessary to sit out bad winter weather, fast-ing in a snug den. In fact, most of the chulos showed some weight loss during the winter, which was not surprising considering that there was less food available and they had to forage harder to find it.

The tribe was out and about foraging in all weathers, in the rain and snow, on hot and cold days. Since in Arizona the chulos were at the northern limits of the species' range and because it has been suggested that climate, particularly low temperatures, may be the barrier which holds them within this range, we watched their reaction to winter weather with particular care. The winter of 1970–71 was a cold one in southern Arizona, with half a dozen days in which temperatures were lower than 15 degrees, many days and nights at our elevation when it was below freezing. However, it was a dry open winter, with only three days of measurable snowfall in Montezuma Canyon. We simply could find no correlation between the tribe's activity and the cold and snow. They were abroad on the coldest days, foraged as usual when snow lay on the ground, showed no obvious signs of being uncomfortable or disliking this sort of weather.

One meteorological phenomenon which we came to feel did have considerable influence on chulo behavior was the wind. It was Ky who first started us thinking about this. One cold, raw, windy February day, we were spread out in the lower half of the canyon trying to pick up the tribe, which we had not seen in two days. We were each up in the rimrock, located so we could watch both sides of the canyon and if necessary signal to each other. Not having seen anything of Ky for an hour or two, I walked down to his station in midafternoon. He was wedged between two slabs of limestone, motionless despite the wind and cold, staring up the canyon.

"No luck?"

"We won't see anything today. The wind is wrong."

"How do you mean?"

"When it's this strong and coming down the canyon, they don't come out—or not very much. Didn't you know that?"

"I guess I hadn't thought."

"Maybe with this wind it's like it would be if it were dark for us."

"I'm not with you."

"Well, maybe the wind messes up all the smells. It's like it was dark or too much noise. They're not sure where they are going or what's around them. Maybe it makes them sort of afraid, so they stay in the caves or right around them."

After he suggested it, we found considerable evidence supporting Ky's observation. Our daily records showed that we seldom saw the animals when the wind was whipping down the canyon. So far as his interpretation was concerned, it was at least a logical possibility that animals as dependent upon their noses as the chulos appeared to be might be handicapped and confused when the wind distorted the scent patterns. A sensible response would be to remain under shelter or, if abroad, to become especially wary and secretive.

When now I try to re-create the feeling of the hours of chulo watching, the remembered sensation of wind in my face is much a part of it. It became almost second nature with us always to approach the chulos, watch them, from a position in which the wind was blowing from them into our faces. Even downwind, given the keenness of their noses, we were not often able to observe chulos without their being aware of us. However, we found that even after we got to know them well, we could usually approach them more closely and disturb them less if we were downwind, rather than upwind, from them. Ky's comparison of our world of light to the scent world of the chulo may be a particularly descriptive analogy. Upwind from us, the tribe knew we were about, but perhaps our presence was blurred, faint, as if we were standing in a shadow.

To repeat, the scent world of the chulo remained a mysterious one. We knew it was there—it figured into many of our calculations, speculations—but we could never make out its shape or substance.

DEFENSE

During the time we watched them, we had few opportunities to see how the chulos would react when forced to defend themselves. In part, this may have been because our presence served to protect them, keep away the few carnivores who might conceivably be tempted to prey upon a chulo. Also nature is not so red of fang and claw as we tend to believe, like to believe, and have recently been led to believe by a series of persuasive, popular essays on animal violence.

It is often assumed that the predators particularly are motivated by feelings comparable to those of a human big-game hunter, that they take pride in making difficult hunts and kills, are stimulated by challenge and risk. Thus a tiger will go out of his way, as in the movies, to take on, say, a python or leopard because they are worthy opponents. In point of fact, the predators are more like the managers of a large corporation, seek to avoid dangerous competition, are always looking for a safe killing, as a rule only enter into confrontations in which they have reason to believe they will be an easy winner. A mountain lion, a wolf, or a coyote would be unlikely to attack even a single adult chulo, much less a full tribe. Physically a lion, for example, is certainly capable of overpowering a chulo, but in the process could be expected to suffer wounds which would be painful and might be handicapping. By the same token, a tribe of chulos might conceivably be able to corner and kill a coyote or even a lion, but the risks would be out of all proportion to the rewards. Species who might be of danger to each other do not go about the countryside challenging one another but sensibly try to avoid confrontations. There was, for example, a female mountain lion who was a permanent resident of Montezuma Canyon—in fact, usually was to be found in the vicinity of the Wedge, the big limestone cliff that jutted out above the cabin and that was often used by the chulos. So far as we knew, the lioness and the chulos never met directly, though they almost certainly were aware of each other's presence. Whatever influence they had on each other was apparently negative, the lion perhaps avoiding ravines in which the chulos were foraging, the tribe giving the lioness a wide berth.

It is of course the defensive potential of a species—along with its knowledge, innate or learned, of the potential of other creatures—which maintains this system of armed neutrality. In this regard, the chulos are formidably equipped. We made no tests, but after having handled, restrained both raccoons and chulos, I thought the chulo was a bit stronger and a much quicker, more agile animal. Furthermore the canine teeth—with which, when it must, the chulo delivers a slashing attack—are exceptionally long, measuring about an inch in the adults. The claws are strong and heavy but designed more as digging, probing tools than as weapons.

One afternoon, John and I found the Bungler, one of the Montezuma males, accidentally trapped inside a garbage can on Montezuma Pass. In the process of being released, the Bungler became enraged, turned on John, and, with one slash of his canines, ripped out the toe of John's heavy work boot. (The boots were actually mine, John having borrowed them while his were being repaired. This was fortunate, since my feet are a size and a half larger than John's. If the fit had been tighter, the Bungler might have removed some toe as well as the boot toe.)

At night when we returned to the cabin, we often let Dain run in the vicinity while we were fixing supper. As mentioned, he would sometimes find and, in a good-natured, unserious way, chase another of the single males, an animal we called the Old Man. However, one evening in January we heard Dain giving his "I've got it treed" bark on the opposite side of the ravine from where he usually encountered the

Old Man. We went to investigate and found that he had, as advertised, treed a chulo, a male who was then a stranger to us but whom we later came to know as Twenty-Seven. Wanting to mark this animal, John ran back to the cabin to get our noose stick while Dain and the rest of us stood guard under the low juniper. Our plan was to rope the chulo out of the tree, then somehow get him into the bag where we could weigh and mark him. However, the chulo was a better climber than we were ropers. Finally Terry volunteered to climb up in the juniper and attempt to move him. Terry was only a limb or so up when the chulo made a great leap over his head, out of the tree, and hit the ground running. I swung with the noose stick, missed, and broke it. Dain wheeled, started in pursuit, and did not miss, grabbing the chulo near the base of the tail. Twenty-Seven turned and, with one slash, laid open Dain's muzzle from just below the eye to the base of his nose. Dain yelped and momentarily released his hold. However, he recovered quickly, and in two bounds, spraying blood as he went, was on the unfortunate chulo, pinned him to the ground by his shoulder, and undoubtedly would have killed him had we not been able to intervene. Fearing for both animals, Ky and I leaped into the melee. More by luck than skill, no one was seriously hurt, and eventually Ky got Dain by the collar and I ended up with the chulo pinned to the ground.

Twenty-Seven had a laceration at the base of the tail, a puncture in his shoulder, but both healed quickly. Dain's gash was ugly but not serious. We took him back to the cabin, stopped the flow of blood, filled the wound with antibiotics. He recovered in a few days but will carry the long scar to his grave, as a memento of his feat of being the only one of us ever to catch a chulo barehanded, so to speak. The incident gave us a rather clear notion as to the defensive capabilities of a thirteen-pound chulo when he is fighting for his life. Also it tended to verify stories we had heard from lion hunters about losing dogs to a group of chulos.

We had some notion as to the probable outcome of a single dog attacking a tribe of chulos from a more or less planned encounter which again involved the patient Dain. Since we had seen defensive behavior only as a reaction to our presence when we were following or trapping the animals, there remained the question of how this apparent system of collective security would function under a real attack. Therefore, on the next to last day that we worked at Kitt Peak, we arranged such a test. When the tribe at full strength came to feed, we trapped one of the cubs but, rather than releasing him immediately, left him in the trap. Blondie, the pugnacious rear leader of the tribe, stayed nearby watching the situation while the rest of the animals withdrew and waited. We then whistled Dain out of the car and he came to the trap, began sniffing, whining at the cub, who showed no great alarm and did not squeal. Blondie, however, reacted immediately and forcefully; she charged out of the bush from which she had been watching. Grunting and snarling, she planted herself in front of Dain, with her head turned to the side, ready to attack. Dain, with his remarkable sensitivity to our wants, was in a more investigatory than hostile mood. He circled around the enraged chulo, barking but keeping a prudent distance. In the meantime, two other females, who had been waiting with the rest of the tribe, turned around and trotted back toward the commotion. Dain and Blondie having moved away from the immediate area of the trap, we pulled the door open and freed the cub, who scampered off, following the path taken by the retreating tribe. Dain turned, took a few steps toward him. As he did so, Blondie and the two other females, who had by then arrived on the scene, rushed at the dog, putting themselves between him and the fleeing cub. Dain made a tentative snap at Blondie, and as he did, one of the other females slashed at his flank. At this point, with Dain more or less encircled by the three enraged females, we broke off the engagement, whistled Dain back, and put him in the car.

The activities and intentions of the three females seemed so obvious that we did not try to repeat the experience, both because we did not want to harass the chulos and because it seemed to be exposing Dain to considerable risk.

We observed only one incident in which chulos met and reacted to a truly feral hunter. In October, Ky and I were working our way along the rim of lower Copper Canyon where it had begun to fan out into the San Rafael Valley. Upwind from us, we heard some stirring on the canyon floor and sat down quickly in the brush, began to search the area through our glasses. After a time, we located the maker of the noise, a coyote who was tugging away at something in the brush. (Later we went down to look and found it was the well-decomposed, almost mummified remains of a deer.) The coyote seemed nervous, wary, which we laid to our presence. However, he kept pausing, staring, sniffing down the canyon rather than in our direction. Shortly, the cause of his concern came into sight, a band of chulos, three adults and five cubs. (After we had returned to the Huachucas in the winter and become better acquainted with local chulo society, we guessed that these animals were the same who made up the small, permanent Copper Canyon tribe.) Without hesitation, the leading female walked directly toward the deer carcass and the coyote, who had withdrawn ten feet away and was sitting back on his haunches. At the carcass, the female assumed a defiant posture, grunted sharply, while the other animals moved up behind her. Without any dispute, the coyote got up and left. We could see him climb out of the low canyon over the rim opposite from us, trot on down into the valley without further pause or reflection.

Certainly it appeared as if the chulos had forced the coyote to move. The coyote made no attempt to resist, and the chulos gave the impression of expecting him to retreat as he did. It was as if both parties knew what was the sensible thing to do in this situation and did it.

We did observe two attempted attacks on chulos, and had

an incontestable account of a third, involving another kind of predator. In late November, while I was sitting on a ledge which looked down into the home ravine of the Kitt Peak tribe, I saw a mature golden eagle sailing along the flank of the Baboquivaris toward Kitt Peak. As I watched, the eagle glided over the ravine in which the tribe was doing a little idle foraging. The eagle ringed high up, perhaps 1,000 feet above the 7,000 foot mountain, waited on, soaring for a time, and then began a long, purposeful, gliding stoop down into the brush. However, as he passed by, he seemed to become aware of me, drew up out of his stoop, soared for a time, and then went on his way.

In December, Terry witnessed a much more conclusive and altogether more curious attack by a bird of prey. Terry was at the mouth of Blue Water Ravine, above the ranger station, more or less surrounded by the entire chulo tribe, to which he was distributing marshmallows. While everyone was so engaged, a red-tailed hawk swooped down and, so far as Terry could see, actually struck one of the juveniles with its talons. Reporting the incident, Terry said, "I don't think the little guy was hurt. He sort of rolled over and squealed. While the hawk was down low, one of the old ladies sat up and batted at him with her paws just as he was coming up from striking at the little one. The hawk flew off and didn't come back."

The first superintendent of the Coronado Memorial was a colorful native of the Southwest named Phil Wells. Phil was born in Chihuahua, the son of a mining engineer, had grown up along the border, and has been variously employed as a prospector, miner, cowpuncher, rancher, hunting guide, border patrolman. He is also an alert and interested naturalist. Phil is now retired and lives near Bisbee, where he works as a gunsmith. He told us that in February of 1956, while driving down from Montezuma Pass toward Park Headquarters, he had witnessed an eagle attacking and killing a chulo. Coming around one of the hairpin curves,

Phil had driven into the middle of the scene. The chulo was crossing the road, the last of a band of them. The eagle dived on, hit the animal, knocked him over, and ripped his side with his talons, killing him. Phil jammed on his brakes but the truck apparently surprised the bird, who rose and flew off. Later the eagle returned and eviscerated the chulo.

Because of both what we saw and heard regarding the attacks of birds of prey on chulos and what we did not see, predation on the animals by other mammals, we concluded that, at least in southern Arizona, the raptors were probably the only hunters who posed a continuing threat to the chulos. Golden eagles are large enough to attack any chulo with good prospects of success. Red-tailed hawks and perhaps great horned owls are well enough equipped to take at least juvenile chulos. Furthermore, the defensive organization and discipline of a chulo tribe would provide little protection against aerial attack.

The vulnerability of a tribe to such predators as eagles, large hawks, and owls may have been a factor contributing to the chulos' obvious preference for thickly covered, scrubby areas. We seldom saw chulos in the open, where they were not protected from view by the chaparral. When they did cross an expanse of bare rock, an open pasture, or a meadow, they never dawdled or foraged, and the tribe or band would lope along under tight discipline. Their resting and socializing ledges were always at least partially covered by vegetation. Since chulo food, particularly grasshoppers in the fall, was often more abundant in clearings than elsewhere, the fact that chulos avoided these clearings suggested that they had a strong reason for doing so. The obvious explanation was that they were most exposed to the big birds of prey in open country and had either acquired or were born with the knowledge of this vulnerability.

Perhaps the most extraordinary chulo incident we observed during the course of the year was not strictly an example of mutual self-defense, but was (or seemed to us to be) a remarkable display of mutual assistance between the animals. Commencing in the early spring, we began, two at a time, to go back to Kitt Peak for a day or two each month, to check on the animals there and also to outfit them with ear tags, permanent metal clips. Our hope was that if we or anybody else had an opportunity to resume the study any-time during the next two or three years, the ear tags would identify the animals, give some information about longevity, as well as changes in or permanence of tribal relationships. One day in late April, Terry and I left the Huachucas in the evening, spent the night in Tucson, and drove out to Kitt Peak early the next day to set up the trap we had left there. In midmorning a band of eleven chulos arrived. In our first attempt, we trapped a nice batch of four animals: three juveniles and one pregnant female, a mid-band animal whom the winter previously we had marked and identified according to our code as Four. The three younger animals were removed, weighed, examined, ear-tagged, and released without incident.

As we worked with the juveniles, Four, remaining in the trap, grew increasingly panicky, tore at the cage desperately. When her turn came, we had considerable difficulty direct-ing her into the bag, and once she was inside it we had to struggle hard to subdue her and hold her while we clipped in the tags. When we finished, opened the bag to release her, she rolled out limp and unconscious. We did not know what had caused her collapse, whether we had actually injured her, whether she had gone into deep shock because of her lengthy struggle, or whether the swoon was connected with her pregnancy. In any event, we felt exceedingly guilty, since this was the first chulo who had suffered any apparent ill effects from our trapping. We carried Four to the shade, where she lay still unconscious but still breathing. We could think of nothing useful to do so far as first aid was con-cerned and so stood watching her, feeling bad.

While all of this had been going on, the rest of the band

had reacted predictably: had retreated when the trap was sprung, were presumably waiting back in the scrub until the captives were released. Blondie, the big, handsome, aggressive rear leader of the tribe, was waiting thirty yards away, standing on a boulder in a defiant position, occasionally grunting. However, since the cubs had not squealed and Four had struggled more or less in silence, Blondie had not tried to intervene, simply waited and watched.

After Four had lain motionless for perhaps three minutes, she opened her eyes, tried to get to her feet, fell weakly, got up again, struggled a few steps, fell again, and lay on her side, panting, too weak or uncoordinated to go farther. Blondie then left her boulder and came forward, and as she did we retreated. Blondie came directly to Four, sniffed at, nuzzled, touched the nose of the prone animal. Then she put her own snout under Four's flank, pushed up, as though trying to lift her companion to her feet. Four responded by rising, but could stagger only another ten feet or so before collapsing again. Blondie walked by her side and, when Four fell, repeated the nuzzling, the lifting procedure. Stage by stage, the two animals proceeded along the main tribal trail toward the chulos' home ravine. As they went, Four fell or had to stop frequently, but she seemed to be growing stronger.

After having watched for a time from the trap area, Terry and I ran to an outcropping of rock which overlooked the chulo trail as it dipped down into the home ravine. From that point, we could see the other members of the band waiting in the scrub below. They continued to wait for at least fifteen minutes, until they were joined by Four, who was still very wobbly, and Blondie, who continued to attend her. When the two females arrived, the band headed slowly back toward the ravine, and after a time disappeared from our sight in the scrub. (We returned to Kitt Peak the next week and found Four fully recovered, apparently in good health.)

The whole incident astounded Terry and me. We had not seen and never again saw anything comparable. The happening is so extraordinary, provides so much substance for sentimental, anthropomorphic interpretation, that it is perhaps best not to try to speculate on its cause, the motives and responses of the animals involved, particularly those of Blondie. However, perhaps more than any other bit of chulo behavior we observed, this incident gave us the feeling that the members of a chulo tribe are bound by ties, innate and acquired, which are far stronger than we had suspected, much more complex than we could or can demonstrate from our other observations.

TERRITORIALITY

Territoriality is a facet of animal behavior which has recently caught the popular and professional fancy. In fact, because of a number of territorial studies and successful popularizations of them, many people seem to have the feeling that most other animals have essentially the outlook and motives of a real-estate agent or investor, that they are forever preoccupied with accumulating and protecting property. This is something of an exaggeration. All creatures are, of course, in one place at one time. (There is a fine Irish teaser which applies: "A man cannot be in two places at once unless he is a bird.") Many animals spend much or all of their life in what seems to us to be a very restricted area. However, it is often for no more esoteric reason than that travel is difficult and dangerous or that everything they need in the way of food, shelter, companionship, sex is near at hand, and therefore it is not imperative that they leave their home place. Some animals seem to become especially attached to and possessive about a particular territory, and much of their behavior appears to reflect their desire or need to protect it against various trespassers. But just as some men are more materialistic, self-righteous, or jealous than others, so some species (and very likely within species some individuals) are more territorial than others.

During the time we were with them, we never saw the Montezuma tribe (except for the Bungler, who sometimes wandered on the west side of the ridge) outside of Montezuma Canyon. However, the canyon contained some 6,000 acres, which probably was enough land to support twenty-four animals in comfort, and there was really little point in going elsewhere. There seemed to be no magical significance to the canyon frontiers, no point in their wanderings, where they reached *terra incognita,* which seemed to alarm or unsettle them. Furthermore it should be remembered that they came into this canyon from somewhere and thus had changed their territory without any apparent damage to their psyches.

Within the canyon, the tribe and single males usually followed well-defined trails between favored foraging areas, rest ledges, caves, water holes. The animals wandered about freely, and if at times they favored one area over the other it seemed to be because of available food. During the winter, when the tribe was usually divided, the two foraging bands showed no possessiveness about a particular territory. They might operate apart for a few days, one at the upper and the other at the lower end of the canyon. Then they might meet and work together for a time, or simply switch positions. When, as they occasionally did, the two bands met during the day, there would be some conversation back and forth, essentially of a greeting nature, but no signs of hostility, no attempt by one to drive away or escape the other. Also there were no specific places—a cave, a rest ledge, a rock or tree—which seemed to "belong" to one band or to a particular individual within the tribe.

During the winter, the adult males displayed a certain amount of what is conventionally thought of as territorial behavior. Each of the five males who lived alone during the winter had a section of the canyon in which he habitually foraged and denned. However, there was nothing sacrosanct about these bachelor quarters. Occasionally a male would leave his customary territory and, for no reason that we could discern, wander through that of another or several other males. No bitter battles or in fact, so far as we knew, battles of any sort resulted. Sometimes the traveling male would return to his original turf, sometimes not, and there would be a general shifting of positions. It may amount to hairsplitting, but we had the feeling that again social rather than territorial considerations determined where the males would be at a given time. They quite obviously did not care for each other's company, were reluctant to meet. The territories simply represented areas in which a male could forage without the risk of running into another male. The boundaries receded and expanded in response to the relative position of the males, and were not arbitrary lines to be defended at all costs. The Supervisor might edge close or cross in to the Bungler's usual territory—not, it seemed, in the hope of humiliating the Bungler or annexing his property but simply because foraging was good. The Bungler would not be physically driven away, but would move on because he found the Supervisor's company undesirable.

Also within their vague territories the males, who seemed to harbor the perpetual hope that they would be allowed to socialize with the communal animals, tended to shift in relation to the position of the tribe or foraging bands. The Supervisor, for example, was usually found in the lower canyon, occupying a territory from the ranger station to the State of Texas Mine, a distance of about half a mile. If a foraging band was active around the mine for several days, then the Supervisor would shift his operations to that subdistrict of his territory. At the same time, the Bungler, who occupied the territory immediately upcanyon from the Supervisor, would come down toward the band, forage on its upcanyon flank.

As noted, there were some chulos in Copper Canyon, which lay directly to the northwest of Montezuma Canyon. We thought there probably were eight to ten animals in this group. We would see them or their signs occasionally, but made no special effort to find or follow them, since keeping up with the members of the Montezuma tribe fully occupied the four of us. We also suspected from scattered reports that there may have been chulos just south of Montezuma Canyon, immediately across the Mexican border. However, even if we had had the time, it would have been complicated, by reason of human territorial behavior, for us to have walked across the border in search of them. In any event, the Montezuma tribe had one and perhaps two near neighbors, and there were at least some meetings between them.

We may very well have missed the most important period of intertribal socializing. In November, while we were working at Kitt Peak, Harry Busch, the Coronado Memorial ranger, several times saw groups of chulos which he estimated to number thirty or forty animals. Shortly after Thanksgiving, he had a chance to make what he felt was a firm count and came up with a total of thirty-three animals in one group. Harry was a good observer and though, as we knew, counting a large number of chulos is difficult, it seems likely that for several weeks he was seeing more animals than we later found to be permanent members of the Montezuma tribe. Harry's observations led us to speculate that when the chulos arrived in Montezuma Canyon from wherever they came from, there may have been thirty or so animals in the communal group. If so, some of these must have moved elsewhere. As a guess, the animals in Copper Canyon may have been a splinter group of the original Montezuma Canyon tribe.

If such a division occurred, it was not, so far as any observations the rangers made, a forcible one. When they saw the large groups, they were foraging, traveling together in apparent harmony. This was in keeping with the two observations we were able to make of intertribal meetings.

In January, John was working one afternoon on the northern side of the canyon in an area where several tributary ravines merged. He was watching the first foraging band from an outcropping overlooking the ravine, and had a good view of the events that followed:

"The Witch stopped foraging, sniffed, then looked up the little ravine that comes in on the left. A couple of minutes later, this new bunch shows up. There were three adults and I think five little ones, but I might have missed one of them. There was a lot of grunting, and a couple of little guys from our bunch ran back toward the Witch as if they were surprised. Queenie and one of the guys from the other gang backed up against a tree and did a little tail lashing. Somebody may have started to ha-ha, but I wasn't sure because there was so much grunting going on. The whole scene was like they were surprised, not frightened—like 'Hey, man, where did you come from?' Then they just sort of got together. They stood around for a while and then went off, with the Witch still behind. They didn't seem to care who was next to who and nobody tried to hassle anyone. I didn't want to follow them because I thought I might spook them. I waited about ten minutes and then started poking around but I couldn't find them."

The next day, we saw both the Montezuma foraging bands, all the communal animals. There were no strangers with them, and though we made a point of looking for them, we did not find the "new guys" John had seen elsewhere in the canyon.

In late March, toward the end of the breeding period, we were surprised one day to find a strange female and a cub with the Montezuma tribe, which was then operating as a single unit. The two newcomers stayed with the tribe for three days, then disappeared. While they were there, they were accepted casually by the tribe, the female taking up a mid-band position, the cub mingling and playing with the Montezuma cubs without incident.

Admittedly we had few observations on which to base conclusions regarding intertribal relationships. Also we were in the mountains at a time when the chulo population was relatively low. It is conceivable that during times of peak population the pressure of and competition between many chulos might influence their behavior toward each other. On the other hand, we had no evidence whatsoever that there was any we-against-them feeling among chulos. Furthermore we had reports from local residents who remembered the late 1950s when the chulo population had been high, a hundred or more animals being seen in a single group. Even adjusting these reports to compensate for the difficulty of counting large groups of chulos, as well as the tendency of people to exaggerate when it comes to size and numbers, it seems probable that there are times when chulos are associated in much larger groups than those we saw. If so, it is likely that these are temporary conventions of several tribes rather than a single permanent tribe. All of which tended to strengthen our opinion that chulo society is not exclusive; that the tribes do not correspond to nation-states, each jealous of its territorial sovereignty; that pacific mingling between the tribes can and does occur.

SOCIALIZING

The tribe was so organized as to be a kind of always ready weapon. It was an instrument with which the chulos could protect their persons and theoretically their property, though we saw little evidence that they valued any particular piece of real estate highly enough to risk much for it. However, so far as we observed the animals at Kitt Peak and in Montezuma Canyon, defensive and territorial concerns did not often or greatly occupy them. Day after day, they spent most of their time, six or eight hours, foraging or traveling between foraging areas. The second most important or, at least, most common activity in terms of time was what might be rather unsatisfactorily called socializing. Since the animals, except for the adult males, were always together while they foraged, traveled, denned, they were never unsocial. However, there were periods during each day which the chulos appeared to devote almost exclusively to the enjoyment or cultivation of each other's company.

There was normally a brief period, fifteen minutes or so, of socializing early in the morning around the cave mouth, immediately after the tribe had emerged from a den, before they commenced foraging. Then, during the middle part of the day, the band or tribe would usually halt on one of the rest ledges, of which there were at least ten regularly used ones in Montezuma Canyon. There they would nap, sun, groom, and the young would play about the ledge, in the tree that invariably grew beside it. They might be so occupied for an hour or more or for as little as fifteen minutes. As the weather grew warmer and the foraging easier, the chulos went oftener to and stayed longer at these rest areas, sometimes taking three or four such breaks in a day.

Mutual grooming was the most distinctive activity which occupied the animals during these social periods. When a chulo grooms another, she does so with her small incisor teeth, moving up her partner's body, generally from tail to head, pulling at the fur and skin with small, quick, gentle nips. Sometimes as she nips, she will also comb her partner with her foreclaws.

Even for a man, being groomed by a chulo is a rather pleasant sensation, somewhat like being given a delicate but prickly massage. We learned how this felt from the four cubs who were born on the cabin porch and whom we brought back with us to Pennsylvania. Among many other things, the cubs taught us that grooming is innate, inherited behavior. When they were two months old, about the time they would have made their début into general chulo society, we found that if we scratched their backs, as one would a puppy, they would respond by trying to groom. At first when they were scratched, the cubs would nip at anything within reach, the arm of a chair, a boot, or for that matter a piece of wood. However, after they were three months old they learned that it was more satisfying to groom living flesh. They would (and still do) pile into our laps and, while we scratched, would nip along our arms and legs. Since they often perched on our shoulders, they discovered that the human ear was an especially convenient and, from their standpoint, desirable appendage to groom. For as long as he would permit it, the cubs would also try to groom Kilo, a young dachshund who was their frequent companion and who, because of his shape and agreeable disposition, we often thought served as a surrogate adult chulo to the cubs.

Other communal animals exhibit behavior which is the equivalent of chulo grooming, some sort of ritualized touching, nuzzling, licking. As it happened, we had in the house another groomer, a spider monkey named Bobo, who has lived with us for four years. Bo uses her fingers rather than teeth to groom, but in at least one respect her response and technique were identical to the chulos'. Both the monkey and the cubs immediately note and persistently try to remove any small blemishes, scabs, scratches they find on our skin. This behavior, typical of most grooming mammals, suggests to most observers that grooming developed and is still, at least in part, carried on for hygienic reasons. Having been groomed by the cubs, having watched wild chulos grooming, we decided, for example, that they would be very quick to find and remove any external parasites from their partners. As it happened, we did not find any such parasites on the chulos we examined, but we had reliable reports that at times the animals were infested with fleas and ticks. That the Montezuma and Kitt Peak tribes were free of these parasites may have been an accidental matter, or it may have reflected the fact that both groups were able to devote considerable time to mutual grooming. Among the chulos, it would also be likely that grooming would serve to remove snarls from the coats, foreign matter from cuts or wounds, perhaps even thorns from the flesh of the animals.

Health and cleanliness aside, grooming or its equivalent seems to have evolved into a ritual activity of great importance to communal mammals. In this respect, grooming among chulos might be considered analogous to the formal or testimonial dinner among men. The habit of eating together in this fashion may have evolved from nomadic hunters gathered around a big kill, feeling proud, thankful for their success. Today we still eat on ceremonial occasions, just as the chulos still clean each other's bodies. However, the purpose of the ritual dinner is more social than nutritional. In the same way, the chulos appear to groom for grooming's sake, rather than for purely hygienic reasons.

There were, so far as we could determine, no hierarchical regulations (such as have been observed in other species) concerning who could groom whom, when. Normally when the tribe or band stopped at a rest ledge, the juveniles would immediately pounce on the adults, sometimes two or three youngsters simultaneously trying to groom one of the matriarchs. In turn, the old females would nibble away at the most convenient portion of the nearest cub. Generally, between adults and juveniles, the adults seemed less enthusiastic about the grooming than the young, which is not surprising since the cubs were rough and inexpert (by adult standards) groomers. After having been mauled for a time by cubs, a female would grow restless, shake them off, move to another place on the ledge, try to break off the session. However, we never saw an adult in this situation behave with hostility—forbid, vocally or by cuffs, a cub to groom her.

The juvenile-adult grooming usually tapered off because of the disinterest of the adults. The cubs would then turn to grooming each other. These sessions often—in fact, usually—degenerated into wrestling matches, games of tug of war, and finally pursuit, a kind of tag. When the cubs became engrossed in their own games, gave them a little peace, adults were able to groom each other. Adults groom each other more carefully, with more concentration than do the cubs, and give the impression that it is a sensuous, luxurious experience. A pair of adults will lie down side by side, the nose of one next to the tail of the other. They will then move along each other's body, nipping and combing as they go. Adults groom each other very slowly, and at times it seems that a grooming pair has entered into a trance-like state.

In the Montezuma tribe, all the adult females except the Witch and Calamity (more of the apparent antipathy of these two later) were grooming partners at one time or another. However, Nancy, the odd adult male who remained with the tribe throughout the matriarchal period, was rarely groomed by the females and then only in a perfunctory manner, as if he were an unwelcome cub. The juveniles, however, did not discriminate sexually, groomed Nancy frequently. Nancy not only tolerated these attentions but seemed more eager for them than did the matriarchs, perhaps because he had so few other chances to take part in grooming.

Little thought or study has been given to the pleasures of other bloods, if and to what extent pleasure-seeking influences their behavior. Among other reasons, there is a prejudice lingering on from the period when we tended to view all other species' behavior in a rigidly mechanistic way. According to the mechanistic approach, all animal behavior can and must be explained in terms of "survival value." Other bloods, so this theory goes, are not, in a sense, programmed to accept or seek such a soft, metaphysical kind of thing as pleasure. Yet in truth all such questions reduce themselves to a matter of motive, and since we are unable to penetrate the inner life of other species, whether or not animals are or can be pleasure-directed remains a matter of speculation.

(There is also the problem of trying to define pleasure, which leads immediately into an even more impassable logical and semantic bog.) However, it would seem that if we, one species of mammal, can experience what we call pleasure, the probability is that other species also do. Furthermore, anyone who has established any degree of rapport with other animals has observed that there are things they seem to like to do because of the agreeable sensation produced, and that they will expend considerable effort to duplicate the experience. I think it would be difficult for anyone to watch a ledge full of grooming chulos without coming to the conclusion that they were enjoying themselves. It seemed to us that it may well be a function of the chulo tribe to give the animals an opportunity to experience this communal pleasure.

EDUCATION

No particular period of the tribal day is devoted to the education of the young, and no particular element of behavior can be isolated and identified as being exclusively educational. However, the education of the juveniles seems to be an important function of the tribal organization, one which is a continuing factor in most tribal activities.

For example, chulo cubs are at first awkward, inexpert, and unsuccessful foragers. Very early, as soon as they are weaned, leave the birth den, they exhibit certain presumably innate foraging behavior. Tiny rat-sized 'cubs will energetically root, dig in the soft earth, make nose holes which are miniature replicas of those made by foraging adults. However, an infant chulo so engaged will often overlook delicacies, either not see or smell them or, as is more likely, not realize that they are edible. Cubs must learn what is good and safe to eat, how to find it. They learn these things by being placed in positions where they can experiment on a trial-and-error basis and where they can imitate and be instructed by the adults. The tribal law which permits a juvenile, up to the time it is six months or so old, to take food literally from the mouth of any adult serves (a) to insure that the inexperienced youngsters will get something to eat, and (b) as a means of instructing them as to what is edible. A cub who takes a beetle from an old female will presumably learn and remember something of the feel, taste, smell of the insect, apply this knowledge when he encounters another beetle as he roots about in a rotten log.

The tendency of a chulo tribe to forage for a time in one spot, then form a line of march and move on to another, is advantageous to all the animals, but particularly so for the cubs, since it puts them in places where, according to the wisdom of the elders, there is a good chance of finding something to eat. When the tribe arrives at a good foraging area, the discipline maintained while the animals are traveling is relaxed. The cubs are then free to scurry about in the litter while the adults, rather than leading, follow them. Again, a result of this behavior is to provide the cubs with learning opportunities.

The four cubs we raised provided us with a good example of how much a chulo must learn about such an elementary subject as feeding. We removed the cubs from Mona, returned her to Kitt Peak, just two days before we left Arizona. At that time, they were partially weaned and showed no inclination to nurse on the rubber nipples of bottles which we offered to them. Therefore we set about finding some sort of soft food which they would take by themselves or lick from our fingers. After a number of failures, we found that canned rice pudding delighted them. Therefore we loaded up on this dessert, fed the cubs rice pudding as we crossed the continent and after we returned and installed them in their Pennsylvania quarters. They thrived on the diet, and since we laced the pudding with vitamins and minerals we were not particularly worried about their health. However, by the time they were three months old, the four of them were eating a case of rice pudding a week, and we decided that expense, if not nutrition, made it necessary that we find some way to vary their diet.

Among other chulo foods in season in the early fall in Pennsylvania were grasshoppers. The overgrown fields next to the house were full of these insects and, knowing that this was a great delicacy for Arizona chulos, we took the cubs into the fields, urged them on after grasshoppers. The cubs had no trouble finding the insects, would pounce on them, play with them, but they apparently had no idea that they were edible. We finally taught them this fact of chulo life, giving them rice-pudding-smeared grasshoppers. Very quickly, they learned to like these insects, became as greedy for straight grasshoppers as they were for pudding. Throughout the fall and winter, we expanded the cubs' diet, often using rice pudding as a lead item. Again and again, we found that the young animals had to be taught that certain foodstuffs were edible.

Young chulos also must learn to use and understand the communicative system, the language of their species. Again, the youngsters come into the world with the innate ability, inclination to respond to vocal signs. The first of Mona's four cubs was born at 10:45 P.M., with the other three following at about ten-minute intervals. Before the last cub had emerged, the first ones had begun to squeal loudly, without much purpose, simply squalling as a newborn human will. While the squeals attested to the vigor of the cubs, they would have been disadvantageous to Mona and the cubs themselves had the birth taken place in normal circumstances. Alone in a den or crevice, preoccupied with the birth process, somewhat weakened by it, Mona would not have been in a good position to defend either herself or her new, helpless young. Anything which attracted attention to the family would increase their risk. Therefore a cub would no more than begin his squeal when Mona would give a sharp, commanding grunt. The cub, though less than a half-hour old, would respond immediately to this signal—instantly, in mid-squall, hush.

Though the cubs inherit certain responsiveness to vocal signals, this innate behavior, like most, was shaped, modified, expanded by experience. Thus when they first join the tribe, cubs will come running whenever they hear a female give the "I have found———" food-identification grunt. However, gradually the cubs become more discriminating in their responses; they learn, for example, when the grunt indicates a lot of food, and presumably learn what kind of food is being announced. The youngsters also must learn the meaning of the elaborate system of warning-alarm-challenge signals. The nose of a juvenile chulo may be as keen as that of an adult, but the young animal appears not to understand the meaning of the scents his nose registers, must be instructed by the matriarchs as to the proper reaction. After hearing a particular grunt given when coyote scent is in the air, after reacting in a certain way because he is directed to do so by the other tribal animals, a cub may begin to attach certain values to coyote scent and associate this scent with appropriate responses.

One day in May, we witnessed a hilarious incident which served as a good illustration of how much young chulos must learn about their language and also that tribal elders appear to recognize that juveniles are students and apprentices. The entire tribe had stopped by the cabin at seven in the morning, looking for breakfast. While they milled about, we sat in their midst drinking our first cup of tea, taking the sun, watching them. Reaching for the sugar, Terry knocked a tablespoon off the bench and it struck Fourteen, a young male, on the nose. None of the other animals were concerned with or even noticed the incident, but Fourteen was naturally alarmed. He scampered away, retreating to the large boulder on the edge of Clark's Ravine, from which he looked down on the cabin yard at the tribe and us. From this

vantage point, he proceeded to run through his entire repertoire of alarm and warning words and gestures. Because of
his youth and excitement, it was apparent even to us that his
speech was slurred, his syntax shaky. Nevertheless his in-
tention was clear: he was doing his best to alert the tribe to
the danger of being smacked in the head by mysterious
pieces of metal. Finally, sputtering, frustrated, Fourteen
began to lash his tail inexpertly, which was a totally in-
appropriate gesture, normally and properly being used when
two adult males encounter each other during breeding season. The tribal response to Fourteen's display was one of
absolute indifference. Though they could scarcely help but
see and hear him, the other animals continued to forage and
feed placidly. Their analysis of the situation was obvious.
Fourteen was spouting hysterical nonsense. In this same
situation, the Witch or one of the other responsible, re-
spected adults could have given a single sign and the entire
tribe would have vacated the premises quickly.

Young animals learn not only from their elders but also, it
is thought, from each other, particularly as they play. If so,
an obvious and important educational consequence of the
tribal organization is that it permits all the chulos born in
the summer to stay together and, among other things, play
together throughout their first two years. A gaggle of chulo
cubs pouncing on rustling leaves, waving flower heads, each
other's tails are not only developing their coordination and
reflexes, but learning the techniques of pouncing and predation. The cubs are great tree climbers, madly chase each
other about limbs. As they do so, they are exploring a new
portion of their habitat, one which is rich in food possibilities. They must learn, for example, by meeting them there,
that lizards are often found in trees and, in time, that they
are edible, can be run out of trees and captured.

Chulo cubs are forever wrestling, mauling each other,
engaging in mock combats. As they harmlessly attack and

earnestly defend against each other, occasionally being separated by the intervention of the adult females, the cubs begin to learn something about tribal etiquette, what liberties are and are not tolerated, the proper forms for cursing, apologizing, surrendering, expressing warning and affection. Among the juveniles, the wrestling matches may serve to introduce the young animals to the satisfaction of physical contact, which in adults is expressed, satisfied by mutual grooming. (There is always a certain chicken-and-egg aspect to behavioral phenomena. Through play, young chulos may learn to groom, enjoy grooming. On the other hand, because the cubs stay together and play together for such a long period, develop such a strong taste for touching and fondling their tribe mates, grooming might be regarded as juvenile behavior which continues on into adulthood.)

So far as their position within the tribe is concerned, young chulos are treated by adults as though they are sexless during their first eighteen months. However, after they are six or seven months old, male cubs will, while playing, often attempt to mount other cubs—of either sex—in a copulatory position. Physically and perhaps sensually, this behavior is meaningless, seems to have very little direct sexual significance. Nevertheless, again through play, the cubs begin to develop adult attitudes and techniques.

In their youth, virtually all mammals spend a great deal of time at what we have come to call play. Certainly this behavior seems to be instructive, helps prepare a young animal for later activities. However, again it is a mistake—or, at least, unnecessarily obscures our understanding of the life style of other bloods—to try to make play more or less than what it appears to be. Young animals, chulo cubs on a ledge, human children at a playground, may indeed be learning things which will be of later value to them. However, there is no evidence that they are playing so that they may survive. The immediate motive and cause of play in young chulos seem to be very similar to that of young children. They play as a means of releasing energy and because the release, the act of play, appears to amuse and entertain them.

PERSONALITY

Throughout our recorded history, presumably throughout our natural history, we have struggled to identify, define, understand personality, to deal with effects of differentiation in our own species. It is obvious that Mary of Scotland and Elizabeth of England were ladies of different character and that the personalities of these two queens directly influenced the behavior of their contemporaries—to an extent still indirectly influence ours. Had the Queen of England welcomed Philip of Spain with a loving smile rather than with Sir Francis Drake, we would all presumably be living in a somewhat different fashion from what we do today.

Each generation has had armies of professional and amateur students, scientists, shamans, statisticians of personality. Yet collectively we have accomplished little more than to compile an enormous personality file. We are still unable to isolate specific personality elements or to demonstrate objectively that a certain such element will have a certain effect on behavior. Today we are as incapable of writing a formula such as Mary $= s \, xy^2 + (y^2-x)$ and Elizabeth $= s \, 2xy - (x^2-y)$ as we were in 1550.

When it comes to other species, our understanding of personality is even more feeble. All or most of the complexities and subtleties which make it difficult for us to deal with human personality problems appear to be present in other species. Furthermore, we communicate with other bloods poorly or not at all, and find it all but impossible to consider them imaginatively, creatively. Yet there is every reason to believe that individual personality differences influence the behavior of other species as, or almost as, importantly as they do our own. Virtually all our understanding, our study, of animal behavior is inadequate at best, very likely inaccurate, because we have not taken and cannot take into account the effects of individual personality upon general behavior.

Academics and scientists who took over the study of other bloods from hunters, trackers, gamekeepers, farmers, menagerie managers have been largely concerned with certain fixed elements of behavior. These—first called instincts, later innate behavior patterns—are inherited, genetically determined responses to certain stimuli, and are identical or very similar in every creature of the same kind. Innate behavior can be isolated, analyzed, occasionally induced laboratory-fashion in response to given stimuli. It can be investigated by traditional scientific methods and it yields graphs, theses, degrees. For these excellent and practical reasons, most formal studies of animal behavior are concentrated in the field of innate behavior. However, scientists—as well as theologians, politicians, and many other idealists—abhor incomplete universals, tentative theorems. Therefore in this area there has been a tendency to treat innate behavior not just as the most studyable facet of general behavior, but as the only element worthy of study. The influence of individual personality has been frequently frostily ignored, often treated as nonexistent. In consequence, the official versions and precepts of animal behavior are likely to be misleadingly mechanistic.

So far as is known, every animal responds individually to stimuli, learns from individual experience. At its upper limits, the capacity to learn is finite, the limit varying from species to species. Thus it is probably impossible for a dog to learn carpentry. However, within specific limits the learning capacity of every individual animal appears to be different, as are the individual experiences, the exposure to stimuli of each animal. The capacity to learn and the nature of instructive experience being unique, so in obvious and subtle ways is the personality of each animal.

The ban against serious consideration of personality differences has been informally, though ferociously enforced by invoking charges of anthropomorphism, the attributing of human characteristics to other species. Generally, serious-minded professionals avoid anthropomorphic thought, speculation, description like the plague, often tying themselves in awkward logical knots so as to avoid even the suspicion of this sin. All of which is often unnecessary and undesirable, an attitude which inhibits rather than promotes understanding of the life styles of other bloods.

Admittedly the anthropomorphic approach can result in great silliness. Faithful dogs and pussycats who, with their liquid and expressive eyes, recite romantic sonnets to their masters and mistresses are fancy, not real animals. However, conscious, restrained anthropomorphism is not in itself vicious. It is an attempt to describe, communicate by analogy, and analogy is at the root of much respectable discourse, including scientific. It is a particularly apt, even necessary, method for describing personality, which we are presently incapable of describing in literal or statistical terms. Since we know virtually nothing about the inner life of another creature, it seems something less than idiotic to report that outwardly a creature in a certain situation appears to respond somewhat as some men might in similar circumstances. It would seem that it is at least as instructive, informative, to describe individual animals analogously as being playful, timid, dignified, elated, anxious, perplexed, jealous, affectionate as it is to insist that they are biological machines whose responses are as rigidly fixed as those of a combustion engine.

Within the chulo tribe, we were constantly faced with examples, reminded of personality differences. The basic vocabulary of chulos of the same age group and sex was largely identical, innate, but there were certain animals who used signal "words" in a somewhat different fashion from others. The peculiar relationship between adult females and males is in the main genetically fixed, universal. However, it was observably modified by certain members of the tribe. The Supervisor was tolerated with more grace by Queenie, the forward leader of the first band, than by Calamity, her counterpart in the second band. Curious or defiant, the Supervisor tended to climb a tree to look over the situation. In similar circumstances, the Bungler was a rock man, preferring to mount a boulder as a vantage point. Though they were engaging because of their playfulness and innocence, the young animals were less personable than their elders. Because of their lack of experience, learning, they were less differentiated in their behavior. One of the pleasures of the year was, as with children, watching the gradual formation of individual character in these young animals, the addition of personal idiosyncrasies to their innate responses.

Among all the chulos we knew well, No. 17, the Witch of the Montezuma tribe, seemed to us to have the most unusual personality, which may be simply another way of saying she was the most learned animal. Terry and Ky were the first to meet her, having on December 17th come on a band of four adults and six juveniles in a wooded ravine a quarter of a mile from the Coronado ranger station. That evening, while we were comparing experiences and collating our notes, they had much to say about one of these adults, who was the Witch (though we did not give the name, were unable to assign her a number, until a month later).

"He really looked bad," Terry said of this animal.

"How do you know it was a male?"

"It, then. It was all beat up. It's got scars on its face, along one side. The fur is messed up like it had mange or something. And it's little. We thought at first it was a young one."

"Did it look sick? Wobble around, seem feeble?"

"It didn't act sick," Ky said, taking up the report. "It acted mean as hell."

"How so?"

"We were sitting on one of those rocks where we find quartz crystals. The band came around a corner in the ravine. This one must have smelled us. It gave some grunts and the rest of them started beating their feet up the ravine. We walked down to see which way they went, but this one just stood there—you know, with its legs spread—and kept snorting at us. It even took a couple steps toward us. We thought maybe it was going to attack, so we waited. Pretty soon it started up the ravine after the rest, but every little bit it would stop, turn around, and snort at us. When it got fifty yards or so away, it ran after the others and we couldn't find them again."

The next day, returning to our open camp, I found it being raided by, apparently, the same band the boys had met. As I approached, the animals ran off, several of them carrying slices of looted bread. Scarface—as, for a time, we called the animal Terry and Ky first described—remained behind, standing defiantly on a sleeping bag, snorting a warning. Scarface held the position until the other animals were out of sight in the brush, then followed them. The behavior of this animal, whom we saw often during the remainder of December and early January, was at odds with anything we had observed at Kitt Peak. The fact that Scarface often hung back from the band, seldom seemed to feed with the others, indicated that Terry may have been right, that it was an idiosyncratic male. However, the small size, the lack of hostility between Scarface and the other animals, suggested a female. We were unable to settle this question and others because Scarface was both aggressive and wary. During the first month after our return to the Huachucas, we trapped, identified, marked most of the animals of the Montezuma Canyon tribe, but we had no luck with Scarface. While the other animals entered the trap casually, fed in it eagerly, Scarface hung back, regarded the device with obvious suspicion. Occasionally the animal would go to the entrance and paw out a bit of bait, but consistently refused to go farther.

On January 10th, Terry and I had the trap duty. It was a

bright day, as always, but a cold one because of a high, sharp wind. Chulo-wise it was a dull day, with no activity around the trap during the first eight hours. By four o'clock, the blue jays had eaten all the dried dog food we used for bait. The sun had dipped out of sight behind Montezuma Pass and the temperature was in the thirties. Cold and bored, we considered packing it in for the day, going back to the cabin and the fire. However, duty finally triumphed and we decided to stay another hour, baiting the trap with marshmallows, a few of which we still had in our pockets. Shortly before full dusk, Scarface and the band appeared. Two juveniles and one adult female rushed into the trap and began to gobble candy. Scarface, predictably, hung back but just outside the trap found a few spilled marshmallows and ate them eagerly. Then, unexpectedly, Scarface walked directly into the trap and, pushing through the other animals, began to feed. Terry pulled the trigger and the door dropped down behind the elusive animal.

By this time, handling the chulos had become routine for us and was usually a quick, smooth operation. Dealing with Scarface, however, was anything but routine. The other three animals in the trap, having all been previously marked, were reweighed and released quickly. In the meantime, Scarface was tearing at the trap, growling, shrieking, bloodying its nose on the mesh. When the other animals were gone, Scarface collapsed in one corner of the trap, panting, heaving, drooling, giving every impression of a terrified animal in an advanced stage of shock. Unable to cajole or prod the hysterical creature into the holding bag, I finally reached into the trap, grabbed the animal by the tail, pulled it out, and dropped it into the bag.

Scarface, it turned out, was a female, but a most unusual one. She weighed 7.9 pounds, almost two pounds less than the next smallest adult. At close range, she was a poorer, more battered specimen than she had appeared to be from a distance. Her right flank, hip, and muzzle were crisscrossed with ridges of blackened scar tissue, over which the hair had grown sparsely or not at all. She was all but toothless, having lost her incisors and canines, some of her molars and pre-molars. The animal was also blind or going blind in her left eye, which was white, filmed over with cataracts. She was probably the oldest chulo we met during the year, certainly the most infirm physically. Yet despite her condition, or perhaps because of the age and experience it represented, she was the most singular.

After she was trapped and released, Scarface—No. 17, as she was then formally identified—disappeared, taking the band with whom she had been foraging with her. Though we scoured the canyons, we did not see either her or the others for eight days. This may have been a coincidental phenomenon, but for whatever reasons it was unusual. We had been seeing No. 17 and the others almost daily up until the afternoon she trapped. All the other animals in the band had been previously trapped, handled. As with other chulos, the experience seemed to have made very little impression on them.

The simplest, most obvious explanation was that the trapping had been traumatic for No. 17, more so than for any other animal. Since the process was all but identical in each case, the difference lay in her character, her sensitivity, memory, perhaps contemplation of the experience. The disappearance of the nine animals with whom she regularly associated was even more surprising and led directly to a corollary deduction. It seemed likely that she had in some manner communicated her reaction to the others and had influenced their behavior.

Sitting one night in the cabin speculating, worrying a little about the chulos we could not find, Ky said, "That old one did it. She looks like a witch and she acts like one." Thereafter, the toothless old crone of the Montezuma tribe became permanently, and it seemed properly to us, the Witch.

When, more than a week after they had split, the Witch and the nine animals came back to the area where we were feeding and trapping, the other members of the band behaved much as they had before they had left, entering the trap casually, feeding there freely. The Witch, however, would not approach within ten feet of it, and gave every indication of having learned that it was a place of danger. She retained her distrust of this wire box throughout the year, even after we had ceased to use it as a trap and had converted it into a feeding station. She entered it much less often than the other animals and, when she did, always seemed to remain on her guard. Otherwise, after her return the Witch grew gradually more accustomed to us and our activities, and in time ceased to be the most suspicious adult, became the one most at ease with us. It was as if while we studied her she studied us, our character and behavior, and sometime in the early spring she decided that we were harmless, if eccentric, and on the whole beneficial creatures. Whatever the cause, it is fortunate, as we discovered later, that we were able to make friends with the Witch, for had we not, we would have seen far less, learned less of the animals than we did. The influence which we suspected she had over tribal affairs turned out to be real and considerable.

Of the two Montezuma tribe foraging bands, it seemed to us that the first, in which Queenie served as the forward leader and the Witch as the rear leader, was more cohesively organized and tightly disciplined. Also there was some evidence that in the tribe as a whole Queenie and the Witch were the principal matriarchs. For example, during the winter months the first band usually foraged lower in the canyon, in the vicinity of the ranger compound, where it seemed to us food sources, both natural and man-created, were more plentiful than higher up in the canyon, where the second band, led by Calamity and Eleven, operated. Twice, both times immediately after snowstorms, the second band divided, one of its females (a different one in each case) taking some of the juveniles and joining the first band below. The chulos, as noted, appeared to us only mildly territorial, but whenever such changes did take place, it always seemed to be a matter of the animals of the second band coming to the first. Also, during the winter and early spring we never saw either the Witch or Queenie with a group of less than eight animals. Invariably when the tribe divided in some way other than its customary ten-eight pattern, Queenie and the Witch were with the larger group.

When, as happened occasionally, the two bands merged and foraged together for a time, Queenie would continue to lead and the Witch to bring up the rear of the combined groups. Calamity and Eleven would drop back or move up and become mid-band animals. This shift in position was never accompanied by contentious squabbling. There was no sense that Calamity and Eleven were humiliated by their new positions or that they were forced to assume them by Queenie or the Witch. There did not seem to be roles amongst the chulos as there are in human organizations. There were only social functions, and one function did not appear to be regarded as more desirable than another. It seemed likely to us that when the bands merged, Queenie and the Witch continued as the forward and rear leaders because by experience they were more firmly fixed in this functional behavior than the other two females. If so, they did not have to prove their talents competitively, as humans might feel called upon to do in similar circumstances. For a chulo tribe, such a role or status struggle would be danger-ous, inefficient. When the tribe was together, the position, function of the adults was determined immediately without dispute, and the decision apparently left no residual dissatis-faction, thwarted desire.

A possible explanation for the Witch's functional role was that she was, among the chulos we knew, an olfactory gen-ius. One morning in February, after the Witch had begun to suffer our presence for longer periods and at closer range, I was sitting on a limestone ledge looking down into the draw we called Blue Water Ravine. The Witch and her band were foraging on the floor of this ravine for early beetles and lizards. She of course knew I was on the rock above, had made certain I knew she knew I was there, having directed a few "Behave yourself, no tricks" grunts toward me, but otherwise showed little concern. Then quite suddenly the Witch rose, wobbled her nose like a probing radarscope, and pointed it straight down the ravine. She sniffed deeply, thoughtfully, then sat down and issued several short staccato grunts, an intermediate warning and command to leave the area. According to the Witch, there was something suspicious below, not danger that required immediate flight but something to which the proper response was an orderly withdrawal. This much I could make out listening above, but it· is not unlikely the Witch passed along more specific information to the others regarding the nature of the danger, its estimated time of arrival. Immediately, the individual animals stopped rooting about in the litter, fell into their traditional marching order—Queenie in the lead; Seven, Nancy herding the juveniles along in the middle; the Witch at the rear—and disappeared out of sight up the ravine.

Curious, I remained where I had been sitting rather than following the chulos. Five minutes later, Ky, with Dain at his heel, came up the ridge to join me. The trail up the Blue Water Ravine is a steep, rough one. Even so, Ky and Dain must have been at least 300 yards away when they were first noted (if they were) by the Witch. Most astonishingly of all, they were downwind from the band.

Later, when we had become more intimately acquainted, the tribe developed the habit of stopping by the cabin for an early breakfast snack before starting off on regular foraging rounds. After the animals had had their ration of dog food, we would throw out a few handfuls of marshmallows. The juveniles, particularly, learned to watch marshmallows in flight, run to where they fell. Occasionally when the candy rolled under the leaves, the youngsters would lose it. The Witch, who perhaps because of her dental problems was something of a marshmallow addict, wasted little effort in attempting to see marshmallows, concentrated on sniffing out their location. To test her, each of us would throw a marshmallow in a different direction, trying to lob them into the thick brush and litter. Unhesitatingly, nose down, the Witch would move from candy to candy, always locating all that had been thrown, coming back to wait hopefully for more after she had found the last one.

Scent being such an important stimulus, all adult chulos often lean back or sit up and raise their noses so as to permit the information-laden air to pass more freely over their sensitive olfactory membranes. As might be expected, the Witch, being a scentmaster, was often so observed in this position, presumably scanning the wind for practical messages it might carry: the presence of danger, food, the location of other tribal members. However, occasionally we felt she might have other motives. Sometimes when the band or tribe was lazing about, resting, socializing on one of their sheltered grooming ledges, the Witch would get up, walk to the rim, sit back, and sniff deeply, slowly. She might so occupy herself for five minutes or so, then rejoin the others without comment or reaction. It may have been that on these occasions the information was all negative, that there was nothing to report. However, she may also have sat high up on the cliff sniffing the canyon below for somewhat the same reasons, in somewhat the same mood, as a man who goes to a gallery or a concert. The scent scene may have instructed, entertained her, given her aesthetic pleasure.

The Witch was also the most articulate of the chulos we knew, her vocabulary being large, her style of delivery apparently incisive. When there were communal announcements to be made, commands to be given, the Witch invariably spoke, gestured, postured first, very likely because she

was the first to possess information by means of her marvel-
ous sense of smell. Furthermore she appeared to communicate clearly, forcefully, for if her message was an action
one, the other animals responded quickly and, it seemed to
us, correctly. In contrast, in the second foraging band
Calamity and Eleven would sometimes repeat signals several times before they were heeded. Also, on occasion, we
saw both these leading animals give simultaneous commands; twice somewhat contradictory ones.

When we first met the Montezuma tribe, the adult
females all regarded us, reacted to us, in much the same
fashion. When we came too close, within 75–100 yards, they
would give the proper warning and retreat signals, hustle
their charges away from us. As the tribe began to become
accustomed to and develop some trust in us, the distance we
could approach narrowed and the range of activities we
could carry on within their presence widened. However,
even after the era of good feeling commenced, we would
sometimes startle the animals, and if we did, the leading
females other than the Witch would react as they had in the
beginning: ordering, stimulating their band to flight. Generally they had only two responses to us, acceptance or full
retreat. With the Witch—and, in consequence, her foraging
band—it was much different. She developed, extemporized
a graduated series of responses to us, used a variety of
modified acceptance and warning signals to express her
reactions and her analysis of the situation to the other
animals. As a result, the Witch and her band seldom gave
way to panic. As a rule, we were able to work closer, stay
longer with her band than that of Calamity and Eleven. The
Witch was constantly alert to our presence, directed a
stream of signs toward us and the members of her band, the
effect of which was to influence the behavior of all parties
and to establish a dynamic and safe (so far as the chulos
were concerned) relationship between us.

Upon meeting, the Witch would acknowledge us with a

somewhat softer, slurred version of the conventional warning grunt. The modified warning, almost a greeting, told the other chulos, in effect, "They are here again—stand by for further information." With this signal, the Witch also informed us, "I know you are there; behave yourselves." Since it was impossible, at least for us, to approach the Witch undetected, openness was always the best policy with her, stealth only serving to arouse her suspicions. Therefore we usually answered her with something pleasant and sincere: "Hello, Witch," or, "Chulo, chulo, chulo." Our purpose was to establish the fact that no trickery was intended—that there was nobody there but us chulo watchers. (We discovered after a time that in dealing with the Witch and her band, total silence was neither necessary nor desirable. A little quiet conversation seemed to reassure her that we had no sneaky intentions.)

The Witch's reaction to Dain was an interesting one. Initially she, like the other adults, was obviously and properly extremely suspicious of the dog, but gradually became less so. In the spring, when the entire tribe began to forage about the cabin, Dain was of course there. If the tribe was in the yard, he would be ordered to the porch, where he lay motionless, tied to the spot more effectively by the command than he would have been physically with a chain. In time, the chulos became accustomed to his presence, but never forgot he was there. When Dain was on it, all the animals avoided the immediate vicinity of the porch, remaining a cautious fifteen feet or so away. The exception was the Witch. After she had been about the cabin and Dain for a month, she would often extend her search for soft food onto the porch itself. Walking boldly through the door, she would, upon entry, assume a defiant pose a few feet in front of Dain, glare balefully at him with her one good eye. Then apparently reassured that the dog would not move, for whatever curious reason, she would serenely make a circuit of the porch, nosing about in the corners and cracks looking for edibles.

It could be argued that the eight-pound Witch flaunting herself before a ninety-pound dog and the manner in which she and the tribe came rather casually to accept us are not indicative of cleverness but of corruption, the overriding of natural and useful suspicion by the desire for soft, sweet food. This is a possible but, we felt, an inadequate interpretation. During this period, we witnessed encounters between the tribe and other people, other creatures, in which there was no evidence that the natural alertness and wariness of the animals had been dulled. It seemed to us that the changing response of the animals to us was evidence of learning. We had the impression, for example, that the Witch came to treat Dain as she did, not because we had made her into a marshmallow addict but because she had properly diagnosed a rather complex phenomenon: that Dain was somehow an unnatural dog, one who in certain circumstances was safe, posed no threat.

If it is true, as we thought, that the Witch was an animal possessed of special abilities, her functional value to the community would in theory be considerable. Because of her keen sense of smell, and to a lesser extent hearing, she provided the tribe with an exceptional early-warning system. Her apparent ability to learn quickly from experience, in a sense to analyze happenings, permitted her and her tribe perhaps greater than average flexibility of response to their environment. Thus the Witch's foraging band fed longer in our presence than did the second band because she seemed to be better able to distinguish between degrees of potential danger than either Calamity or Eleven. The apparent boldness of the Witch did not result in her and her band taking greater risks, but rather entering without risk into situations which lesser animals, ones in whom the other members of the community had less confidence, avoided. In almost any activity of any creature there is an element of risk, against which the possibility of reward must be balanced. The more precisely this risk-reward equation can be calculated, either because of what an animal has learned or because of what she innately is, the more successful she is likely to be. Again in theory, it would seem that risk-reward matters would be of special importance to communal carnivores such as a chulo tribe whose foraging activities are largely extemporaneous, investigatory.

Despite our view of the Witch's abilities, a disclaimer regarding our analysis of her position within and value to the tribe is perhaps in order. We tended to think of her, treat her, as a leading animal. However, and this is the great danger of the anthropomorphic approach, our notions about leadership are deeply, inevitably stained by our experience with leadership in human society. Our experience, definitions simply may not be applicable to a chulo tribe. Thus it is conceivable, beginning with a different set of premises, that the Witch did not function within the tribe as she did because she was superior, but because she was inferior. Vigorous adult chulos may express the reality of their fitness by forcing older, weaker animals into more exposed, less desirable functions. Thus the Witch, as the rear leader of the tribe, often had less opportunity to feed than the other animals, and should the tribe be stalked by any terrestrial predator, she would normally be the first to encounter or be surprised by it. It could be argued from the grim logic of survival that the tribe could better afford the loss of the old, enfeebled Witch (unless of course, as we thought, her years and infirmities had equipped her with special talents) than that of, say, Seven, the youngest of the mature females. On much the same grounds, a Martian behaviorist, for example, conducting a field study on this planet might come away with a view of the human hierarchy far different from that which we conventionally hold. The men and women whom we regard as leaders, who hold positions of authority, might from another viewpoint be regarded as defectives. Through the efforts, pressures of "normal" individuals, the leaders are exposed to assassins, heart attacks, humiliations, with the functional effect of protecting those they theoretically lead, promoting their survival. It is a possible explanation, but on the whole I prefer the alternative: that the Witch, for example, was truly a leading member of the chulo tribe—among the least, rather than most, expendable.

The personal life of the Witch, in contrast to her public activities as a tribal administrator, was also unique in several respects. Just as strong-willed, clever old ladies are sometimes regarded as difficult within our society, so at least one of the other adult chulos—Calamity, of the second foraging band—seemed to regard the Witch. To say that the two animals were enemies is too strong, too anthropomorphic, suggesting motives and an intensity of feeling that were probably nonexistent. However, the two had an observable, recordable, unique disinclination to associate with each other any more closely than was absolutely necessary. The final summary of our daily records showed that the Witch and Calamity were together in the same group only 30 percent of the time they were observed. In contrast, the Witch was with Queenie 75 percent of the time, with Seven 68 percent and Eleven 45 percent.

Even when the entire tribe was together, as it often was in the spring, the Witch and Calamity seemed purposely to avoid each other, usually feeding, foraging with the other animals between them. On four occasions, we observed face-to-face meetings, which seemed to occur either accidentally or out of forgetfulness. In all these instances there were signs of a hostility which was difficult to explain, since no juveniles or other adults were involved. Each time, the Witch turned quickly on Calamity, hissing and growling at the younger, larger animal in a peculiar manner which we never saw duplicated in relationships between females. (Its closest counterpart was the reaction of a male toward another of his sex during the post-breeding period when several might be simultaneously foraging with the band.) On each occasion, Calamity deferred, withdrew a few steps.

These passages, though peculiar, were brief and infrequent. We might have dismissed them as accidental had it not been for a final, more serious exchange between the two. On March 29th, Terry and Ky spent two hours with the entire tribe, which was foraging in a small side canyon between the State of Texas Mine and the ranger station.

"The Witch and Calamity really had it out," Terry, who had been the closest at the climactic moment, reported. "Calamity was eating and the Witch walked up. She grunted a couple times, and Calamity grunted back. They stood there facing each other like two males and began to growl. Then the Witch ran at her, knocked her over. They were tumbling around squealing almost like juveniles. Then they rolled apart and Calamity walked away. There might have been a little blood. The Witch stood defiant until Calamity was a good ways away."

"What did the others do?"

"Seven and three young were the only ones really close. Their tails went up and they ran back like they were frightened, but as soon as it was over they went on feeding."

"Was there a male?"

"The Supervisor. He was fifty feet away. He didn't do anything. Didn't even seem interested."

That evening, the tribe divided into its usual foraging bands, both of which we found before noon the next day. The Witch had a deep, bloody gash high up on her scrawny right flank. In the second band, Calamity was limping, unable to put any weight on her left forepaw. ("If the Witch did it, she must have used karate," Terry commented. "She'd have a hell of a time getting Calamity's foot between her molars.")

That afternoon, the Witch entered the feeder and for the second and last time we trapped her, for the purpose of examining her wound. (Since we did not have to weigh, bag, or handle her and since we were by then on terms of some intimacy, she showed little fear and none of the traumatic aftereffects of the first trapping.) The gash was a half-inch deep, four inches long. It seemed most certainly to be a chulo slash, similar in position and character to those which males inflict on one another. It had already begun to fester and had an ugly, infected look to it. Therefore, abandoning the role of dispassionate observer, working through the wire mesh, I cleaned it with a swab and filled it with an antibiotic ointment, which seemed the least we could do for the Witch considering what she had done for us. Whether it was because of this treatment or simply natural healing, the Witch's wound mended during the next week, leaving only another ridge of scar tissue on her battered hide. Calamity limped about for a few more days, but also recovered completely. We saw no other hostile encounters between the two during the rest of the year.

It is possible that the two animals did not injure each other, that between the passage Ky and Terry observed on the afternoon of the twenty-ninth and the time when we saw them again on the morning of the thirtieth, Calamity and the Witch coincidentally were injured through some other agency. However, it seemed more likely either that the brief, quick scuffle between the two had been more serious than it appeared to Terry and Ky or that later, sometime during the night, the two matrons had had at it again. In any event, this was the only time during our year of chulo watching that we saw or found a wounded female, and it was the only instance we observed of actual physical violence between mature females. Perhaps the battle resulted from the crossing of innate, fixed responses and drives, was inevitable because of their age, sexual condition, or other factors. However, again it seemed to me that there was a simpler, if more anthropomorphic, explanation: between the Witch and Calamity there was bad blood. It was a personal matter and, if so, their animosity was probably acquired, not inherited.

Less dramatically, the Witch also seemed to have what might be called a friend, Queenie, the forward leader of her regular foraging band. When the band was foraging for any length of time in a good place, these two females often seemed to seek out each other, feed companionably side by side. On rest ledges after the juveniles had finished helling around, had had enough grooming and had lain down to nap, Queenie and the Witch frequently moved next to each other and indulged in a long, luxurious mutual grooming session. Statistically they were a grooming pair almost twice as often as any other two adults.

By June 13th, the disintegration of the tribal matriarchy was well advanced. The females, their time of delivery near, were heavy, irritable, and often left the band to forage alone. In the early evening, Queenie, who had been in the lower canyon by herself since the previous morning, climbed slowly up the ravine to the feeder behind the cabin. John and I were alone that night and, having done nothing of importance all day, I decided to follow Queenie when she had finished feeding, leaving John with his aftersupper tea and a panful of dirty dishes.

Queenie waddled up Clark's Ravine, panting heavily, stopping often to rest in a thicket. At the point of the Wedge, she took the East Ravine. I guessed that she was planning to go to its head, drink from the tiny spring that was still running there. I set off cross-country, climbed up to and sat down on the small ledge on the far canyon wall from which we so often watched the tribe when it was on the Wedge. In a few minutes, Queenie came lumbering along the floor of the ravine. While watching her, I caught a glimpse of movement higher up on the face of the Wedge. It was the Witch, purposefully scrambling down the rocks toward the ravine. The Witch did not forage on the way down, descended directly, rather quickly, considering she, too, was gravid. When the Witch was fifty feet away, Queenie turned, sniffed, then waited (there was no doubt in my mind as to the purposeful nature of the activities of both) for her old companion, from whom I knew she had been separated for at least thirty hours, perhaps longer. When they met not far from the spring seep, both began to chirp, sounding the chulo pleasure trill. Then deliberately, delicately, they touched and rubbed their long muzzles. In a brief grooming gesture, the Witch nibbled for a moment at Queenie's flank. Then, side by side, the two heavy, awkward animals walked to the spring, drank, climbed slowly up the side of the Wedge, disappearing from my sight into the dusk and jumble of ledges at the summit of the Wedge.

I claim nothing more for or about this moment than that it was one which charmed and moved me, as I sat on a ledge at dusk in June in the Huachuca Mountains. I do not know what, if anything, it signified for the two chulos.

9

The Males

The name, coatimundi, by which chulos are generally known throughout their range, is a misnomer of sorts, based on inaccurate observation and understanding of the sexual relationships between adult animals. The word "coati" is of Indian origin, meaning "belt" (*cua*) and "nose" (*tim*), and was apparently given to the chulos because they often sleep curled in a ball with their noses on their stomachs. "Mundi" is a corruption of the Portuguese (who first met the species in Brazil) *mondi,* or solitary. Coatimundi was first used to refer only to the single males, but later came to be used to designate all chulos.

The peculiar social arrangements of the chulos, the segregation of the adult males and females, has apparently long been noted and has long confused naturalists. As late as this century, chulos, or coatimundis, were classified as being of two distinct species: *Nasua sociabilis,* the social chulo; and *Nasua solitaria,* the lone chulo. This error suggests among other things that nineteenth-century students did not do much field work so far as the chulos were concerned. A little collecting would have shown that all *Nasua solitarias* were males, a fact which should have given pause for thought.

The confusion concerning the relationship between adults is in other respects understandable, since their sexual relationships are among the more unusual of the mammalian world. In some species, males and females remain together throughout the year. In more cases, they are together for only a few days or weeks, during a brief period of courtship and/or copulation. After these sexual encounters, the sexes separate, have little influence on the affairs of one another. The chulos, however, are in a midway position. The males leave—or, more accurately, are driven from the group by females—in the late summer. For the next six or seven months, the males lead largely solitary lives. They rejoin the tribe in March, commence to court the females, but do not (or, at least, did not as we observed) leave the tribe, as they are generally thought to do, after copulation occurs. Both in Montezuma Canyon and at Kitt Peak, the males remained with the group until midsummer. During the post-copulatory period, the males are an integral part of the social organization, important potential protectors of the gravid females, the inexperienced juveniles. When the females leave the tribe, go off to bear their cubs and then nurse them along, the males remain with the juveniles, in a sense assuming the responsibilities of parenthood a year after their offspring are born.

By and large, we reached conclusions concerning the function of the males in the tribal organization that were much different from those of other observers. The conventional view is that the adult males are generally solitary, social only during a relatively brief period of sexual activity. Our feeling is that this is an oversimplification of a much more subtle and remarkable arrangement. In the first place, the males (or at least—again to qualify—those we observed) are intensely social, very much part of the group for four or five months of the year, from early March until late July. Secondly, even during the matriarchal period, when they are physically separated from the tribe, the males are strongly influenced by the activities of the other animals, and to a lesser degree influence the behavior of the females and the young. It seemed to us that during the fall and winter months the communal group, females and younger animals, might be thought of as a planet and the nearby males as satellites orbiting around it. Throughout the year, we thought of the males as part of the tribal unit; that, to continue the analogy, the tribe was a single system composed of both a planet and satellites.

The curious divison of the tribe during the fall and winter inevitably sets one to wondering about why it exists—what, if any, benefit the arrangement has for the tribe. A variety of explanations occurred to us, all of which are tentative and speculative, as all answers to questions regarding the cause of, motives for, behavior must be.

Until more and better information is available, it would seem that so far as the males are concerned, the best possible explanation is the simplest. They appear to orbit around the communal group because they have an urge to be part of it. It is not difficult to think of reasons for this urge, if it indeed exists. For the first two years of their life and thereafter for four or five months of the year, the males are social animals and regularly associate with the other members of the tribe. Being a member of a group seems to be a desirable thing for chulos, seems to provide animals of both sexes with a sense of security and satisfaction, and improves their foraging opportunities. Also, only in the group can an animal regularly groom, touch, play, converse with other chulos. If not pleasures, these are at least habitual activities. It would not be surprising that the males, having become accustomed to communal living, have a sense of deprivation when they are ostracized from the tribe, that this sense is strong enough to hold them near the group, to make them try to force their way back into it.

Another possible, diametrically opposed explanation occurred to us. It may be that the males lurk about the edges of the bands, seek to join them, not for reasons of affection but in the hope of preying on the cubs. Predation by adults, particularly males, on young is not unknown among mammals. However, we saw no evidence, had no impression that the males were so motivated. On the very few occasions during the fall and winter when we observed encounters between cubs and males, both parties seemed startled—the males, if anything, more so than the cubs. Furthermore the cubs are not appreciably larger, better able to defend themselves in March, when the males are permitted to rejoin the group, than they are in January and February, when the males are excluded. The cannibal theory suggested itself because it was possible, and because throughout this period the females consistently treated the males as though they were dangerous enemies.

(There was a small roadside zoo near Bisbee. The owner had obtained two female chulos and, in an effort to breed them, had twice introduced males into their enclosure—in both cases during the winter. The females had promptly killed the males. Caged animals are inclined to be unbalanced, psychotic, unpredictable. However, these incidents are the only absolutely verified cases of chulo murder we know of and indicate that such acts are at least possible.)

From the standpoint of the group, the reason often advanced for the exclusion of the males is that in this way the inexperienced cubs are protected from having to compete against males for food. It seemed to us that while this might be a partial explanation, it is not an entirely satisfactory theory. In Arizona, the sexually mature males are driven from the group in the late summer. Then and for the next three months, food, at least chulo food, is at its most abundant. Furthermore, if it were entirely an economic matter, it would seem that the males would be further removed from the tribe than we observed them to be. As it was, though they were separated from the cubs, they hunted at different times in the same territory and were, in fact, direct competitors of the other animals. (All of which introduces another line of speculation. We observed the males to be more closely, intimately associated with the communal animals than have others who watched the animals in the more tropical portions of their range. Perhaps, because of local climate, available food, food preferences, there is less reason for the segregation of the sexes, and thus in Arizona the segregation is less rigidly enforced.)

Another conceivable advantage stemming from the exclusion of the males during the fall and winter is that in an involuntary, accidental way the males may contribute to the security of the communal animals. Scattered as they are around the groups, the males might represent a kind of outer picket line. They do not warn or directly defend against intruders, but the chances are that a wandering predator entering the tribal territory would first encounter a single male or at least his scent trail. In such circumstances, the male might distract, lead away, or even drive off the threat before it reached the females and the cubs. At the very least, the response of a threatened male might serve as an early warning to the matriarchs.

The males may also serve the communal animals (again unwittingly) as scouts and pioneers. There were few places within Montezuma Canyon, for example, where the matriarchs might lead their foraging bands that they would not cross scent trails laid down by the satellite males. Presumably these trails led to and from good food sources, open water, rest ledges and dens. In any given area, a leading female could navigate using a kind of olfactory map created by the solitary males.

It is conceivable, if speculative to the point of being esoteric, that the tension created by the males attempting to join the band, by the refusal of the females to permit them to do so, is of value to the tribe for its own sake. Konrad Lorenz, who has perhaps thought more deeply than anyone else about these matters, has suggested that social aggression, the stimulation that it provides, is a kind of cement which holds animal societies together. For some reason, a combination of reasons, the males may represent a kind of low-grade but continuing threat to the other animals, provide pressure which contributes to the cohesiveness, discipline of the tribe.

About the best that can be said about the origin and function of most behavior patterns is that they are complex, and appear to be too complex for us presently to comprehend. Such an intricate arrangement as the partial segregation of male and female chulos most assuredly does not exist for any one reason or to serve a single need and is the product of the interaction of many cause-and-effect patterns.

PERSONALITIES

The personalities of the adult males were as varied and interesting as those of the other chulos, and in some respects they were easier to become acquainted with, particularly during the winter period. Perhaps because they then had no tribal responsibilities, could deal with us more or less on a man-to-man basis, the males at first tended to be less spooky and suspicious, more ready to accept us, even seek us out. Among the six adult males who were members of the Montezuma Canyon tribe, we became best acquainted with and most interested in three of them, animals we called the Supervisor, the Bungler, and Nancy.

The Supervisor was a large, strong, sixteen-pound animal, the dominant male of the tribe, though this did not become evident until the sexual competition between males began in the spring. During the fall and winter, his territory was in the lower part of the canyon and included the picnic area, ranger station, and residence, all desirable foraging areas.

Both of the communal foraging bands often worked the same territory, and the Supervisor was nearer to the band for longer periods of time than any of the other solitary males. Once in December and twice in January, we saw him do what no other male either in Montezuma Canyon or at Kitt Peak was observed to do—succeed in actually joining a foraging band. It is true that he did not stay long, fifteen minutes at the most, and was eventually forced to retreat— on all three occasions by the Witch. However, he did actually mingle with the other animals, confirming our impression that he was the least segregated of the solitary males.

The Supervisor was one of the first members of the Montezuma tribe we trapped and one whom the experience seemed to faze very little. He soon discovered that the traps were also feeding stations and visited them regularly. Often he would be in or around a trap when a band arrived. He would withdraw, but gave no impression of panic. Frequently on these occasions, the Supervisor would retire a hundred feet or so, climb a tree, sprawl out on a limb, and watch the group as it fed. He gave the impression that while he was a solid citizen, he felt obliged to respect only the letter of the tribal law, was free to interpret the spirit of it to suit himself.

In his relationships with people, the Supervisor was an animal of touchy dignity and boldness. He was easy to watch and follow because he could handle any problem we might present. Of all the chulos, he was the most likely to stand his ground when we met, to issue grunting challenges rather than deferring to or fleeing from us.

One day in January, the Supervisor gave a demonstration of how casually he regarded us and, at the same time, permitted us to observe a chulo in the throes of what can best be called a temper tantrum. Mary Jane and Kate were visiting, sitting with me at one of the traps on the edge of a small ravine in the heart of the Supervisor's winter territory. We had been there only a short time when the Supervisor ambled up, entered the trap, and began to eat. Since it was time for his monthly weighing, I trapped, bagged, hung him on the scales. When I dumped him out on the ground, he did not run, but rather shook himself, grunted a few challenges, and then began to nose around the trap. To see what he would do, I reopened and reset the trap. The Supervisor immediately entered it, began to feed, and I retrapped and released him. Again I reset the trap, and again he entered. In the course of fifteen minutes, we repeated the routine half a dozen times. Then, since it seemed the Supervisor was prepared to be trapped as many times as necessary to get all the bait, I shut both the doors and we stepped back a few paces. The chulo walked around the box, scratched at both doors, then took hold of the cage and began to tear at the mesh, trying to force his way inside. The longer he worked, the angrier he became. The Supervisor then began to rock the twenty-five-pound trap violently back and forth, to grunt challenges at it as if it were a live thing, and in general to work himself into a lather. Finally, to save the trap and to save the Supervisor from apoplexy, I opened both doors and let him clean out all the dog food.

Shortly thereafter, the Supervisor learned that there was more than one way to get dog food out of a trap—or, at least, get dog food that had been in a trap. There was an energetic rock squirrel who persistently raided our bait, carried it away a kibble at a time, and cached it in a rock-slide which was a hundred feet or so from the entrance to a small cave where the Supervisor often slept at night, napped during the day. By February, when all of us—chulo trappers, chulo, and squirrel—had established our routine, the Supervisor on first emerging from the cave would go to the squirrel's stash, as John called it, roll away the rocks, and eat whatever dry dog food the rodent had accumulated. The squirrel would move his hiding place from one crevice to another, but always used the same rock pile, never seemed to be discouraged by the repeated robberies.

The Bungler was also a large male—in fact, a bit larger than the Supervisor—but his personality was much different. He was, from our standpoint, an ingratiating, entertaining animal and seemed to be a very clever one, but he lacked a certain self-confidence, even arrogance, which the Supervisor had. For example, when we met, the Supervisor might withdraw a bit or, more often, hold his ground, challenge us in a no-nonsense way, but whatever the response we always had a feeling of confrontation, a certain test of will. The Bungler's inclination seemed to be to avoid any showdown. If we surprised him, he often tried to ignore us. If this was impossible, he might put on a much more artistic and, to a stranger, more ferocious challenge display than the Supervisor, often calling ha-ha, lashing his tail at us, as well as grunting. However, we soon learned—and it seemed that the Bungler had learned that we had learned—that this was almost entirely pretense. If we ignored him, he would quickly stop his posturing. If we gave any indication of returning his challenge, spoke sharply or made as if to approach him, he would retreat apologetically. Often when his bluff had been called, the Bungler would suddenly stop, look the other way, and begin to root about frantically in the ground in a burst of what seemed to be face-saving displacement activity.

Like the Supervisor, the Bungler was attracted to the communal animals, but he had no stomach for arguments with the females. Several times, we saw him sauntering toward one of the bands, with the air that his mind was elsewhere. However, at the first sign of any hostility by one of the matriarchs, the Bungler would run. He never gave the enraged ladies a chance to close in and discipline him, and kept running until he was a long way away from the band, farther than custom demanded.

We gave him his name because his intelligence and self-indulgence often led him into predicaments that a duller or more conventional animal would have avoided. For example, there was a Park Service garbage can in the parking area at Montezuma Pass. It was equipped with a lid fixed on an axle, so that it would swing in when you wanted to dispose of trash but would not open from the inside. It was in effect a chulo trap or, more accurately, a trap for the Bungler, who, so far as we knew, was the only member of the tribe who visited it or at least learned how to operate the swinging door. If the can was full, the Bungler would climb on top of it, push the door open with one paw, reach in with the other, and fish out bits of edible garbage. However, if he saw or smelled something particularly desirable in the bottom of the can, he simply dived in after it and, once the door swung shut behind him, was trapped. Five times during the winter and spring, either we or Alphonso, the park garbage collector, found the Bungler in the can and released him. It was our feeling that it was his cleverness, not stupidity, which got the Bungler into these difficulties. In other situations, we saw him learn so quickly that it was unlikely after one or two experiences that the Bungler did not understand this trap. Rather it seemed possible that he had learned that the warm dry can, filled with the remains of exotic food, was a convenient place to wait until a man came and released him.

All the chulos in time found our cabin, began stopping by either regularly or occasionally for food. The Bungler, whose winter territory butted on the cabin yard, was not only one of the first to make this discovery but again elaborated on it in a creative way. By mid-February, he had apparently reached the conclusion that it was a waste of effort to commute back and forth between the cabin and the ridge of limestone a quarter of a mile away in which his regular den was located. He simply packed up, so to speak, and moved in with us, taking up residence in a small crawlway area under the cabin foundations, and became the cabin chulo. There were from the Bungler's standpoint certain inconvenient features to his new apartment. He had to keep a sharp eye and nose on Dain, sometimes had to stay inside while the dog was prowling. When we stayed up late at night, or had visitors, we sometimes heard the Bungler rustling around underneath the floor, presumably because we had interrupted his sleep. Occasionally he would go off elsewhere for a time, but until courtship competition began he was more often under the cabin than not, the proximity of the basement to our kitchen apparently compensating for the disadvantages.

He most certainly enjoyed our garbage, but we also had the feeling that the Bungler came to enjoy our company, as we did his. He often wandered onto the back porch, the rickety door to which he quickly learned to open. He would eat anything he found but, even after he had cleared away the scraps, would continue to poke about as though to satisfy his curiosity about our belongings and affairs. The door to the cabin proper had a better latch on it, and we tried to keep this shut to keep out dust, flies, chulos. However, if this door was not tightly closed, the Bungler could and would open it, come in and snoop about inside. One day when he came in is—and, I think, will long be—memorable for me, since it is a kind of pleasant summation of our life at the cabin in the midst of a chulo tribe. It was a warm afternoon in April and I was alone, working on notes at the long table in the front room. The Bungler apparently entered very quietly, because when I finally turned around he was lying on the cool stone hearth of the fireplace, sprawled out dog-fashion, giving every indication that he had been there for some time watching and contemplating me. I grunted to him softly, "Chulo, chulo," then turned back to the table, since to have stared at him would have made him uneasy. He remained a quarter of an hour longer, caused no trouble, then got up and quietly left the room. I have thought about the incident frequently and with pleasure. I would give a great deal to know what his mood and motivation were—what, if anything, was in his mind.

Nancy, the mature male who spent the fall and winter with the communal members of the Montezuma tribe, usually with the first foraging band, was altogether the most perplexing chulo of either sex we met in Arizona. His position within the tribe was different from that of any other animal we observed—also, so far as we know, different from that of any chulo observed by others.

Since he was a somewhat furtive animal who remained toward the rear of the foraging band, we noted Nancy shortly after we began working with the Montezuma tribe, but were unable to trap and examine him until January. Before we got our hands on him, we assumed that he was a female, as were all the other fully grown animals in the bands. When we finally captured him and found him to be a fully mature male, the information confused rather than clarified our understanding of his behavior. After mulling over the matter between ourselves and with others it seemed and still seems that there were only two possible explanations of why this one male should remain with the communal animals. The first was the easier: Nancy was a special case. Due to some abnormality of physique or personality, he was not or was not regarded as a truly adult male. The second possibility is more complicated. Perhaps, in addition to juvenile, subadult, and adult males, there should be another category, animals which for purposes of speculation we called "virgin males." Nancy was the only member of this hypothetical group that we encountered, but we could conceive of circumstances in which such a category might be created. Normally males become mature at the end of their second year; that is, in June or July, at about the time when cubs are born. When the females return with their new offspring, join the other family groups to reconstitute the matriarchy, they drive all the sexually mature males from the group. Occasionally, however, a male such as Nancy might be born late in the year or might develop very slowly. Therefore when the tribe is re-formed in August or

September, such an animal may not yet be sexually mature. If not, he is tolerated by the matriarchs throughout the fall and winter, even though he becomes fully sexed during this period. There are many objections to this notion, the most obvious being that one case, Nancy, is a flimsy support for such an elaborate theory. Secondly, if the mature males are, as they seem to be, an abomination in the sight of the females during the matriarchal period, why would they not drive a late maturer, such as Nancy, out of the group when he eventually did mature in October or November?

Whatever the reason, Nancy was always with the communal animals from December, when we first met them, until mid-March, and as noted was most often a member of the first foraging band. He foraged toward the rear or perimeter of the group, hung back while the other animals fed, was never allowed to share their food. As often as not, when Nancy did find a bite to eat it was taken from him by a cub. He never resisted or tried to defend himself or his belongings. He was very seldom groomed by the adult females, but was often mauled by the cubs in what passed with them as grooming. The matriarchs, particularly the Witch, browbeat, bad-mouthed, occasionally swatted at Nancy. All in all, he seemed to have a poor time of it (again from our viewpoint), and we often thought that Nancy would at least have eaten better, had a much more peaceful life, had he taken to the woods with the rest of the menfolk. However, he stayed on, diffident, humble.

Nancy's subsequent history was also unique, worth recording here, out of chronological sequence. During the second week of the courtship period, the Supervisor encountered and badly drubbed Nancy, physically and psychologically, driving him from the group. It seemed unjust, for reasons that Terry expressed succinctly if not very elegantly: "He took all that shit all winter and now he doesn't even get any when the females are ready."

Thereafter, so far as we observed, Nancy was never again

with the tribe chulos, in fact seemed intentionally to avoid the other animals. Soon after courtship began, the entire tribe moved its center of operations upcanyon to the vicinity of our cabin and the Wedge. Nancy, however, remained below, slinking about in the thin oak scrub east of the ranger station, at the mouth of the canyon where it fanned out into the high, all but treeless desert. He was on the extreme tribal frontier and, it seemed to us, in the least desirable, most exposed portion of the chulos' regular territory.

We saw him seldom, since he became timid and secretive and also because our attention was centered on the affairs of the other animals in the upper canyon. Occasionally he would appear, usually very early in the morning in the ranger area, and during August, Ky, who was then the only remaining full-time chulo watcher in the canyon, saw him twice. In early September, after we had all left, the rangers once saw and twice had reports of a single chulo whose description fitted Nancy (he was an exceptionally dark, bushy-tailed animal) and who was seen wandering about near the mouth of Ash, the next canyon north of Montezuma on the east slope of the Huachucas.

All of which suggests that if Nancy's rather sad history was not unique, if there are from time to time other Nancys in the tribes, then the virgin males may have at least one rather specialized function. If our theories had any relation to fact, there would never be many virgin males, but for purely statistical reasons the larger the tribe grew, the more of these animals there would tend to be. According to logic, if not fact, an increase in population would increase the reason and need for the tribe to pioneer into new areas, perhaps divide into smaller units. If so, the virgin males might serve as a kind of catalytic agent in this process. Harassed in the original tribal area by more experienced males, wandering alone, excluded from social activities at a time when all animals, including the males, were most social, the Nancys might drift out of the old range. Then in the fall when the females and young reconvened, a matriarch leading a foraging band, perhaps pressed because of the number of chulos in the old territory, might strike the scent trail of a virgin male, follow him into new territory, in effect create a new tribe. Again it is obviously sheer speculation, as are at present all notions about how, why, and when a chulo tribe divides, colonizes new territory. However, for sentimental reasons alone, it was an appealing theory. If it were true, then some of our old friends from the Montezuma Canyon may have organized a new tribe in Ash Canyon or elsewhere, and it is conceivable that in the new community Nancy would be a principal male.

10 | The Mating Season

In the mountain islands along the Arizona-Sonora border there are days, often several successive ones, in January which are like spring, even summer, according to the standards of the rest of the country. The sun is hot, with the temperatures in the eighties. Rock and seep plants come into bloom. Lizards and insects are active. On the other hand, there are winter days with ice on the water, snow on the ground, in April and even May. In consequence, there is not such a sharp sense as elsewhere that on one day, during a particular week, the season has changed. It is rather that it becomes gradually apparent that there are more spring days than there are winter ones.

Personally, because it was the first day on which I thought much about it, it seemed to me that sometime before March 2nd spring arrived in the Huachucas. On that afternoon, I had found a very comfortable niche in a ledge overlooking a cave in which the Supervisor was napping. I was reclining on the ledge, shirtless, sunbathing, lazily re-reading the *Sand County Almanac* while waiting for the Supervisor to make his appearance. As I read, I kept brushing away a largish sphinx-like moth which was flying around my head. Eventually I turned my attention to this persistent bug. He was not, it turned out, attracted to me but to the book, a paperback edition, the back cover orangish in color, from which the moth, apparently under the impression that it was an early flower, was trying to extract nectar. Since this was something which I had never seen before and which seemed especially symbolic, considering the subject of the *Sand County Almanac,* I stopped trying to read, began to watch the moth, look around, think about where I was and what I was doing. It was in these circumstances that I was first consciously aware that there was a faint rusty-reddish tint to the Emory oaks, the principal tree of the scrub forest which filled Montezuma Canyon to the rimrock. This was a definite—if, from a Northeasterner's point of view, perverse—sign of spring. The oaks stay green throughout the winter, but in the spring new red leaves emerge, forcing the old green ones from the branches. Thus in the Huachucas the foliage turns color in the spring rather than the fall.

Shortly thereafter, I saw a truly spectacular springtime happening. A pair of golden eagles swept into view and for fifteen minutes or so dived, twisted, pirouetted, presumably courting, over the canyon. On my way back to the cabin late that afternoon, I stopped by the State of Texas Mine and passed the time of day with Tommy, the eldest of the Embers, a collective name that we inevitably gave the Sparks children. I told him about the two eagles and Tommy grew excited, saying he thought he had seen them, too, just after he had returned from school. We checked the circumstances and decided we had both been watching the same birds at exactly the same time, from different points within the canyon. For some reason, this coincidence pleased us both.

We had, of course, been thinking in an abstract way about the coming of spring, wondering what changes might occur in the affairs of the chulos, how and when they would be manifested. Most particularly, we thought we should begin to see signs of sexual activity. As with so many other matters concerning the animals, there were few previous observations to guide us. However, working back from the information we had collected at Kitt Peak regarding the pregnancy and presumed birth dates of chulos there, and based on the observations of others that the gestation period for chulos was between seventy and seventy-five days, we guessed that copulation must occur sometime in March or April. It also seemed that because of the segregation of the adults, there would be a getting together, a courtship period, which should begin even earlier. In anticipation, we had begun to follow the males closely, because they were easier to keep under surveillance than the matriarchal bands and because it seemed to us that they were more likely to go to the bands, initiate whatever activity was to occur, than it was that the bands would seek them out. With the great good luck which continued to accompany our chulo work, things worked out more or less as we had hoped and we were able to observe what was very probably one of the first sexual incidents which occurred in the Montezuma tribe that spring.

On the morning of March 8th, Terry and I were in the lower canyon, hoping to locate and follow the Supervisor. I was on a low ridge dividing the main canyon bed and a tributary ravine. Terry was a quarter-mile below in the oak scrub just to the west of the ranger station. We both were carrying, keeping in touch with, walkie-talkies. About nine o'clock, Terry called to say he had found the Supervisor, who was heading up the canyon toward me. After finding the Supervisor, seeing the direction he was moving, Terry left him and started to make a big circuit so that he could get above me and pick up the chulo again after he had passed my station.

As I sat waiting, I kept sweeping the area through my glasses looking for the Supervisor and whoever or whatever else there was to be seen. In one of these passes, I caught a bit of movement, 200 yards away, low on the south slope of the main canyon. Focusing in, I found the first band foraging in and around a large windfallen sycamore which lay at the edge of a small thicket of oak. There was a den cave often used by the band a quarter of a mile farther up the canyon slope from this spot, and I had the feeling that the animals might only recently have left it. They were doing as much sunning as foraging, gave the impression that they were still getting themselves together and had not yet begun to hunt in earnest. Suddenly a long brown shape rushed—in fact, leaped—out of the brush at the chulos. I was astounded and yelled through the radio to Terry, "A coyote has jumped them!" Almost immediately thereafter, I realized my error, saw that the attacker was the Supervisor. What followed occurred very quickly, in less than thirty seconds, but because it was so extraordinary in terms of what up to then had been normal chulo behavior, it took me much longer to sort out my impressions, to comprehend what I had seen.

So far as I could see, the Supervisor appeared to have surprised the other chulos and, if so, it was the first and only time we saw this happen to a band in which the Witch was present. Landing in the middle of the group, the Supervisor pounced on and tried to mount a female juvenile. He assumed a copulatory position but maintained it for only a few seconds. The juvenile squealed and almost simultaneously the Witch, Queenie, and Seven all rushed toward the Supervisor, snarling and screaming. He released the juvenile and fled down the canyon. Chulos are normally not sprinters but can cover ground rapidly, in a long bouncing lope. However, on this occasion the Supervisor opened his stride and ran almost like a dog, skimming over the rocks and brush. He gave every impression of an animal who was using every bit of speed he was capable of—was running, if not for his life, at least for vital parts of his person. All of which was quite out of character for the normally bold and dignified Supervisor. The three females continued the chase for fifty yards or so. Then as the Supervisor disappeared, giving every indication that he was going to keep on running for some time, they rejoined the group. For a time, the band milled about in apparent confusion, the adults grunting, the juveniles giving an occasional squeal. Finally they organized, marched hurriedly back up the canyon slope, and we did not see them (or the Supervisor) again that day.

Based on what we later learned about the courtship of chulos, what I saw on the morning of March 8th might best be described as an attempted statutory rape. The Supervisor was apparently so stirred by his desires that they overwhelmed his sense of what was proper and prudent. Since he was with the band for only a few seconds, the fact that he grabbed a juvenile, or even a female, may have been more or less accidental. Any—the nearest chulo—body might have served his purposes as well as another.

After this first incident, we never saw a similar one and so concluded that the Supervisor's behavior was idiosyncratic, an outburst of premature sexual activity. However, as always, there is at least one other, quite different possibility. It seemed unlikely, but perhaps such quick, unsuccessful attacks occur normally, in effect announce and call attention to the fact that the period of sexual activity has begun.

The Supervisor's extraordinary (so far as we observed) attack aside, the courtship of the chulos is still another phenomenon which illustrates the exceptional influence of the community on the affairs of individual animals. The males do not woo a female or females, but rather the entire community, and they are not accepted sexually by the females until they have been accepted socially by the community. The first necessary step for a male in a courting mood is to join the communal animals. Often he is not initially successful, as the matriarchs, accustomed to dominating the opposite sex, may rebuff him. However, as the season progresses and presumably in response to glandular changes within the females, this hostility lessens, is replaced, if not by affection at least by tolerance, and the more persistent males edge their way into the community. Entering the group, they do not give any immediate indication of their "maleness." They travel, forage, groom with and as the other animals do, do not engage in any overt sexual activity. The males may leave the group from time to time, but once they have been accepted—after a week or ten days of casual association—they are reaccepted on their return. Only after a male has in a sense introduced himself to the group, been associated with it for a time, will he copulate with a female.

Though the other animals seemed to regard his first assault on the band as outrageous, the Supervisor was apparently soon forgiven. He was the first male to be accepted by the communal animals, and the male most often with them during the courtship period. By March 20th, he had, as previously described, met and defeated Nancy, who then left the tribe—never, so far as we knew, to return. Thereafter the Supervisor was more often with the tribe than he was alone. At about the same time, there was an important reorganization of the tribe, which may or may not have been caused by the approach of the sexual season, but which definitely affected the courtship style and behavior of the animals in Montezuma Canyon. The two winter foraging bands combined, shifted their operation up the canyon to the vicinity of our cabin. From then until late May, the tribe seldom and then only briefly divided into two bands, was usually together as a single unit, and usually to be found near the cabin or the Wedge. After the bands joined, not only the Supervisor but all the other adult males, with the exception of Nancy, drew in from their solitary winter territories and also moved toward the cabin area, where they circled in tight orbit about the tribe, made attempts to join it and become involved in the courtship proceedings.

So far as we observed during this period, only one male at a time could or would associate with the communal animals. Since the tribe was usually together in one group and since all the males appeared to be eager to join it, competition was inevitable and a situation was created in which there were bound to be what amounted to winners and losers. The resulting rivalry between males produced the only truly violent incidents we observed within the chulo tribe.

One evening in late March, just before dusk, all four of us watched a classic confrontation between male chulos. The Supervisor was with the tribe which was foraging in Clark's Ravine, immediately behind the cabin. While they were so engaged, the Bungler slipped quietly into the cabin yard, having apparently been lurking in the scrub thickets lower down on the slope. The Supervisor immediately came up out of the ravine into the clearing. The two males halted fifteen feet apart, faced each other, and began grunting terrible threats and curses. Both assumed the bowlegged, head-lowered defiant posture. The tails of both were held upright, were fluffed out like those of angry cats. After two or three minutes of this display, the Supervisor began to advance in a methodical, step-by-step fashion. As he came forward, the Bungler just as slowly retreated. Both held their heads to one side, almost parallel to the ground, an awkward contorted-looking position but one in which they were ready to deliver a slashing attack. When he was within ten feet of the Bungler, the Supervisor made a quick rush at his opponent. The Bungler turned, fled, retreated perhaps twenty feet. Again the Supervisor began his advance, and again launched himself into a charge. The Bungler held his ground for a moment and the Supervisor ran into him, bowled him over. Then the Bungler flattened, prostrated himself on the ground, dropped his tail, and began to squeal piteously, as would a juvenile calling for help. The Supervisor stood over him, canines bared, growling low in his throat. The Bungler continued to squeal but otherwise was motionless, almost rigid. By this time, the maneuvering of the animals had brought them so close to where I was standing that I could have reached out and touched either of them. However, neither of the males paid the slightest attention to me. In their aroused state, my presence was apparently of no more concern to them than that of a rock or tree stump.

The Supervisor stood over the thoroughly cowed Bungler for perhaps a minute, then turned and, stiff-legged, walked away. He whirled once and glared back at the Bungler, who had stopped squealing but remained frozen in his position of surrender. Not until the Supervisor had walked slowly back to the edge of the ravine, had begun rather contemptuously to paw about in the litter as if foraging, did the Bungler stir. Then he got up, turned around, and walked directly out of the cabin clearing, without pausing or looking back, as though this is what he had intended to do all along.

The complex bluff-challenge-surrender behavior, of which the passage between the Supervisor and the Bungler was a kind of textbook demonstration, has been observed in other mammals. A male dog in similar circumstances will roll on his back, sometimes urinate, which is again juvenile behavior used to break off a fight. A wolf wanting to surrender to another will turn his head, expose his throat in a gesture of helplessness toward his opponent. In all cases, it is assumed that the function of this behavior is to inhibit intraspecific violence. If there were no method of doing so, each conflict would presumably have to be carried to a bloody, sometimes fatal conclusion, a situation which would obviously be disadvantageous to the species.

However, no system is infallible. (Among other things,

the mysterious element of personality tends to modify and distort inherited behavior patterns.) On three occasions among the twenty encounters we observed between male chulos, we saw the ritual break down, with the result that real fighting occurred. The most notable of these involved the Bungler again, and a smaller but equally aggressive male, Twenty-Seven. It occurred on April 5th in Clark's Ravine, a day when Ann and I were fortunately in the right place at the right time to record most of the affair with a movie camera.

The Bungler had been with the tribe while they fed in the cabin yard, but remained behind when the other animals departed. A few minutes later, Twenty-Seven appeared at the edge of the ravine. He was immediately spotted by the Bungler. (It is conceivable that the Bungler waited behind for the meeting, since we never observed serious encounters between the males occurring in the immediate presence of the females and the young.) The Bungler advanced toward the newcomer with a stiff-legged gait. Then he charged, hit Twenty-Seven, and the impact sent the two rolling down the side of the ravine. When they regained their feet, Twenty-Seven showed no inclination to quit. Both animals stood more or less toe to toe, growling deep in their throats, jaws agape, batting at each other with their forepaws, sparring-fashion. (This latter was a kind of shadowboxing in which no contact was made.) Then Twenty-Seven returned the charge and the battle was joined.

Chulos do not (or, at least, those we observed did not) seek to grab their opponent, hang on and maul him—as a dog, for example, will. Such a technique would be ineffective, considering the shape of their long narrow jaw. Both the Bungler and Twenty-Seven fought in typical fashion, more like duelists than wrestlers. Each would try to rush the other, deliver a few slashes with the formidable canines as he came in, and, if he succeeded in knocking over his opponent, cut him again while he was down. The animal being charged would feint, bob, deliver counter-slashes. After a few such thrusts, they would separate, resume the maneuvering, sparring, get ready to charge again.

The fighting between the Bungler and Twenty-Seven was not continuous, but because of the exertion, and perhaps emotion, both were exhausted after fifteen minutes. They heaved and panted; their muzzles were covered with saliva and both were bloody. The Bungler had a gash on his left hip, Twenty-Seven a cut across the top of his skull, several smaller nicks. As they grew more tired, the periods between charges became longer. The animals drew back farther and farther from each other, began to scratch at the ground as though foraging (again a good example of displacement activity). Finally both turned and staggered off in opposite directions, their battle having been, we thought, a draw.

There were certainly other and more violent encounters between the males which we did not observe. Except for the Supervisor, all the males bore slash wounds before the end of the breeding season. The worst of these, a gaping hole which exposed his rib cage, belonged to Twenty-Three. All the wounds drew flies, and those of Twenty-Three and Twenty-Seven became noticeably infected. In general, the wounds the males inflicted on each other were the most serious problems of what might be called a public-health nature that we observed in the Montezuma tribe. There were no fatalities among the tribal males during the spring, but we heard several stories which we considered reliable of a male elsewhere killing another. Based on our own observations of the way the males fought when the surrender ritual failed, it seemed to us that such outcomes were possible.

Whether it had been determined long before or was quickly established during the first days of the courtship period, it was apparent that there was a hierarchy of rank, status, prestige among the males. There were many indications that the Supervisor was the dominant male in this hierarchy. Assuming that being with the tribe was a desirable position for the male to be in at that time, the Supervisor most frequently occupied it. Between March 8th and April 10th, the principal period of sexual activity, we found a male with the tribe on twenty-four occasions, and twelve of these times the male was the Supervisor. The Bungler was with the group five times; the male we called Twenty-Seven three times; and Twenty-Three, the Old Man, only once. (Nancy, the odd male, was with the group three times, early in the period, before being ejected.)

Also, in confrontations between males, we never saw the Supervisor lose. He was not the largest animal, being somewhat lighter than the Bungler, nor did he seem to be more agile than the other males. He had, to put it simply and not entirely anthropomorphically, more character and confidence. Except for the early encounter with Nancy, which was more a police action than a true battle, we never saw the Supervisor forced to fight physically. On the five other encounters we observed, his opponent surrendered as did the Bungler, before it came to sparring and slashing. For some reason, the other males seemed to regard the Supervisor as the better man, an opinion which he appeared to fully share. He was so pre-eminent that Nineteen and Twenty-Three never, so far as we knew, even tried to challenge him. On a total of three occasions, the Bungler tried to face down the Supervisor, and each time the result was as described, a humiliating (or so we might have thought it) defeat for the Bungler. We saw Twenty-Seven twice challenge the Supervisor, unsuccessfully. Otherwise the Supervisor was able to rest, in a manner of speaking, on his laurels, go serenely about his business of ingratiating himself with the tribe and the matriarchs.

Aside from Nancy, who after the first week was not involved in the male rivalry, the lowest-ranking animal was Nineteen. Even during the winter, he had seemed to be exceptionally timid and we never became well acquainted with him. During the courtship period, Nineteen would occasionally be seen trying to insinuate himself into the band, but as soon as another male approached he would slink away even before the posturing, challenges, and cursing began. However, at some time he must have found courage enough to make at least one stand, because in early April he received a bad slash wound, one that all but severed his left ear, sliced open his neck.

(Because he was so often absent and because we frequently saw him high up on the ridge which separates Montezuma and Copper canyons, we thought it possible that Nineteen might spend some of his time with the small tribe in Copper Canyon—in effect, functioning as a link between the two groups.)

Twenty-Three, whom we called the Old Man, had a more competitive spirit than Nineteen, but in practical terms was not much more successful. He would challenge or stand to be challenged by both Twenty-Seven and the Bungler, but always, so far as we observed, lost. In consequence, by the end of the courtship period he bore more serious wounds than any other male. One afternoon, we watched a free-for-all between these three animals in which the Bungler again demonstrated his well-developed survival instincts. The encounter began when the Bungler met Twenty-Three, challenged him. These two had only begun to swear at and size each other up when Twenty-Seven came into the clearing and, without much preliminary posturing, charged Twenty-Three. The males began to maul each other while the Bungler prudently withdrew beyond the immediate area of combat but continued to grunt, lash his tail, let out a few ha-has. Twenty-Seven, as usual, routed Twenty-Three but had little opportunity to savor his success. The Bungler charged him, and perhaps because he was exhausted by the previous battle, confused or surprised by the fresh attack, Twenty-Seven immediately fled without either surrendering or fighting.

Generally the Bungler and Twenty-Seven were the most

evenly matched of the males. Twenty-Seven was much smaller, almost four pounds lighter than the Bungler, but he gave the impression of a hard-working, gritty, if not very ingenious, athlete who makes the most of his limited talents. In encounters between the two, the Bungler usually was the aggressor, but the outcome was never assured. The Bungler seemed to be more articulate, superior at psychological warfare, and could sometimes bluff Twenty-Seven into surrender or retreat. However, if the ritual failed and it actually came to hand-to-hand combat, Twenty-Seven was likely to be the winner. We observed six encounters between these two and judged the Bungler to be the victor in three of them, Twenty-Seven the winner in two. The sixth engagement was a draw, the memorable one previously described.

COPULATION

Copulation, which in a certain sense is the objective of the rivalry between males, was something of an anticlimax so far as we observed it. After a male had established his credentials with the group, associated with it for a time, he might simply walk up to a female and mount her. There were no special circumstances in which mating occurred, nor was there any preliminary activity which we could observe indicating the intentions of the male, the receptivity of the female. This behavior or lack of special behavior again underscored the communal nature of the courtship proceedings. It was as if, having once worked his way into the group, the male had fully declared his intentions, performed all the self-introduction necessary.

To copulate, the male half-stood, mounted the female's hindquarters, and grasped her flanks with his forepaws, then made a few pelvic thrusts, very quickly, and within five seconds or so released his partner, went on about his business. The females seemed unconcerned to the point of oblivion, would stand passively in their original position during the brief moment of actual mating. (We had a report of the mating of a pair of captive chulos in which, while she was being mounted, the female continued to eat from her food pan.) Occasionally a female would shrug aside or even direct an absent-minded cuff at a male who was attempting to mount her. However, in general the matriarchs seemed to have a somewhat Victorian attitude toward sex. They may not have actually found it distasteful, but they gave no indication of eagerness or that it was a matter which greatly concerned them. It was, we thought, a rather curious response for these matriarchs who at other times were so domineering and forceful in their social relations.

So far as our observations went, we saw the Supervisor copulate with Queenie, Calamity, Eleven, and on two occasions with Seven. The Bungler mounted Calamity, and otherwise we did not see any of the other males or the Witch engage in direct sexual activity. Considering the degree of his dominance, it seemed that the Supervisor might well have prohibited all other males from associating with the group or mating with the females. However, now and then for a few hours or days, he would leave the group, apparently voluntarily. When he did so, another male would usually take his place with the tribe, though even during the height of the courtship period there were times when the females were unattended by a male. This temporary faltering of interest or purpose was typical of all the males. After having finally won his way into the tribe during the absence of the Supervisor, even a lesser male might after a time relinquish what seemed to be a hard-earned prize and wander off by himself. Perhaps the presence of the other males circling nearby intimidated the animal with the tribe, made him reluctant to remain for long in a position where he was vulnerable to challenges from every direction. Also it sometimes seemed to us that the males who had been bachelors all fall and winter may have found the joys of communal life, traveling with other animals, sharing food with them, not so desirable as they had anticipated. Whatever the reasons, the tendency of the males to refrain from monopolizing the tribe may have certain functional advantages. For one thing, it would seem to be another behavior factor which helps to suppress violence, reduce confrontations between males. Also it may promote a kind of genetic mix—for example, allowing the other males, who could not have physically dislodged the Supervisor, to copulate, presumably impregnate some of the females in the absence of the dominant animal.

Twice when he left the tribe, the Supervisor went in company with a female, and these occasions came closer than anything else we observed to representing intimate, private courtship behavior. Once, the Supervisor took a walk or perhaps stayed in the den with Eleven, the winter rear leader of the second foraging band. Both animals were with the tribe early one evening but were absent the next morning, reappeared together in midafternoon. On another day, John, Ky, and I found the Supervisor and Seven, the youngest of the matriarchs, walking together up a small ravine, at the head of which was a limestone cave often used as a chulo den. The pair walked slowly, the Supervisor in the lead, but were not foraging. When they reached the cave entrance, they paused for a brief grooming session, then went underground, remained there for three hours. We were not certain of what went on in the cave, but, eavesdropping at its mouth, we heard considerable grunting, chirping, a ha-ha or two, and some faint squeals. Everything considered, we thought it most likely that they had mated, perhaps frequently. The pair left the cave separately, Seven emerging a half-hour before the Supervisor. Without being coy about it, both looked tired and disheveled when they appeared. Also both the Supervisor and Seven did exactly the same thing when they came out of the cave—walked directly to a small seep spring and took a long, apparently refreshing drink of water.

Because of this incident and because of what we knew

and guessed about the life style of the tribe, we had the feeling that we did not, could not, observe much of the sexual activity which occupied the animals during March and early April. We knew that males were sharing dens with the tribe during this period, and suspected that in the privacy and intimacy of the caves the chulos might be both more social and more sexual than we observed them to be aboveground during the day. In any event, the period had to be counted as a success from the chulos' standpoint, since, as we later learned, all the eligible females had become pregnant by April 10th.

11

Snow, Anarchy, Fire

SPORT

A creature who was often about the cabin during the winter was Sport, an old pinto gelding who, ownerless, untended, wandered about Montezuma Canyon. Sport was as poor a looking horse as I have ever seen, rheumy-eyed, all ribs and skull, staggering about the mountain on obviously aching legs. He was grotesquely senile. "I remember cutting the stud who sired him," George Brown, the rancher, told me one day. "That was the year the war broke out, so it was 1939. That Sport has got to be at least thirty-one, maybe thirty-two years old."

Sport, surprisingly, made it through the winter but just barely. On April 16th, all of us went back to Tucson, the last time until we left in August when at least some of us were not in the mountains chulo watching. We returned on the nineteenth in the midst of a late spring blizzard that laid down five inches of wet snow at the elevation of the cabin. As we eased the van up the slippery cabin trail, John yelled from the back seat that the old horse was lying in the bushes along the road. Not being able to stop on the way up, John and I, after unloading the van, walked back from the cabin yard. Sport was dead, having apparently, since there were only a few weak scuffle marks in the snow, dropped quietly to the ground, never to rise again.

The rest of us had felt that Sport—stumbling through our sleeping bags, pawing at our garbage—was something of a nuisance, but John had liked the old beast, talked to him, petted him, saved out potato skins and other tidbits for him.

"Jeez," said John, looking down at the carcass. "That's terrible. He was sort of a buddy. I should have left more food out for him."

"Hell, he was so old he was a freak," I said. "He just died. He'd had a pretty good time just roaming up here for fifteen years, nobody working him, beating on him. Anyway if he had to die he did it in a good place. The carrion should give us some good observations on scavengers."

John, giving me a look of absolute disgust and horror, said nothing. We walked back to the cabin, where Terry and Ky had started a fire, commenced making supper. John and I sat with our feet on the hearth steaming our boots. Then John got up, got his guitar, returned to the fireplace. He sat plucking at it moodily.

"Has that got something to do with the old horse?" I asked him finally, nodding at the guitar.

"Yes. This is a horse requiem." This also is John Thomson.

Post-Courtship Anarchy

The snowstorm and the death of the old horse coincidentally marked the end of courtship and sexual activity. From our standpoint, the period that followed was a confusing one which resists neat classification and description. From mid-April until mid-June, the members of the Montezuma tribe, including the males, were often together. However, there were many indications that the tribe was not so tightly organized, structured as it had been in the fall, winter, and early spring. Some of the customs of the matriarchal period lingered on, but there was a sense of things becoming unglued, as if some dynamic principle had been lost or forgotten. After we had accumulated a variety of observations, records, impressions, we came to think of it as the period of anarchy. With all the distortions of analogy admitted, anarchy at least gives the sense of social disintegration which seemed to occur.

In an objective way, three new social phenomena were of paramount influence during the late spring and early summer. The adult females commenced to withdraw from tribal affairs and by the end of the period had withdrawn completely. The adult males, sometimes two or three at a time, regularly associated with the communal animals. The juveniles were forced more and more on their own, were weaned socially.

The change in behavior, and perhaps the reason for the change is most obvious in the adult females. After the period had ended, we were able to reconstruct the time sequence and concluded that by April 10th at the latest, all the Montezuma matriarchs were pregnant. By May, the condition of most of them was apparent, their increased bulk and weight having begun to show and begun to affect their movements. From then on, the females continued, in a certain sense, to be the most influential animals in the tribe, but unlike the previous months when they had dominated, commanded, directed tribal affairs, their influence became increasingly negative. The other animals had to adjust their behavior to compensate for the social lethargy and ennui of the females.

The withdrawal of the females from tribal affairs was an erratic process which may have confused the other animals almost as much as it did us. More commonly during late April and May, but occasionally even in June just prior to the time they gave birth to their new cubs, the females would be with the tribe, function, lead the other animals as they had during the days of the matriarchy. However, the interest of the females in the tribe was capricious, undependable. Early in this period and with increasing frequency as it advanced, a female, some of them, or all of them might wander off, leave the communal animals to their own devices. Even more surprisingly, we saw many instances in which the females, though with the tribe, refused, forgot, or simply did not care to function as leaders. For example, having found a good food source, a female was much less likely than she had been to inform the other animals of her discovery; she would eat what she wanted and then go about her own foraging. In moments of alarm or potential threat, a female might withdraw, flee without first informing the other animals or giving any instructions as to what they should do. Often we saw Queenie, who had always been the responsible forward leader, simply wander off from a foraging group without alerting the other animals or without any apparent concern as to whether or not they followed her. In the same vein, when the tribe moved on, the Witch, the former ferocious rear guard, might choose not to leave with the others or even to walk off in a different direction.

There was also a marked change in the mood of the females. In the fall and winter, they had been permissive, patient in their dealings with other tribe members. In the late spring, they became irascible. If, when she was feeling touchy, another animal of any age or either sex tried to share her food or even came close to her, the matriarch would grunt sharply and, if the warning did not suffice, cuff or even snap at the offender. When the tribe arrived at the cabin, a female would often walk into the trap-feeder first, commence to eat, and would not let any other chulo enter until she finished. Several times in what seemed to be a display of sheer termagancy, we saw the Witch, having eaten as much as she wanted, turn around and lie down in front of the door of the trap, refuse to allow any other animal to feed on the remaining scraps.

Even grooming sessions were affected by the change in attitude of the females. As they became larger, clumsier, perhaps more uncomfortable with their unborn cubs, the females were more and more inclined to groom with each other, less tolerant of being mauled by the cubs. A juvenile who had the temerity to try to groom a female when she was in a bad mood ran considerable risk of being slapped across the face, even nipped.

The hostility of the females was of a low-grade sort, not so sharp or ferocious as they displayed toward the males during the winter. It could perhaps most accurately be described as bitchiness. The effect of their behavior was as if they had decided that they would wash their hands of tribal responsibilities, had announced, "We've taken care of the lot of you for damn near a year. We are tired, peckish, and are now going to take care of ourselves. Don't come to us with your problems."

Because of the rather abrupt change of behavior and attitude of the females, the late spring must be a particularly hard time both physically and psychologically for a juvenile chulo. On the first of April, for example, the cubs are still enjoying the favored position which they have occupied since they were born the previous summer. They are the pampered darlings of the tribe—constantly supervised, protected by the adults—to whom nearly all liberties are permitted. By the first of May, they have been given to know in a series of humiliating, even mildly painful lessons that they are second-class citizens whose welfare is of not great concern to their elders. Most noticeably the cubs had difficulty accepting, adjusting to their new status when it came to feeding. Time and again, we watched cubs try to do what they could have done with impunity a few weeks earlier—shoulder their way into a place where an adult was feeding or try to take food from her. Invariably the female turned, smacked, drove the cub away. At first, the cubs would squeal as they had previously when they were rebuffed, but they found that now this was no longer a breach of tribal ethics and law, that no adult would come to investigate, correct the injustice. Gradually learning that times had changed, the cubs ceased to squeal or protest when attacked in this way. More important, they became careful about giving their elders an excuse or opportunity to punish them.

As the females became irascible, the cubs became timid. In the fall and winter, a chulo cub is one of the most open and trusting of creatures (as they should be, considering how beautifully they are cared for and educated), but by late spring the youngsters had become shy and furtive. They hung back in the group, deferred, often to the point of cringing, before adults. We noticed that even in dealing with us their confidence appeared shaken; they were more spooky, less tame and open.

During this time of change, the cubs showed an almost pathetic nostalgia for the good old days, as well they might. For example, they appeared desperately eager to follow an adult chulo, preferably a female, but even a male if he was all that was available. In June, when the females were often alone, jealous of their privacy, we would sometimes see a group of youngsters pick up the scent trail of one of the matriarchs and follow it as if she were their prey, as in a certain social sense she was. Scampering along, the agile youngsters had no difficulty catching up with a gravid female. However, when they did, they were likely to be driven off with grunts and cuffs. About the most they could hope for was to be permitted to tag along behind without receiving much in the way of encouragement or affection.

Largely ignored—almost, it seemed, despised—often abandoned by the matriarchs who had directed their activities, the juveniles of the Montezuma tribe formed what amounted to their own version of the winter foraging bands. The twelve cubs divided into two equal groups, which we began to call teen-age gangs. In the first there were two young males and four females, and in the second a single male and five females. Between the two gangs there was some transferring, and particularly when adults were available they would often unite, but generally the grouping was a stable one. A cub or two might join the other gang briefly, but as soon as the opportunity presented itself they tended to rejoin their original associates.

The teen-age gangs seemed to give the juveniles the companionship which they craved, but otherwise they were ineffective models of the matriarchal bands. Though we watched carefully, we did not find any of the cubs emerging as precocious leaders. Who went first or last, the order in which they traveled and foraged, appeared to be a matter of sheer accident. In consequence, the teen-age gangs were often scattered, the members tending to stray and lose touch with one another. Also they were very skittish, since there was no authority to stabilize them. Startled, all the cubs might make alarm and warning signs, not infrequently conflicting ones. Lacking dependable intelligence, they were apt to flee in different directions, simply reacting to each other's fright.

It seemed to us that if records were kept over an extended period, the late spring might prove to be the time of highest mortality for a chulo tribe, with the juveniles accounting for most of the losses. At this time, the cubs are inexperienced, unaccustomed to fending for themselves, and are not individually formidable. In May, the Montezuma cubs weighed between five and six pounds, and though they were agile their permanent canine teeth, the chulo's principal weapon, had only begun to poke through their gums.

The only "natural" fatality among the Montezuma chulos occurred during this period, and was one for which we felt indirectly responsible. On the morning of May 5th, Ky and Terry were working in the West Ravine along the side of the Wedge when they surprised (as they would not, had an adult female or even a male been present) one of the teen-age gangs. The youngsters scattered and fled, each cub for himself, and the boys made no attempt to pursue them. That afternoon when the gang showed up at the cabin, one of its regular members, a male, Six, was missing. We thought that he might have blundered onto and temporarily joined the other group. However, we never saw him again and, though we did not find his remains, could only assume that alone, confused, perhaps searching about for companions, he had met with foul play.

This period when the cubs appear to be most vulnerable corresponds with the period when what we thought were potentially their most serious enemies, the big hawks and eagles, are feeding their own young and have the most need and motive for preying on a chulo. For example, a pair of red-tailed hawks, both large enough to dispatch a five-pound juvenile chulo, had nested on a spire of rock 300 yards from the cabin. By May, they were hunting hard throughout the canyon to feed themselves and their single chick. One morning, I was sitting behind the cabin and saw a teen-age gang come pelting down the slope on the far side of Clark's Ravine. Presumably they were hustling down to the cabin for breakfast, but in their haste and greed they had chosen a route across several hundred yards of rocky, almost bare mountainside over which no matriarch would have led them. As I watched, one of the red-tails came from behind me and swooped at the chulos. By this time, the animals were in a position where a small ridge blocked my vision, but apparently the hawk missed, for she rose twenty feet in the air, pounced again. I heard a high-pitched chulo squeal and assumed that the hawk had been successful. Thinking that the hawk was by then feeding on or attempting to dismember the carcass, I edged down into the ravine and therefore missed what probably actually happened—the hawk rising into the air a second time. However, as I moved surreptitiously toward the scene of what I thought was the kill, the gang of cubs came down into the ravine from the other side. All were present, but Three, a female, had a long bloody furrow along her ribs. I assumed she had been struck by the red-tail but had managed to wriggle free before the bird could lock its talons in her flank. The incident confirmed our suspicions that while chulos might not be the easiest prey for a raptor the size of a red-tail, the birds regarded them as at least potential quarry and may at times have hunted them successfully.

From the narrow standpoint of an individual animal, the springtime change from the tightly organized community of the fall and winter might seem to be disadvantageous, a retrogressive development. Yet in terms of the complete chulo cycle, the tribe, the species itself, it is apparent that this period is necessary and progressive; that the behavior of the individuals and of the group is the product of many forces and needs, ecological pressures and opportunities, innate and learned responses.

The "disintegration" of the former tribal organization takes place at a time when chulo food is abundant and the weather is mild. The chulo cubs cannot be protected and guided by the matriarchs indefinitely. (A changeless relationship is impossible—in fact, literally inconceivable—in the dynamic biological system of this world.) Having been protected and cared for during the harsher winter, the spring is the best, the easiest time for the cubs to be forced to fend for themselves, in a sense to test the survival responses they have or should have developed. Operating independently in circumstances where only they themselves are penalized for their errors, the cubs are prepared for the time three or four months later when the matriarchy is reorganized and they, then yearlings, must assume subadult status and responsibilities. As subadults, they lose most of their juvenile privileges, must defer to the matriarchs and new cubs, must begin to contribute something to the security and welfare of the tribe. They began to form the required attitudes and develop the necessary skills during the difficult (for them) springtime period.

The social weaning of the cubs occurs simultaneously with and very likely because of the pregnancy of the females. If it can be considered a kind of fundamental function of chulo society to provide for the welfare of its youngest members, then the reason for the change in relationship between the females and the juveniles becomes evident. The change occurs at almost precisely the moment when the juveniles, then ten months or so old, are no longer the youngest animals. They have been replaced in this favored position by the embryos which the matriarchs are carrying in their wombs. After they have conceived, the females, when it comes to foraging, security, defense, show an increasing inclination to put their own interests, and by extension those of the unborn young, first—to risk and give up less for the cubs of the previous year. In a sense, they have done all that biological justice permits them to do for the juveniles, and now must begin to devote their attention and energy to the interests of the embryos. There is no evidence that these changes are made consciously, the new arrangements entered into knowingly. The chulos are simply responding to fixed rhythms which dominate their lives. Yet, whatever the motive, the propriety and effectiveness of the responses is impressive, thought-provoking.

(After this period was over and we were able to speculate about it with the advantage of hindsight, we wondered what might be the behavior and function of an adult female who did not conceive. Would she behave as the pregnant matriarchs of Montezuma Canyon did? Withdraw from tribal affairs simply because it was the season for her to do so? Or would she, not being physically changed by pregnancy, continue to provide some matriarchal guidance and organization for the juveniles? It had to remain, of course, an entirely speculative matter, since all the females we observed were pregnant.)

The adult males were also caught up in and affected by the subtle, shifting pattern of springtime behavior. They did not leave the communal animals, return to solitary status, after courtship and copulation, but rather became more social, in an asexual way, during April, May, and June. Most surprisingly so far as we were concerned, the males became much more tolerant of each other than they had been previously. During the courtship period, only one male at a time would or was able to be with the communal animals. However, in the late spring, when the disintegrating tribe was together, there was usually one male with it, not infrequently two, and on half a dozen occasions three of the five (excluding Nancy) patriarchs attended the females and the young.

When they met in these circumstances, the males did not seem to take any particular pleasure from each other's company, but their hostility was less intense than it had been during the breeding season. If two males were with a group, they tended to remain some distance apart from each other—at opposite perimeters of a foraging area, for example. When they did meet, tempers might flare, but things seldom progressed to the point of actual combat. The ritual of bluff-and-challenge usually served to settle the matter. The passages were brief and less passionate than they had been, and often the loser, who would withdraw only a short distance, was not required to leave the group.

In this period, the males held the same rank they had in the hierarchical system which was established during the courtship period. If, for example, it came to a showdown, the others always deferred to the Supervisor. However, none of them were so quick and anxious to challenge as they had been. Also the Supervisor and the Bungler, formerly the two leading males, seemed to have lost some of their interest in tribal affairs. Both were less often with the communal animals than were Twenty-Three and Twenty-Seven, though these two lesser males would retreat if the ranking animals insisted on exercising their rank. It almost seemed as if Twenty-Three and Twenty-Seven, who had been thwarted earlier in the sexual period, took the opportunity to satisfy their social desires later in the spring when passions had cooled.

There was a curious bit of behavior involving adult males and females which we observed on three separate occasions. In each of these instances, two males had begun to challenge each other and the exchange had grown heated to the point where it appeared it might become violent. However, before either one could launch a charge, a female, twice the Witch and once Eleven, broke up the brawl by attacking one of the males. Even more peculiar (or so it seemed to us), in each of these cases the female attacked the higher-ranking of the two males, in effect came to the aid of the underchulo. This may have been coincidental or may have had something to do with the personalities of the three animals. On the other hand, this sort of police action might be a regular function of the females, might have evolved because it was of value to the community as a whole. Based on our observations from the courtship period, the males, once they had closed with each other and begun to fight in earnest, were oblivious to everything but the combat. Later in the spring, when two or three of the males were with the tribe at the same time, such fights might have accidentally involved innocent bystanders among the cubs and females. To have two males slashing away at each other in the midst of a foraging or resting group could have been as dangerous for the other chulos as a brawl between knife fighters would be to patrons of a family restaurant. By halting the quarrels before they became violent, the females functioned to reduce this sort of risk.

By and large, the pregnant females treated the males as they did the cubs, not so much as a threat but as an annoyance. They were not—breaking up fights aside—openly hostile, but displayed their irritability in many ways, pushing them aside from food, grunting, slapping, nipping at them if the males came too close or otherwise crossed the matriarchs. As had been so throughout the year, the males always deferred to the females, never attempted to resist or retaliate when they were objects of the matriarchal ire.

During this period, the relationship between the adult males and the cubs seemed, as did so much other chulo behavior, to depend upon the position of the animals within the group. If the tribe was assembled at more or less full strength with at least several females present, the cubs were more likely to act aggressively toward the males, contend with them for food or position. The males in these circumstances were inclined to back down in any dispute with a cub. If, as was often so by June, a group contained only cubs and a male or two, they treated each other as peers. The outcome of low-level disputes depended on the particular circumstances, perhaps the personalities of the disputants. Cubs and males would forage and feed together. If a cub found a tidbit, a male might investigate, but if it was firmly in the cub's possession, if there were other cubs around, the finder retained his prize. Cubs might try to shoulder a male aside but were seldom successful, usually were forced to retreat by a grunt or a slap from the male. However, if a cub and a male had a difference of opinion and there were no other animals in the immediate vicinity, the cub invariably gave way, as if realizing that without group support it was both imprudent and impractical to challenge an adult. Sometimes in these meetings there was a hint of the challenge-and-bluff pattern which occurred between males. A cub might stand for a moment, head lowered in defiance, grunting at a male. However, if the male indicated that he took the matter seriously, if he began to advance, the cub would squeal and retreat. Nevertheless, except for an occasional cuff or a swift pinching nip, we never saw a male launch any serious attack against a cub.

Late in the spring, when the females had all but abdicated

their tribal functions, males often accompanied one or both of the teen-age gangs, but the association was casual and irregular. For example, two males might be with six of the cubs while the other six were alone, or the males might transfer from one group to the other, or all the males might wander off on their own. When they were with one of the teen-age gangs, the males were just one of the group, did not show particular concern for the welfare of the younger animals, did not provide the sort of leadership and direction which the females had. If such a group was startled, the male might voice his alarm, prepare for defensive action, retreat, but appeared to act as a free agent, paying little attention to the response of the cubs.

What little cohesiveness there was in the association between the males and the cubs seemed to come about because of the wistful desire of the younger animals to associate with adults. The males did not lead as the females had in the fall and winter, but the cubs still had the habit of following. Given the chance, they would tag along after a male, even though whether they did or not seemed to be a matter of indifference to the older animal. It could scarcely be called cooperative behavior, but it may have had the effect of easing the cubs through the difficult period in which the old matriarchal organization was disintegrating. The males did not appear to take their social responsibilities very seriously, but they were older, more experienced animals, and cubs following one of the males probably had a better chance of foraging successfully, were less vulnerable to surprise and danger, than if they had been entirely on their own.

In the same coincidental way, the presence of the males may have contributed to the security of juveniles and even the matriarchs. In the late spring, the tribe, so far as self-defense was concerned, was at its weakest. The females who previously had functioned as tribal warriors and guardians were heavy, gravid, lethargic. The cubs were confused, inexperienced, still developing physically. Thus the males were the only remaining mature animals of unimpaired vigor. It did not seem to us that they would risk much, as the females had in the winter, to protect the other members of the community, but at least they were there and as capable as ever. Motives and intentions aside, their presence with the tribe may have tended to act as a deterrent to potential enemies.

GESTATION

We had learned early in our acquaintanceship with the tribe that it was hopeless to try to keep up with chulos when they wanted to be rid of us. Once they began to run or just to lope, there was no way we or even Dain could keep them in sight. It was not so much a matter of sheer speed as it was their ability to slip through thickets which we found all but impassable, to scramble up and over cliffs and ledges where even with ropes we would have found it hard and slow going. In the late spring, we came to a point with the females when they simply did not want to be bothered with us and so were not. Though the gravid matriarchs were heavier and clumsier than they had been, they were still better bushwhackers than we were. We shortly learned that whatever success we had had earlier in following the matriarchal bands was due not to our skill but rather to their tolerance. When this tolerance evaporated, there was nothing we could do about it. No techniques or tricks of trailing, relaying, lurking worked very well or for very long. The females were still sometimes with the tribe and still came to feed in the cabin yard, but when they left the tribe or the cabin we thought it a great feat if, between the four of us, we could stay with one of the ladies for as much as a half-mile. She would either outleg or outthink us. Time and again, all four of us, working in country that by then we knew well, would surround a thicket into which a female had disappeared and there lose her completely. Even our good friend the Witch had little time for us and, in fact because of her keen nose and general wisdom, could, when she chose, shake us from her trail quicker and more effectively than any other female.

The desire for privacy was understandable in light of the new needs and attitudes of the matriarchs but was a frustrating development for us. Having gone as far as we had with the chulos, we wanted—and, in a curious way, felt entitled—to observe what was obviously to be the next major phase in the cycle: the birth of the cubs. However, unless there was some drastic and unexpected change in the behavior of the females, it was apparent that our prospects of even finding a birth den, let alone being able to watch what went on inside it, were extremely poor. The problem was further complicated because we were not able to fix the time when the females had been successfully impregnated (we remained unable to do so until after the fact of birth) and thus did not know when they might bear their young.

In consequence of these difficulties, we finally agreed after considerable soul-searching to take a pregnant female and keep her for observation. Not wanting to disrupt the affairs of the Montezuma tribe, about which we had accumulated so much information, we decided to take an animal from Kitt Peak, where there were more mature females and where there was in one sense an excess of chulos. Though we no longer were as intimately acquainted with them as we had been, we had been going back, two at a time, to the Peak once or twice a month, and knew that courtship and copulation had occurred there at the same time it had in Montezuma Canyon.

On the evening of May 24th, Terry and I drove into Tucson, got up early the next morning, and were at the Peak with our trap set by eight o'clock. Shortly before nine, a female, whom in the fall we had designated as Seven, came alone to the kitchen area and entered the trap, where we took her. Seven was two pounds heavier than she had been when we had last weighed her in December; she seemed plump and her nipples swollen. Not wanting to risk any detailed examination because of the possibility of miscarriage, we decided from these superficial signs that she was probably, if not certainly, pregnant. We put her in a small wire carrying cage, over which we draped some burlap to give her some sense of security, and started the long drive back to the Huachucas.

Ky and John had been waiting impatiently and had held up supper for us. Before we ate, we installed the female on the back porch of the cabin which we had converted, hopefully, into a chulo nursery, blocking the outer door, covering the floor with leaf litter, furnishing a nest box, water, and food pans. When we opened the carrying cage, she walked onto the porch, found the water tray, took a quick nervous drink, then retreated to the far corner, where she sat down and studied us speculatively, without exhibiting any panic.

"I think we had better call her Mona. It's a very good name," John said, as though he were announcing that water was wet. Nobody ever thought to ask John how he knew Mona was the right name, but on the other hand nobody tried to call her anything but Mona thereafter.

In a day or two, Mona had settled in comfortably, ate well, became tame enough to eat from our hands, showed no desperate desire to escape from the porch. Despite the equanimity with which she accepted her fate, we were never completely happy about her—or, more precisely, about ourselves. At one ethical level, we knew that there was no defense for abducting a citizen of another community and imprisoning her. There was no excuse for our behavior, only the explanation that our curiosity was stronger than our scruples.

Though she did not outwardly pine or decline, it is of course impossible to know what Mona's inner feelings were, if she had a sense of being restrained and if it disturbed her. On the whole, and not entirely as an exercise in rationalization, I suspect she did not find her circumstances too hard. They were similar in several important respects to those she would have sought had she been free. We provided her with a variety of natural chulo food, and so feeding was easy for her at a time when the feral females seemed to lack either the strength or inclination for long, hard foraging expeditions. The porch was cool and secluded, gave Mona the privacy and security which seemed so important to the females at this time. Her major lack was perhaps the companionship and stimulation of other chulos, but again, at this particular time of year, the females were minimally concerned with social matters. She seemed mildly interested in our comings and goings, may have found the attention we gave her a partial substitute for that which she would have received from other chulos.

We watched Mona often and carefully, looking for any physical or behavioral changes which might indicate she was preparing to give birth. However, through the early weeks of June her activities were unremarkable, not at all suggestive. Rather than using the box we had given her for a den, she raked a pile of leaves into one corner and used this as a napping and sleeping pad. The kind of food and the amount of food she ate did not change. She spent a good bit of her time, two or three of the daylight hours, napping, perhaps because she had nothing else to do.

The matriarchs of the Montezuma tribe, so far as we could observe them, appeared to share Mona's mood and behavior pattern. Except when we tried to follow them (when they could run like goats, disappear like ghosts), they moved slowly, rested often, panting in the shade. They seemed to be especially thirsty and in general to be uncomfortable because of the heat, fatigue, and their condition. By mid-June, they were seldom with the tribe and hardly ever all with the tribe at the same time. Occasionally a pair of the ladies would travel together for a time, almost as if they found some satisfaction in sharing their mutual problems and discomfort. Frequently a female might disappear (so far as we were concerned) for three or four days, and we would begin to speculate that she had borne her young at a time and in a place which we had missed. Then she would waddle back, still gravid, and the suspense would be prolonged for both her and us.

DROUGHT

The two-and-a-half-month period of tribal anarchy and gestation commenced with one impressive natural happening— an April blizzard—and coincidentally ended with another— a raging fire. The blizzard came as a surprise but the fire was all but inevitable—a phenomenon which we waited for, if not looked forward to, from the first of June onward.

Late spring and early summer is always drought season along the border, but the spring of 1971 was dry even for that time and place. No measurable precipitation fell after the April snowstorm until June 24th. The resulting drought was reported by local residents to be the worst in fifty years. Whether it was or not—there is an inclination to exaggerate at such times—it was God-awful dry and gave us a taste of the harshness and downright ferocity of this country which previously we had found so agreeable. Day after day, out of a clear cloudless sky, the sun beat down through the thin air on the mountainsides. The new succulent growth and flowers of March and April withered, turned brown and brittle. The skin of the earth cracked and scored, turned to powder. Even ground-feeding birds as small as towhees kicked up tiny puffs of dust as they scratched on the baked ground. One by one, the seeps and springs dried up, turned first to mud, then adobe, and finally also to dust. By mid-June, an artificial pond behind Park Headquarters and our spring-fed stock tank were the only open sources of water remaining in Montezuma Canyon. No matter what their feelings toward us, the other inhabitants of the upper canyon were forced to share the cabin area with us because we were squatted by the water. The javelina band, a dozen deer, the lion, the chulo tribe, and many lesser creatures drew in toward the water and around us.

Two or three times a week, a few hopeful-looking black clouds would pile up on the horizon, but all they produced was dry lightning, which, so far as breaking the drought was concerned, was worse than nothing. Where the lightning hit, a fire usually followed and after a time there was a faint but perceptible haze in the air from fires in Mexico, from both the San Rafael and San Pedro valleys, from the northern Huachucas, the Santa Ritas, and the Chiricahuas. Chuck Shipp, the forest ranger from Patagonia, stopped by one afternoon, bleary-eyed from a week of fire fighting, to tell us that the Huachucas were being closed to the public and that we should proceed carefully with our chulo work, be ready to evacuate quickly.

The fire for which everyone was waiting started on June 13th. Following the Forest Service lead, Hugo Huntzinger had closed the memorial except for the picnic area, which was heavily used by local residents looking for shade. On this particular Sunday, two boys had slipped away from their families in the picnic grove, gone back in the chaparral to set off a few firecrackers. Ten minutes later, the fire had taken hold, and half an hour later fifty acres were ablaze in the lower canyon. The fire that swept across the scrub-choked slopes acted in one sense as a scavenger, cleaning out dead and decayed matter, opening the land to new species and ecological communities, and generally had (or would have in time) an invigorating effect. However, in the presence of a wildfire it takes a very cool and dispassionate ecologist to think of these things. We were not that cool, and as soon as we saw it going down into the lower canyon, we threw ourselves into the fire fight and stayed with it for twenty-four hours. Before it was under control the next day, the Montezuma Canyon fire engaged some hundred and fifty men, several bombers dropping loads of fire-retardant slurry, a helicopter, and a lot of other ingenious devices. We worked with the fire crews because all our friends at the ranger station and the State of Texas Mine were fire fighting and we would have felt like slackers had we not joined them. Also we had a stake in stopping the fire before it reached our cabin and our chulos in the upper canyon. But mostly we worked for the excitement.

The attraction of fire fighting is strong and underrated. It provides the pleasure of war without most of the dangers of war. Ecological principles aside, fire is an obvious and open enemy, and stomping it out gives everyone a righteous common cause. There is a delicious sense of crisis about fire fighting, which tests both the mind and the body. "We've got to hold it at that last ravine or just as sure as God made little green apples it'll jump the road, and that'll be all she wrote." A fire fight also gives satisfying opportunities to play at grand strategy and field tactics. "Now, listen. The chopper is going to drop some of the Sierra Vista crew up above in the rimrock. We want you to work up toward them. If we can pinch off that little tit of brush halfway up, we've got ourselves a good line. If you get in trouble, we can get the bomber to give you another shot of slurry."

It has always seemed to me that the authorities might give some thought to devising a system whereby every male from, say, the age of twelve to sixty might be offered the opportunity to fight at least one fire a year. I do not know how much aggression and violence would be sopped up by such an experience. However, it seems likely that it would provide at least as much wholesome entertainment and genuine stimulation as throwing balls, picketing politicians, or mugging bus drivers.

12

Birth and Infancy

DELIVERY

On Monday afternoon, a day after it started, the fire was still smoldering but had been officially declared controlled. The outside crews and much of the equipment were released, sent off to other fires which were breaking out every day or so in southern Arizona. Ky and Terry drove back to Tucson to get cleaned up, sleep for a day, and tell the girls about their adventures. John stayed with me and worked the next three nights with a local crew which patrolled the burn, mopping up the remaining hot spots. Having had almost all the fun I could stand with the fire, I slept on Monday and went back to watching chulos.

On Tuesday evening, June 15th, John was sleeping on the front stoop of the cabin and I was reading by lantern light in the kitchen, having promised to wake John in time for him to get down the canyon and report in to the midnight fire crew. About 10:45, I heard some faint chirpings from the rear of the cabin and at first paid little attention to them, thinking they were made by night birds or bugs. Then the possibilities of the sounds, their significance, suddenly occurred to me. Grabbing a flashlight, I rushed out to Mona's quarters on the back porch. Mona was on her pad of leaves, hunched over, calmly licking a small black object from whence came the chirps. I ran around to the front of the cabin, shook John, and shouted, "We're having babies!" John was groggy, having had very little sleep for the past three days, but he got up immediately and delivered one of the best lines of the year: "Get the hot water and clean sheets."

We tiptoed back to the porch and stood in the far corner, motionless, trying to breathe as little and quietly as possible. Occasionally, for a few seconds at a time, we would shine the flashlight toward Mona, at first not so much to see what was happening as to reassure ourselves that something had happened, that there was indeed a cub.

Judging from the sounds I heard while reading in the kitchen, the first of the cubs must have been born about 10:45. For a time, Mona licked and nuzzled this infant, which lay largely concealed, protected by her arched body. At about eleven o'clock, Mona lay on her side, the first cub cradled between her forelegs, and began to heave and pant. The second cub emerged five minutes later. The two remaining cubs followed at fifteen- to twenty-minute intervals. As noted previously, it seemed to us that the most remarkable feature of the whole process was the almost immediate responsiveness of the cubs to their mother. In each case, after a cub had been licked and cleaned, welcomed into the world, it would attempt a sharp, piercing, surprisingly strong squeal. Immediately Mona would give a premonitory grunt and the cub would break off, stifle the sound. These commands and responses were repeated throughout the night as the cubs learned their first lessons in communication and discipline.

After we watched the birth of the second cub, John and I got out, hooked up a battery-powered movie light which we had borrowed and kept on hand just for this occasion. Being fearful of disturbing Mona, interfering with the birth, we floodlit the scene only intermittently and briefly, eventually exposing about thirty seconds of movie film. We probably could have photographed the entire birth sequence, since even when the light was on Mona seemed unconcerned, accepted it as she had so many other peculiar happenings.

By midnight, when John went off to the fire crew, Mona seemed to have finished her work and the four cubs were nestling underneath her body. I watched until about 12:30 and then, feeling that no useful purpose would be served by further direct observation, I left, got my sleeping bag, and unrolled it outside, against the corner of porch where Mona and the cubs lay. Though I had no notion of what emergency might arise or what I would do about it if some crisis did occur, it seemed that I should be close at hand. There were, as it turned out, no problems whatsoever, except that I was too pleased and excited to sleep much. I lay awake throughout most of the night, listening to the rustlings, the bird-like chirpings of the new cubs, thinking that I would probably never hear such sounds in such circumstances again, being grateful that I was where I was.

At daylight when I got up, Mona was lying on her side with her long tail curled toward her nose, in effect hugging the cubs to her body. Since they were shielded, I could catch only a glimpse of the babies but they seemed to be well and to be nursing successfully. During the day, we (Ky, Terry, Kate, and Mary Jane arrived at noon from Tucson) watched the new family continuously and attentively. Mona may have left the cubs during the night, but during the day she did not leave them until late afternoon, until almost eighteen hours after they had been born. Perhaps our presence affected her behavior but, considering how placidly she accepted us, it seemed likely that she stayed with the cubs for reasons other than protecting them from us. In any event, when she got up, leaving the cubs in a squirming ball, she walked across the porch, took a few sips of water, nibbled on some food. Her meal was interrupted, as most of them were during the next few days, as a cub began to squeal. Mona immediately stopped feeding, returned, and wrapped herself around the babies.

On the second day, we decided to take the risk of disturbing the family long enough to examine the cubs, make a few measurements of them. Having no idea how Mona might react, we devised an elaborate scheme. When Mona left the cubs to feed, Ky would try to distract her, offer her some marshmallows and grapes (her favorite sweets) while I picked up a cub and passed it out to Mary Jane, who with Terry would weigh it on a letter scale and measure it. John, with assistance from Kate, would man the cameras. As it developed, the plan was unnecessarily complicated. Mona walked over toward her food and water pans in midmorning. Ky and I approached and she studied us for a moment without signs of hostility or panic, then accepted some grapes from Ky. I passed back one cub, returned it when the measuring and photography was finished, took another one. Mona was unconcerned until we were replacing the third cub, who began to squeal. Mona's reaction was immediate and belligerent. She rushed back toward the nest pad, and as Ky tried to intervene, she snarled, slashed at him. I laid the cub on the leaves, made no attempt to take the fourth, and both Ky and I retreated hastily. As soon as the cub stopped squealing, Mona's rage disappeared. She nuzzled, licked the infants experimentally, and seemed satisfied. Then she curled up around them and they began to nurse contentedly. During the next three weeks, we took the cubs every two or three days to examine them. We did so easily, with, so to speak, Mona's permission. As on the first day, there was no difficulty until one of them squealed. (They did so less frequently as they became more accustomed to handling.) Then we had to unhand them immediately and get out of Mona's way.

When we first measured them, thirty-six hours after their birth, Mona's four cubs each weighed between 5 and 5½ ounces. From nose tip to base of tail, they were approximately 200 mm. long. The tail, in comparison to the proportions of adults, was stubby, measuring only about 110 mm. (The infants had good muscular control of the tail, on their third day being able to hold it upright.) Mona's four cubs were well furred, almost coal black in color. There were faint ghost traces of the lighter facial masks and tail rings. They were blind, their eyelids sealed, and, though active, squirmy, could not stand upright or walk.

Even we, who were of course much prejudiced in their favor, could not claim that the four cubs were beautiful babies. Rather they were peculiar to the point of being grotesque little beasts. Their heads were huge, accounting for almost half their body length, and the skulls were high-domed, bulbous. Not only did the outsized head give them a deformed appearance, but it also seemed to affect their early movements. Even after they had begun to toddle about unsteadily, the cubs staggered under the weight of the head, walked nose down—more, it seemed, for support than any other reason. An anatomical investigation aimed at determining the utility and function of the disproportionately large head with which young chulos are born might be an interesting one for a physiologist. We, of course, could not make such an interior examination, and would not have even if we could.

So far as the chronology of their development was concerned, the sealed eyes of Mona's four cubs began to open at about eight days, were fully opened by two weeks. At one month of age, about the time when young chulos would naturally be venturing out of the birth caves, Mona's cubs seemed to have as good eyesight as adults. As noted, they were vocal from the beginning, but confined themselves to squeals and squeaks until they were about five weeks old, when they made their first tentative grunts. At two weeks, they could totter about unsteadily on the porch, and by the time they were five or six weeks old (the development of the cubs varied from individual to individual) they could run and climb actively, if awkwardly. They doubled their weight during the first ten days, and by a month each weighed about one pound. They fed exclusively by nursing for their first forty days, and then began to make ineffectual attempts at mouthing, lapping up semisolid food. By this time, their milk teeth had emerged and Mona began to leave them for longer periods of time, show more restlessness when the cubs nursed, perhaps because of the sharp needle-like teeth. We felt that, under natural circumstances, after the fifth week the cubs may be allowed to nurse less frequently and probably are weaned by seven or eight weeks of age. At six weeks, Mona's cubs when placed on the ground would begin to root energetically. The impression was that this was innate, almost reflexive behavior, since the cubs gave no inclination that they were purposefully foraging. Often on discovering an edible tidbit they ignored it or were not able to deal with it.

TRIBAL BIRTHS

Mona's litter was especially valuable to us because, as best we could later determine, hers were the first cubs born that spring in Montezuma Canyon. Beyond giving us an opportunity to observe the birth process and the maturation of her own cubs, Mona's splendid performance served as a kind of model from which we could deduce what was happening among the feral females.

During the first ten days of June, the five tribal matriarchs, though secretive, continued to operate in the upper canyon, in the vicinity of the cabin and the Wedge where they had been since mid-March. However, in the third week of June they dispersed. The Witch and Queenie, the two long-time companions, went back to the lower canyon near the ranger compound, where they had often foraged during the fall and winter. At the same time, Seven and Calamity staked out territories halfway down and on opposite sides of the canyon, at about the elevation of the State of Texas Mine. Only Eleven, the former rear leader of the second foraging band, remained in the upper canyon in the Wedge area. On the morning of June 18th, having been absent for two days, Eleven showed up to feed and drink at the cabin. She was gaunt and thin and, based on Mona's post-partum condition, we thought it almost certain that she had whelped, probably on the night of the sixteenth or on the seventeenth of June. From similar observations and circumstantial evidence, we concluded that Seven and Queenie gave birth on June 19th; Calamity on the 20th; and the Witch on the 23rd. It was quite possible, considering the difficulty of observing the matriarchs, that we may have been mistaken by a day or so on these dates. Even so, the fact that all the females whelped within one week of each other was striking evidence of the precise rhythmic workings of the cycle which dominates chulo society and the lives of members of a chulo community.

In comparison to their erratic, listless behavior during the last stages of pregnancy, all the Montezuma females settled into a similar and, it seemed to us, purposeful routine following the birth of their cubs. They would leave the area in which we assumed their dens to be located early in the morning and late in the day. They were seldom abroad or foraging at other times, or at least we did not observe them to be. Queenie and the Witch began to come to the ranger area to forage on scraps and handouts as they had in the fall and winter, while Eleven continued to use our feeding station at the cabin. Though we were usually able to see these three animals once a day when they foraged, we continued to be thwarted when it came to trailing them back to their cubs. We were, for example, particularly eager, for practical and sentimental reasons, to find the Witch's nursery. The four of us, often with assistance from the rangers and the girls from Tucson, spent a good many frustrating hours waiting for the Witch, trying to follow her unobtrusively. Despite the effort, the man and girl power, the best we were able to do was narrow down the area in which her den was located to a hundred-square yard patch of rocks and scrub located in a ravine which joined the main canyon just above the park picnic area. Time and again, we would see her appear from this thicket and return to it, but though we examined the ground literally on our hands and knees, we were unable to determine which of the many available crevices the Witch was using as her den. We might have been more successful had we used Dain to trail the Witch, and though we considered this tactic we never tried it, since we had the feeling that the Witch would rightly regard it as an unfriendly act.

Though we worked at it almost full time, we managed to find only one of the five dens, that of Queenie, who, like the Witch, came regularly (but at different times) to forage at Gil and Margaret Withers's house. When Queenie left the feeding station at the ranger's house, she headed up the Blue Water Ravine, which was directly across the canyon from the area in which we guessed the Witch had denned. The Blue Water Ravine was a narrow, brush-choked defile, the southwest wall of which was formed by a prominent ridge of limestone. In this ridge, 200 yards or so up from the ranger houses, was a cave which we knew well, since it had often been used by the chulos during the winter and was one of the few den caves large enough for us to enter. The main passage slanted 75 yards down and back into the ridge. The walls of the cave were honeycombed with small solution holes and crevices. Many of these, while big enough for a chulo, were so small and irregular that we had no notion of how far they extended.

When it became apparent that Queenie was operating in the vicinity, we, of course, thought of this cave system as a possible den site. However, we never saw her entering or leaving the main passage, even though the mouth of the cave was large and situated so that we could observe it easily. When she left the ranger compound, we could sometimes follow or relay Queenie for a short distance, but invariably she either passed the cave entrance or we lost her in the scrub thickets which choked the ravine below it. Again we spent some time crawling over the sharp limestone, looking for a crevice that might have served either as a den site or as an inconspicuous secondary entrance to the main cave. If there is such a hole, we never found it.

Though we could not catch Queenie going to or coming from the cave, it seemed like such a promising spot that every now and then one of us would crawl in to investigate. Twice, on separate occasions during the second week in July, both John and I, while sitting toward the end of the passage, thought we heard sounds, rustling and squeaks, coming from somewhere farther back in the maze of limestone. However, we were not certain of what we heard or, in fact, that we had heard anything. The total darkness and silence of a cave plays strange tricks on the senses, particularly when one is straining to find or hear something. Odd as it may seem, it is possible in such situations to hear your hopes.

On July 16th, the matter was settled. That afternoon I decided to check the cave again. The entranceway is very narrow and, in fact, is a kind of dry-well shaft dropping almost straight down for six feet, then turning in to the main passage, which is wider, less precipitous. To enter the cave, we customarily went headfirst through the entrance well, slithering on our stomachs. I had just completed this maneuver, had come to the elbow turn but was still close enough to the entrance so that a little natural light reinforced the flame from my carbide lamp, when I met Queenie. Though she had certainly heard me coming, she had apparently been unable or unwilling to get out of my way because she was holding a cub in her mouth. (She was carrying the cub as a cat will carry a kitten, by the nape of the neck.)

Since the passage was narrow and I was headfirst, we met almost face to face. Queenie glared at me, which, encumbered by the cub, was about all she could do. She turned quickly in to a small side passage to her left. I wiggled ahead quickly enough to shine my light down this hole in time to see Queenie disappearing and to catch a brief glimpse of another cub being herded in front of her, hear the squeak of at least one other farther back in the crevice. Later when we talked it over, we thought of several possible explanations of the incident. Queenie may have heard me entering the cave and been trying to move the cubs to a more secure area. Or I may have interrupted her as she was moving the family for reasons which had nothing to do with me. Terry ingeniously suggested that if this latter possibility was true it might be that within the caves the females regularly moved the cubs, bringing them progressively closer to the light as their vision improved, as they had more use for light.

Finding Queenie's den more or less by accident gave us a better understanding of why we had so little luck in finding those of the other four females. Assuming that she had been using the cave since the cubs were born, Queenie had gone to considerable lengths to keep this information from us. Apparently she had refused to enter the cave when there was any chance of our seeing her do so, and on many occasions had led us past and away from the entrance, waiting until we had left to return. We had the suspicion that if Queenie was capable of this behavior, a more devious animal such as the Witch might and probably did mislead us in more elaborate ways.

So far as we knew, the females during the first six weeks after the birth of their cubs never or only very briefly associated with other members of the tribe. Even the Witch and Queenie, whose relationship had always been most amicable, were never, so far as we knew, together even though we thought their birth dens to be only a quarter of a mile apart and they often foraged in the same area. In their case, where both animals were using much the same area, it seemed to us that the fact that they did not meet was more likely a matter of intent than accident.

We observed no meetings between the females and the adult males, who by July were themselves becoming increasingly solitary. Twice we saw a casual meeting between Eleven, the only female who denned in the cabin area, and a group of juveniles, who by that time might more properly be called subadults. On both occasions, Eleven was feeding behind the cabin when the younger animals arrived. There were no apparent signs or sounds of greeting, and when Eleven left the teen-agers made no attempt to follow her, as a month earlier they might have. During this period of the chulo cycle, it seemed to us that one of the most important of tribal laws was "The privacy of the females and the cubs is inviolable."

Again working from the premise that the welfare of its youngest members is of paramount importance to a chulo tribe, the compelling (or so it seemed to us) desire of the females for privacy makes considerable practical sense. While the all but helpless cubs are in the den, anything which might attract attention to their location would be disadvantageous. For example, if the teen-age gangs had continued or been permitted to continue dogging the footsteps of the females, we would have had a much easier time finding the birth caves than we did. So, too, of course, would have any other hunters who had designs on infant chulos. Also, being alone, the females when they emerged from the dens on their daily foraging trips may have been able to feed better, more quickly, return sooner to the cubs than would have been so if they had had to compete with the rest of the tribe. As it was, the males and the teen-age gangs were seldom seen in the areas where we thought the birth caves were located. The effect, though unlikely the intent, of this dispersal was to preserve otherwise unused foraging territories for the exclusive use of a single female.

RAIN

There is a belief along both sides of the border that the first real rain of the summer will fall on St. John's Day, June 24th. Since in 1971 the drought was so severe, relief from it so eagerly awaited, this bit of folk meteorology was frequently cited during June. Much to the satisfaction of traditionalists, the first rain, a general gully washer, fell on the afternoon of June 24th. However, at least in Montezuma Canyon, the triumph of the folklorists was somewhat spoiled by Harry Busch, the ranger at the Coronado Memorial. Harry, a matter-of-fact young man, went back through the weather records kept at the ranger headquarters and found that it had rained on previous St. John's Days—but on only four out of the last fifteen of them.

The rain broke the drought and considerably reduced the threat of fire. Also the St. John's Day deluge, and those which thereafter fell almost every afternoon, greened, flowered up the countryside in spectacular fashion. However, like many things, the rain was a mixed blessing. As the moisture in the air and the ground increased, so did the midsummer temperatures. Having become accustomed to the dry heat of late spring, we found it hard to cope with the humidity. We dragged about, bitching about the weather as if we had not spent most of our lives in the muggy, subtropical climate of the Atlantic coast.

On June 27th, disgusted with the way in which we were letting the weather affect us and not having seen either of the teen-age gangs since the first rain, I routed everyone out of bed early, said we were going to do some serious chulo hunting no matter what the heat or humidity. The boys decided to sweep the canyon from the cabin to the ranger station. I said I would go up to the pass, follow a trail from there up to the ridge which divided Montezuma, Copper, and Ash canyons, work along the ridge eastward, and then bushwhack down the side of the mountain to the cabin. Ann, whose birthday it was, decided to celebrate by coming along, and of course Dain went with us.

The slope up from the pass to the top of the Huachucas is steep, crossing a series of high meadows and boulder fields in which there is virtually no shade. By the time we reached 7,500 feet, Ann had come to the conclusion that climbing a mountain through thin air and under a sun that had heated things up to 95 degrees or so was not a good way to spend her birthday. She turned down a javelina trail that led back to the cabin. Having talked so much in the morning of mind-over-weather, I continued on, and Dain, being what he is, had no real choice but to follow me. Acting on the premise that a little hardship was just the tonic we all needed, I had brought no water, planned to get a drink at a small seep spring which the last time I had been that way was still oozing in a saddle at the top of the ridge. When we reached the saddle, the spring was bone dry and at about that time I began, belatedly, to worry about Dain. He is a big, heavy dog and all the way up the mountain he had been panting hard, slobbering profusely, losing a lot of water. By the time we reached the defunct spring, he was wheezing deep in his chest. Shortly thereafter, we came across an abandoned mine shaft which had been bored some fifty feet back into a face of rock. Normally, Dain will follow me anywhere except into a cave or a cave-like hole; he has always drawn the line at underground adventures. However, when we reached this place, he went ahead of me, directly into the dark, cool shaft where he lay down on the floor heaving. This odd—for him—behavior convinced me that he felt the time had come for extraordinary survival measures. We sat for ten minutes cooling ourselves, but there was no water in the cave, so eventually there was nothing to do but go back out into the sun. At this point, I should have headed directly back toward the cabin, but again stubbornness overcame good sense. We continued on along the ridge at more or less 8,500 feet until we reached a point where it was intersected by the shoulder of the Wedge. From there we could see the cabin a mile away by the path but a half-mile directly below us. We started down through the thorns and bush, across the cliffs and slides. Before we were halfway home, it was apparent that we were in trouble. I was giddy from heat, fatigue, and elevation. Dain was staggering, seemed almost blind and deaf. Encouraging, dragging, sometimes half carrying him, and stopping when we found a little shade, I finally got him and myself back to the cabin six hours after we had left it. Dain flopped or fell on the cool cement of the front stoop, and I brought him a dishpanful of water. He was so exhausted that, still prone, he hung his head in the water, drank a gallon or so, threw it up, drank some more which he kept down. Thinking that that was that, I went inside to break off some ice to make myself a drink. When I came back outside, Dain tried to rise but fell back on his side unconscious and began to quiver convulsively. For a moment, I was numbed by fright, a feeling almost immediately replaced by self-loathing as I thought how I had imposed on this friend who would follow and perhaps had followed me to his death. Finally we pulled ourselves together and began some frantic first aid. Ky and Terry brought the water barrel outside and John got a sleeping bag, which I soaked in the water and then wrapped around Dain. Then we slowly poured water on the bag and dog. After a few minutes, he regained consciousness, was able to focus his eyes on us, give a couple of feeble, apologetic thumps with his tail.

As he lay recovering (Dain eventually recovered completely, but for the next two days was too stiff and dispirited to leave the cabin), I sat holding his head, talking not so much to say anything but to soothe us both with sound. At one point, I said, "We're both getting too old for this nonsense." John immediately and excitedly broke into the monologue, as if words had provided him with a clue to some puzzle we had all been trying to solve.

"It's like falling off a high building. The older you get the faster you fall, and there is no way you can stop. You don't know what's at the bottom but it's probably no good."

I was so surprised by John's remarkable comment that for a moment I forgot about Dain's and my troubles.

"What in God's name are you doing thinking about that? You're nineteen."

"I think about it a lot," John said with dignity. "Sometimes I dream about it."

Since then, I have often thought about what John said, not so much because of the substance, which was odd enough, but because in a weird free-form way it seemed to summarize and symbolize the mood and circumstances of our last weeks at the cabin. Like a collective case of flu which we could not shake, we were affected by a sense of terrible loss, of things we valued flying away from us. The aching ailment, like a fever, seemed to eat away at our vitality, addle our wits, and above all sour our luck.

The causes of the malaise were not mysterious, but they were various. The steamy weather, the daily rainstorms probably contributed. Also we had the feeling that we were being rejected by the chulos. The females obviously wanted to keep their distance from us and were usually successful in doing so. The teen-age gangs were shy and moved about the canyon erratically. Some days they would hang around the cabin for several hours, seem to enjoy their old playground, even our company, but then they might disappear for several days. Since they were so spooky, we did not want to follow them, fearing that we might unintentionally scatter them, make them more vulnerable to predation. Among the males, we seldom saw Nineteen, who we guessed was somewhere up on the ridge above Copper Canyon, or Nancy, who still lurked at the mouth of Montezuma Canyon—trying, it seemed, to avoid both men and other chulos. The Supervisor had drifted down the canyon toward his winter territory, would occasionally feed at the ranger station, but spent much of his day napping in caves, resting in trees, apparently being primarily interested in beating the heat. Perhaps for the same reason, seeking coolness, the Bungler had moved upcanyon toward the pass. We were left in the cabin area with Twenty-Three and Twenty-Seven, who would still occasionally associate with one or the other of the teen-age gangs. Both these males tended to do their foraging late in the day, often after dark. They would come to the cabin, feed, and leave quickly. After months of being constantly with chulos, often knee-deep in them, we sometimes had days in July when we saw none at all, and even when we were with them, the old sense of intimacy had disappeared.

There was also the matter of saying goodbye to friends we had made in the Huachucas, people who had become interested in and helped with our work: Van Horn, Chuck Shipp, George Brown. One evening during our last week, the park rangers and the State of Texas Mine crew threw a big steak and beer party. It was, because of the occasion, a predictably depressing affair. Mutually we vowed to keep in touch, see each other again, and knew as we promised that we would not, that once we pulled out of the canyon it was most unlikely we would ever again be vitally associated with, be concerned with, care for each other as we had.

Above everything else, we were bothered and depressed by the thing that John had tried to describe, by the sense of time running out, of being helpless to do anything about it. In the evenings after the thunderstorm had passed, we would sit outside the cabin, looking down into the canyon from which hot mist and vapors rose, and talk about things we had not talked about all year—about what we had not done, were never going to do. During the last three weeks or so, I think that daily each of us, for one reason or another, was reminded that we had one day less than we had had yesterday, that we were one day closer to the end.

One afternoon, I rode into Bisbee with Hugo and tried to explain the feeling. "It's like we can see this big hand reaching out of the East for us. Behind the hand there is somebody saying, 'O.K., you had your fun; now it's time to get back to the real world. Gotcha.' "

"Well, you all had a great year," Hugo counseled. "You know, a lot of people never get even two weeks in their whole lives like the year you've had."

"I know we've been lucky. I'm not really bitching. I wouldn't do it any differently. It's like one of those fly-now, pay-later things. We don't want to pay."

MONA'S CUBS

Of all the partings, the one with Mona was the most difficult. Our decision to take her cubs with us, leave her behind, was another of the sort that can be explained more easily than it can be defended. The official reason for taking the cubs was that observing their maturation might shed further light on the matter of acquired and inherited chulo behavior, since the four young animals would have had little opportunity to learn from adults. There was another, less rational, but more compelling reason. Having been thinking about chulos, looking for and at them, living with chulos for nearly a year, we could not bear the thought of being without them. We did not have enough character to kick our chulo habit by suddenly and completely withdrawing from the animals. We thought we could install the more or less malleable cubs as house and yard chulos back in Pennsylvania, create a life style for them which, if not natural, would not be disagreeable. We did not think we could do the same for Mona. We thought that if we took her she would probably end her days as a caged animal, a situation which we felt would be intolerable for an adult feral animal, intolerable for us.

For these reasons, we went out onto the cabin porch on

the morning of July 25th and lured Mona into the carrying cage. Ky and I loaded her into the van, drove her back to Kitt Peak. Around noontime, we set her free behind the kitchen area, where we had trapped her two months before. Stepping out of the box, she looked, sniffed about for a minute, then trotted off through the brush, following the main trail of the Kitt Peak tribe. We did not see or hear of Mona again. However, I suspect that her enforced separation from the tribe, even from her own cubs, did not have a marked effect on either her or her position within the tribe. We had taken Mona from Kitt Peak during the period when she would normally have withdrawn from the chulo community and association with the other animals. She was returned at about the time when she would naturally have rejoined the group. It is true that she did not have her own cubs with her, but this may have made less difference to a chulo than it would have to a female of another species. Within the tribes, the matriarchs seemed to make little, if any, distinction between "yours" and "mine" when it came to caring for, being responsible for cubs. We thought it likely that Mona, after rejoining the tribe, would take up her matriarchal duties without much sense of loss or frustration.

Back at the cabin in the Huachucas, the cubs were confused and appeared to be lonely for five or six hours after Mona was taken from them. However, by the end of the day they seemed to have adjusted completely to their new status as foster infants. They came to us (and also to Dain and to Kilo, the dachshund puppy that the girls had acquired in Tucson) to play, be fondled, for affection and warmth. By the second day, they were eating regularly and greedily, seemed anything but cowed or despondent. On July 27th, we started across the country with the cubs in an elaborate traveling box. They rode easily, the movement of the van seeming to lull them to sleep, and enlivened the vacations of a number of tourists who gathered around them at roadside stops where we took them out to exercise on the grass.

In Pennsylvania, we built a large indoor-outdoor run for the cubs. Also, when somebody is around to keep an eye on them, they are free to roam through the house, in the yard, in adjacent fields and woodlots. As this is being written, the cubs are ten months old. None of the four have been sick and they have not, so far as we can tell, suffered psychologically, being bold, outgoing, busy little animals. However, it would be dishonest to omit the unpleasant fact that we have not been able to protect the cubs as well as a chulo tribe would have. Our failure was in a sense predictable, since despite our interest and affection we have other interests and affections, while for the tribe the welfare of the young is the paramount concern. Two of the cubs were killed when dogs broke into their outside run. The two fatalities are clearly my responsibility and they weigh heavily on my conscience.

The development of the cubs is somewhat aside from the purpose of this book, which is intended as a description of our experiences with and observations of feral chulos. However, briefly and very generally, the cubs seem to have inherited most of their basic skills. They climb Pennsylvania locusts as they would have Arizona oaks, root about in our loam as their contemporaries presumably are in the Huachuca scree. They are startled by the same sort of loud noises as the wild animals are; follow the same pattern of daily activity; play, groom, investigate curiosities much as we had seen cubs doing in the Arizona mountains.

The greatest differences between the Pennsylvania and the Arizona chulos is, not surprisingly, in their social behavior. Lacking adult supervision and instruction, our four cubs have been much more inclined to wander off on their own, are more individualistic than wild cubs. Also they are much less communicative than the feral animals. From time to time, we have heard or seen them make most of the signs appropriate for their age, but they use them less frequently, less meaningfully. The cubs are like children who have grown up associating only with other children, if such a thing is conceivable. In consequence, they have had no opportunity to overhear adult chulo conversations, to observe, imitate, and learn the meaning of adult behavior. They lack not only the opportunity to develop socially but also the need, since they are our wards, not responsible for their own fate. Therefore while they are content—even, if such an anthropomorphic expression can be excused, happy —they are, as all domesticated wild creatures inevitably are, somewhat retarded. Our experience with the cubs has confirmed the impression we formed in Arizona that without a tribe a chulo is something other than a chulo—or, perhaps more accurately, an incomplete chulo.

13

The Last
Chulo Watcher

When we left Pennsylvania in the summer of 1970, it seemed that a year would give us time to do anything that we wanted or could reasonably expect to do so far as chulo hunting was concerned. We could have arranged to stay in Arizona for thirteen months, fifteen, eighteen, but twelve seemed like a good round, sufficient number. Suddenly, in the summer of 1971, we found ourselves stuck with this arbitrary decision made a year earlier in ignorance. All manner of arrangements, leases, money, school, promises to other people hinged on our leaving by July 15th. We twisted and turned, prolonged our stay another twelve days, using up, in regard to our commitments, all the margin of safety we had, but the grubby hands from the East had a grip on each of us and we could not shake free.

We knew we would be leaving behind us all manner of unanswered chulo questions (in those last weeks we talked often about what we could do, now that we were introduced to the animals, if we had five years to live with them), but, most frustrating of all, it became apparent that we would not be able to complete our observations of the basic cycle of chulo activity. Leaving as we had to in the last week of July, we would not see the new litters emerge, see if and how the tribe was rejoined. Having done much more than we had thought we would, we all had the feeling that for the lack of a lousy three or four weeks, we were going to leave a year of good work hanging, loose ends flapping like an unfinished piece of macramé.

Because we bitched and moaned so much about it, the rangers at the Coronado Memorial were well aware of our problem and in a sense shared it, since they were by then almost as curious about the chulos as we. They had promised to continue to watch the animals, make notes on what they saw (a promise which they kept throughout the following year), but the rangers were busy running their park and did not have the same intimate knowledge of the chulos that we had. Neither we nor they had much confidence that they would have time or expertise enough to collect the information that was needed to complete the observation of the chulo cycle. With all this in mind, Hugo, a week or so before we were to leave, said that if it would help any he would be glad to have one of the boys stay on at the memorial, live with him and his wife Ja, and continue the study until the end of the summer. I said that we'd think about it and changed the subject, not wanting any of the boys to be caught in a quick decision, to agree to stay behind out of a sense of obligation. That evening, Ky came to me alone. "If you think I can do it, I'd like to stay. I'm the only one who hasn't been alone this year."

"How do you mean?"

"I mean without my family. I guess I mean mostly without my old man."

I told Ky he had a good point, but to think it over for a day or two; that being the last one was going to be painful. I said there was no way he was not going to be lonely, but that if he could stand it, it might be an instructive experience; that until you learn to cope with loneliness you cannot be your own man, are always a ward of whoever protects you from loneliness.

After the decision was made and announced, Ky was excited, keyed up, not because we were leaving but because he was getting ready, talking himself into doing something hard. It was clear that standing alone waving as the rest of us pulled out of the canyon was not going to be easy or fun, but it was going to be a challenge, like climbing a bad cliff—something that a man could take pride in doing or even volunteering to try. We had been so close that the rest of us had no difficulty imagining the loneliness Ky was going to have to endure, and in the last days we were especially solicitous of him, freeing him from the worst packing chores, working on his gear, giving him things of ours we thought he might need or like. John, Terry, and I were somewhat in the position of a support party, a little envious of but also concerned for the climber who is going to make the final assault on a peak.

The last day at the cabin was bearable chiefly because we had left most of the packing until then, were too busy to brood. Ann, Mary Jane, Kate, Lee, the spider monkey Bobo, the black cat named Christy had headed East the week before. John, Terry, Lyn, and I were left to arrange ourselves, Dain, Kilo, the four chulo cubs, a coyote pup named Shad whom Lyn had acquired, as well as a mountain of gear, notes, film, and specimens in the van. In the interests of space, we ruthlessly threw away and burned the heap of treasures and mementos which make a cabin a Shangri-la. By late afternoon, the place was clear except for John's guitar, which we left behind as a kind of monument-sacrifice, along with a note telling any stranger who walked in to play the guitar, have a good time, that we had had a lot of them in that place. We ate a cold supper, and afterward I walked up Clark's Ravine, sat on the side of the Wedge in a niche where I had sat often. Just before dark, I saw the second teen-age gang scramble across the limestone below me, disappear into the brush. They were the last wild chulos I saw or have seen since. It seemed like the right, if not a good, time to leave.

After we left, Ky continued to keep the daily tape-recorded log we had used throughout the year and also called in several times a week to let us know how things were going, to talk over chulo business. During the course of one call, I asked him what was happening, who was left in the cabin area.

"I don't know. I went up once, took along a lunch. I was going to stay all day, but I couldn't do it. I felt like bawling all the time. Everything was so empty."

"Don't try it. Stay away from there—that's too much."

"Way too much."

Ky

Despite the practical and emotional difficulties of working alone, Ky did a fine job of winding up the chulo study. Before we had separated, we had talked over what he could reasonably expect to do and decided that, being alone, he should concentrate on the two outstanding problems: finding out how many cubs had been born to the tribe; if and how the tribe was reunited.

On August 3rd, one of the Sparks boys saw a chulo with a single cub. He got in touch with Ky, who came in time to identify the female as Calamity. A day later, Ky found Seven, also in the vicinity of the State of Texas Mine and also with a single cub. On August 7th, Ky had his best day, as he reported in his tape-recorded notes:

"This was a really good morning. I went out before breakfast to put some chulo chow out behind Gil and Margaret's house. I was sitting on the woodpile and who pokes her head up out of the ravine but the Witch. I was really glad to see her, because I hadn't seen her for two days. She looked around and I know she saw me. She grunted a little bit and then came up in the clearing, and right behind her were three cubs. They were really cute. They were about rat-size but they were very active. The Witch led them right past me and didn't seem to be worried at all. They were only about twenty feet away. The Witch started to feed. The little ones sort of nosed around, but I don't think they ate any of the dog food. Two of them were playing with and batting at a flower of some kind. The Witch fed for about ten minutes. Then she grunted again, and the little ones got behind her and they all marched back into the ravine. I didn't try to follow, because I didn't want to frighten her so she wouldn't come back."

Thereafter Ky saw the Witch and her brood almost daily until he left; he said that sometimes if he was in the right place at the right time, the cubs would play—were permitted by the Witch to play—around his feet. Ky described one such incident over the phone and I passed on the information to Terry, who came by the house daily to hear about how things were going in Montezuma Canyon. "It makes me sick to hear about it," Terry said glumly. "I really wanted to see the Witch and her kids."

On August 10th, Ky saw Queenie, who had with her, as we had suspected because of our meeting in the cave, three cubs. Ky saw Eleven, the remaining female who had stayed in the vicinity of the Wedge, only once, in the brush above the State of Texas Mine. So far as he could observe, she had no cubs with her, but he caught only a brief glimpse of her under poor observation conditions.

With Eleven's contribution being uncertain, there were, as best Ky could determine, eight cubs born to the Montezuma tribe that summer. Considering that all five of the females had been pregnant, this was not an impressive record. A possible explanation was that more cubs were born but that some of them may have drowned during a series of exceptionally violent flash floods which ripped through the canyons in the first two weeks of August. The fact that Seven and Calamity both appeared with only a single cub did not prove this assumption but gave some weight to it. Both Ky and Hugo reported that on several occasions after a downpour, the water rose with astonishing suddenness in the narrow ravines, so fast that a matriarch caught with her cubs in a flooding cave might have had time to move only one of the youngsters to safety. However, though he spent considerable time looking for the remains of cubs, Ky found none, and thus we could only speculate about why there were so few youngsters or if indeed the number was abnormally low.

Generally, as Ky observed them during August, the chulos seemed to be moving down the canyon. By the first of August, four of the five females were using the territory between the State of Texas Mine and the ranger station. The Supervisor was in the same general area, had more or less re-established himself in the territory he had occupied the previous fall and winter. Several times, Ky caught glimpses of both teen-age gangs in the brush on the canyon slopes, but their movements still seemed to be erratic, not centered in a particular territory.

Though the tribe seemed to be drawing together, it was not until August 13th that Ky observed a true reunion. Late on that afternoon, he found Queenie and the Witch with their six cubs together at the feeder above the Blue Water Ravine. While he was watching, they were joined by Calamity and her single youngster.

"They were jumbled all together," Ky reported. "I couldn't tell from the way they acted which of the babies belonged to which mother. Nobody made a big thing about it and I had the feeling they had probably been together before, but this was the first time I saw them together."

After a while, the combined family groups returned to the ravine. ("What order?" I asked Ky over the phone. "What else—Queenie in front, the Witch behind, Calamity and the cubs in the middle.") They stopped in the thicket not far from the entrance to the cave where I had seen Queenie and her cubs. As they milled, played, foraged in the thicket, the teen-age gang made up of five of the former juveniles, now subadults, came down over the side of the limestone ridge and joined them.

"There was some grunting between the teen-agers and the females," Ky said, "but no trouble. It didn't seem to me that the cubs and the teen-agers had much to do with each other, but you know how thick the brush is there. I couldn't see all that well. They hung around for a while but the Witch knew I was there. Pretty soon, she did some grunting and they took off up the canyon, Queenie leading them."

"That's sort of where we came in, isn't it?"

"I guess."

"It's a good time to pack it in. You still coming on Monday?"

"I guess I should. I got a lot to do if I'm going to get ready for school, but I don't know how I'll like it."

"Worry about that when you get to it. We'll see you at the airport."

The last of the chulo chasers came through the gate carrying his camera cases and tape recorder, yelled out, "I saw the Witch this morning before Hugo brought me into Tucson. I told her goodbye for all of you, too." Then we took each other's hands, two shaggy-haired sunburned freaks, and, having no words suitable for marking the absolute end of the chulo year, stood grinning idiotically at each other, which at least was better than crying in the middle of the D.C. National Airport.

Index